Sangu is Managing Director of Africa Health Holdings focused on "building Africa's healthcare future" and Chairman of Golden Palm Investments Corporation, an African venture capital firm. GPIC portfolio companies have raised over $500 million in the last five years. Delle has been named Africa's "Young Person of the Year", a TED Fellow, a Tutu Fellow and one of Forbes' "Top 30 Most Promising Entrepreneurs in Africa". Sangu is a Trustee of the Peddie School, an Advisory Board member of Harvard University's Center for African Studies and a member of Harvard Medical School's Global Health Advisory Council. Sangu graduated with a BA, a JD, and an MBA from Harvard University.

T0247409

"In this ground-breaking book, Sangu Delle has profiled different innovators on the continent collectively creating prosperity for millions of people. This is both inspiring and essential reading for anyone who cares about Africa's progress."

– Efosa Ojomo, Co-author, *The Prosperity Paradox: How Innovation Can Lift Nations Out of Poverty*

"Sangu awakens a desire to get your boots on the ground and engage with the thriving African entrepreneurial champions and communities as he brings to life the potential of the continent through its rich culture, history and teeming population transitioning from mere consumers to formidable producers of all manner of goods and services."

– Tokunboh Ishmael, Co-Founder and Managing Director, Alitheia Capital

"If the youth drive tomorrow, we better get ready for Africa to take centre stage in our global future. This excellent book shows vividly the entrepreneurs who are shaping the future of the dynamic continent. It is a must read for those who want to understand global entrepreneurship and how we can make the 21st century a prosperous one for all people."

– William R. Kerr, Dimitri V. D'Arbeloff - MBA Class of 1955 Professor of Business Administration, Harvard Business School

"Sangu Delle takes us on an inspiring journey to discover some of the great entrepreneurs who are not only shaping Africa's boosting digital ecosystem but also writing a new narrative for the whole continent."

– Thomas Buberl, CEO of AXA.

"*Making Futures* is a fascinating book about entrepreneurship on the African continent. As an entrepreneur and investor, Delle is uniquely positioned to tell the story of an emerging digital Africa and its incredible entrepreneurs like Gregory Rockson of mPharma who are building life-changing enterprises enabled by technology."

– Jim Breyer, Founder and CEO, Breyer Capital

"Sangu Delle's *Making Futures* should be required reading for all college students in Africa. And I especially hope educators across the continent will all get to read it. The stories in this book serve as an eternal reminder to everyone who reads them that there is a lot for Africa to be hopeful for. It has been a real delight savouring each one."

–Patrick Awuah, Founder and President, Ashesi University

"This book captures the vast array of innovation occurring across the African continent - the ingenuity that is going to transform Africa's challenges into African and global opportunities."

– Fred Swaniker, Founder, Africa Leadership Group

"In *Making Futures: Young Entrepreneurs in a Dynamic Africa*, Sangu Delle gives reason to be be bullish about Africa's future. With its demographic projections, concern has been expressed over whether Africa is growing fast enough to avoid a demographic disaster. By 2050 Africa will have the largest youth population in the world. It takes a young entrepreneur like Sangu Delle, enmeshed in the emerging entrepreneurial ecosystem to open our eyes onto a different Africa that is emerging over the 21st century. *Making Futures* provides an informed basis to be excited about Africa's future."

– Emmanuel Kwaku Akyeampong, Ellen Gurney Professor of History and African Studies at Harvard University and Oppenheimer Faculty Director of the Center for African Studies

MAKING FUTURES

YOUNG ENTREPRENEURS IN A DYNAMIC AFRICA

SANGU DELLE

FOREWORD BY HENRY LOUIS GATES JR.

ABUJA – LONDON

First published in Nigeria and the UK in 2019 by Cassava Republic Press

Abuja – London

First published in the USA in 2020 by Cassava Republic Press

A CIP catalogue record for this book is available from the National Library of Nigeria and the British Library.

ISBN 978-1-911115-88-5
eISBN 978-1-911115-89-2

Book design by R. Ajith Kumar
Cover & Art Direction by Seyi Adegoke

Printed and bound in Great Britain by Bell & Bain Ltd., Glasgow
Distributed in Nigeria by Yellow Danfo
Distributed in the UK by Central Books Ltd.
Distributed in the US by Consortium Book Sales & Distribution

Stay up to date with the latest books, special offers and exclusive content with our monthly newsletter.

Sign up on our website:
www.cassavarepublic.biz
Twitter: @cassavarepublic
Instagram: @cassavarepublicpress
Facebook: facebook.com/CassavaRepublic
#MakingFutures #ReadCassava

*This book is dedicated to a friend, a brother and
a beloved mentor, the late Komla Afeke Dumor.
An extraordinary African journalist who was the face of
BBC Africa, Komla was our very own prince,
who narrated our stories with nuance, passion and pride.
He inspired an entire continent. He always taught me that
we Africans have a responsibility to tell our own stories.
Komla, I hope I do you proud.*

CONTENTS

FOREWORD

AT TEN YEARS OF AGE, I EXPRESSED MY FASCINATION WITH Africa by memorising the name of the leader of each new African nation – when Africa was still only a book and a nightly newscast to me. During my undergraduate years at Yale University, my own initial encounter with Africa began as I spent half a year working in an Anglican mission hospital in the centre of Tanzania and ended with my trip across the equator, travelling from the Indian Ocean to the Atlantic. Despite my many extensive visits to the continent in the decades following, Africa remains endlessly mysterious and intriguing to me, and I eagerly awaited this new volume, *Making Futures*, as an account of the work of young entrepreneurs transforming their societies.

During my career in academia, I have had the honour of chairing the Department of African and African American Studies at Harvard, including the African Language Program which offers 40 different African languages. This expansion of our faculty's mission provides an Africa curriculum spanning both the social sciences and the humanities to Harvard graduate and undergraduates. As a student at Harvard, Sangu Delle, the author of this book, was one of the two top undergraduate students our department has ever produced. I do not exaggerate Sangu's merits; he is the rarest of young people, filled not only with formidable intelligence but also with fire and compassion, including a tremendous will to make a difference in his communities. He founded Cleanacwa, a non-profit that focuses on bringing clean water and sanitation to 200,000 people across 160 villages in Ghana; I proudly serve on its board.

Rather than write about his own extraordinary achievements, Sangu has chosen to tell the stories of 17 other young entrepreneurs, a task that led him to travel to 45 African countries where he interviewed over 600 entrepreneurs and business leaders. As a counter to the old images of an Africa shackled by poverty and darkness, a new narrative has emerged of "Africa Rising", stories of booming prosperity and an emerging middle class. The "Africa Rising" narrative has given a great deal of hope and projected a more positive – and in many ways fact-based – perspective on African development. However, as Sangu relates, this new narrative is also flawed, "complicated by the reality of its diversity." Recent scholarship has shown that both of these narratives hide significant and important aspects of the trajectories of African societies, flattening their often-staggering diversity in theory and reality.

One of the most salient of these factors is the incredibly high and rapidly growing population of Africa's youth. Images of malnourished children readily come to mind on one side, and the young, tech-savvy entrepreneur is held up on the other. The rapidly rising youth population presents perhaps one of the greatest sources of potential *and* disaster for most African countries as youth unemployment continues to rise. Nigeria's President Muhammadu Buhari unwittingly created a controversy in 2018 by implying that the country's youth were lazy, kick-starting the #LazyNigerianYouths hashtag which drew attention to the ways Nigerian youth were turning to entrepreneurship on many levels to make a viable living for themselves. These events epitomised the competing narratives, often internalised within Africa itself, and the ambiguous nature of development, wealth creation, and entrepreneurship with respect to Africa's youth. To these conflicting narratives, Sangu brings a nuanced view of young African entrepreneurs, tracing both their triumphs and failures in their specific circumstances.

Resisting each polarised narrative, as well as standard narratives of development and economic models that have repeatedly failed to offer Africa an equal position on the world stage, *Making Futures* provides a balanced but optimistic window into the way some of the greatest strengths of Africa's youthful entrepreneurs are drawn directly from their challenges as well. While the book is centred around exciting and exemplary African entrepreneurs, it also ensures that Africa's great diversity is showcased on multiple levels: regional and ethnic, economic, political, social, artistic, historical, and in terms of gender. This last area is one that receives the close attention that it deserves, with many female entrepreneurs featuring prominently alongside the ways that technology and integration into the broader global economy have often been a mixed bag from a gendered perspective. As Sangu notes early on, "technology is a means to an end and not an end in and of itself," offering a warning to those too eager to embrace technological innovation without realising the ways it often perpetuates gender and economic inequality if not designed and harnessed properly.

Each section and entrepreneur offers insight into how and why Africa has become the world leader in entrepreneurship, how entrepreneurship is being enlisted to solve critical social problems, how Africans' creative vision and voices are shared with the world, and how fascinating new technologies are being generated. Taken as a whole however, they also present relatable real-world experiences that have great implications for policy, investment, and entrepreneurial strategy. The book provides important signposts for navigating the dangers and promising opportunities of Africa's youth and future, offering an inspiring and even emotional journey that a diverse audience including Africans, entrepreneurs, techies, Africanists, economists, politicians, and many more besides will surely enjoy and find useful. Written with clarity and precision, each story unfolds a fascinating new view of Africa today.

Henry Louis Gates, Jr.
Alphonse Fletcher University Professor
Harvard University
August 2019

INTRODUCTION

I GREW UP IN ACCRA, AND I HAD THIS TRADITION WITH my father: on the drive to school, he would buy newspapers and magazines from the street hawkers as we turtled through traffic in the city centre. I had to read them as quickly as possible before I was dropped off. My favourite was *The Economist*. At age 13, it did not win me any cool points with my peers, but in a world predating social media, it expanded my horizons and gave me a window into the rest of the world. I was enamoured. I can never forget one day in May 2000, when I glanced at *The Economist's* cover.[1] The page was pitch black, emblazoned with the contours of my continent, and a man holding a grenade launcher, with three words that forever haunt: "The hopeless continent". 'Why do they think we are hopeless?' I remember asking my father.

In 2050, there will be about 2.5 billion Africans in our world.[2] By then, Africa's youth will account for over 60% of the world's young, with over 1 billion people needing jobs. With 6 of the 10 fastest growing economies in the world over the next decade in the region, Africa is becoming today what China was a couple of decades ago: the next frontier of strong economic growth.[3] Until 2015, *Forbes* magazine did not feature a billionaire's list for Africa. In 2018, that list featured 23 billionaires with a combined wealth of over $75 billion.[4] *The Economist*, presaging this change in fortunes, heralded an "Africa Rising" on its cover in 2011.[5]

This "Africa Rising" narrative is complicated. As the eminent African historian and Oppenheimer Faculty Director of Harvard University's Centre for African Studies, Emmanuel Akyeampong argues, 'The "Africa Rising" story of booming economies and growing middle classes is important in correcting the global perception of Africa, for Africa has not always been in decline. The 500 years after European arrival in Africa saw an increasing integration of Africa into the global economy, but often on terms which worked against Africa's interests: the slave trade through the end of the 19th century, then European colonial rule to the 1960s. The challenge of development has been the story since, as Africa struggled with the legacies of colonial rule, its marginal share of global trade, and corrupt and dictatorial leadership.'[6]

This reversal in fortunes and economic surge of the region has been uplifting for the continent, and for me as an African whose childhood perceptions of identity were mired in tropes of poverty and darkness and magazine covers declaring us hopeless. Africa's rising is, however, complicated by the reality of its diversity. A Deloitte report on the continent's economic outlook noted that 'The Africa Rising narrative was always flawed. Africa is so diverse that it has always been simplistic to have a single view of the continent. The vast geography, nascent markets, lack of connectivity, very low regional integration and lack of trained people and knowledge networks make a more nuanced view of a multi-speed Africa more appropriate.'[7] We also have to contend with the rising inequality that has accompanied much of the economic growth. While we are proud of having some of the fastest growing economies in the world, we are also home to seven of the ten most unequal countries in the world.[8] Africa may be rising, but not every African is rising. Whether or not you believe our economic growth is sustainable, what is undeniable is that the continent is growing and is doing so at one of the fastest rates in the world.

My friend and Business School classmate, Irene Sun, in her book *The Next Factory of the World* argues that 'Chinese factories in Africa' are 'the future that will create broad-based prosperity for Africans.' She adds: 'I finally understood that the future of Africa depends on industrialisation. This is what will allow Africa to follow in the footsteps of Japan, South Korea, Taiwan and China: to employ its booming population, to grow world-class firms, to raise living standards across the bulk of its populace.'[9] I adore and respect Irene, but I do not fully agree with her conclusion. There is no question that industrialisation must play a key role in Africa's transformation. However, instead of following in the footsteps of China, the digital technology revolution allows for a different model and a different story for Africa, one that can be pioneered internally, not by the Chinese or the Europeans, but by us Africans.

The technology revolution, coupled with globalisation, has ushered in a new era for the continent, exemplified by an economic leapfrogging aided by the mobile phone, which has underpinned an explosion in innovation. After a decade and a half of rapid urbanisation and strong economic growth, digital Africa is emerging. In Africa's major cities, 50% of consumers have internet-enabled devices with 3G networks. Across Sub-Saharan Africa, smartphone adoption is at 34% (compared to 57% in Asia-Pacific, 70% in Europe and 61% in Latin America), and is forecasted to reach 68% by 2025.[10] Infrastructural development and the fall in global smartphone prices have contributed to millions of Africans going online.[11] In 2018, the number of Africans online was estimated at 453 million with a current penetration of 35% (compared to a global average of 54%). While the rest of the world experienced a growth rate in internet penetration of 89% from 2000 – 2017, Africa grew at an exponential rate of 9,942% over the same period, albeit from a much smaller base.[12]

Of course, this leapfrogging and growth in telecommunication did not occur in a vacuum. It was enabled by billions of dollars of investments in telecommunication infrastructure in the African continent over the past two decades. Approximately $70 billion has been invested in the telecommunications sector in Nigeria alone.[13] These investments are still not enough. Most African countries lag other emerging markets in infrastructure. Electric power consumption in Africa is on average 632 kilowatt hours per person compared to 2,622 in Brazil, Russia, India and China, and Africa's demand for electricity is forecasted to quadruple between 2010 and 2040.[14] Road density in Africa is a paltry 97 kilometres of road per square kilometre compared to 485 in Brazil, India and China.[15] Many African countries need to address the infrastructure gap (estimated at $350 billion annually) to create the enabling environment for technology to flourish: the road and transportation networks to power e-commerce deliveries, reliable energy to power computers, hospitals, schools among others.[16]

The digital infrastructure has sparked a new wave of innovation as young entrepreneurs leverage the digital economy to create for profit, non-profit and hybrid enterprises to change their communities. Research by McKinsey points to internet-related services as a driver of economic growth and social development. 'An increase in a country's internet maturity correlates with a sizable increase in real GDP per capita. As countries go online, they realise efficiencies in the delivery of public services and the operations of large and small businesses alike.'[17] The internet is estimated to have contributed more than 10% of total GDP growth in China, India and Brazil over a five-year period.[18]

Technology and globalisation are transforming the African continent and are equipping young entrepreneurs with tools to build enterprises that could not have been possible decades ago. At the same time, technology isn't a panacea, and there are many young entrepreneurs solving important challenges on the continent that aren't dependent on digital technologies, such as Bernice Dapaah who founded the Ghana Bamboo Bikes Initiative, hiring young women to use bamboo to create environmentally friendly bicycles or Bilikiss Adebiyi who founded Wecyclers, a social enterprise empowering low-income communities to turn 'trash into cash' by offering convenient household recycling services using a fleet of low-cost cargo bikes.[19] Technology is a means to an end and not an end in and of itself.

Our history in Africa is rife with extraordinary personalities. In 1324, the Muslim king of Mali, Mansa Musa, embarked on a legendary pilgrimage to Mecca. Musa, who is considered by some historians to be the wealthiest individual in history, and his entourage are alleged to have given away so much gold during their stopover in Cairo that the price of the metal was depressed in the region for decades. Stories of Mansa Musa's wealth went global. When Angelino Dulcert of Majorca created a map of the world in 1339, for the first time ever, Mali was featured.[20] In recent times, Mali has dominated the news media for different reasons, in reports on civil conflicts, food insecurity, and poverty. Yet, I met many young entrepreneurs determined to build a new narrative for Mali: from Aliou Yattasaye who developed the first Malian smartphone, the YuvSmart (which is distributed throughout the country in partnership with Orange Mali) to Issam Chleuh, an impact investor and Tutu Fellow who is building incubators in Bamako to support the next generation of start-ups.

This book is the product of spending seven years, from 2012 to 2019, traversing the nooks and crannies of my continent, visiting 45 African countries, and interviewing in depth over 600 young entrepreneurs. It is an attempt to capture the Africa being built through the eyes of the new generation of young Africans: the aspiring Mansa Musas (without his excess), the young women and men who are taking charge of their destinies and building business enterprises and innovative non-profits to radically change their lives and the lives of their communities. It is telling the stories of markets being created, industries being disrupted, and theories being challenged, and describing the challenges and opportunities of making futures on a continent so complex and diverse, and exciting. The hope of the continent, and the future of its trajectory, lie in my generation and with these iconic young entrepreneurs.

While I would have loved to write about all 600 interviewees, a scale of that nature would have turned into a ten-volume, five-year writing project. Although all the entrepreneurs informed and shaped my thinking, this book focuses on 17 of those entrepreneurs who represent the breadth of diverse entrepreneurial journeys on the continent, organised across four broad sections: The Aspiring Moguls (general business entrepreneurs), The Sociopreneurs (social entrepreneurs), The Creatives (entrepreneurs in the creative economy), and The Techies (technology entrepreneurs). The 17 entrepreneurs profiled in depth are a mélange of eight women and nine men from 13 countries spanning North, West, Central, East and Southern Africa. Their stories are inspiring and uplifting, a testament to a new age and new possibilities for the African continent. I daresay the 21st century could be the African century, driven by its young people. Unlike most of the rest of the world which will have an ageing demographic, the continent of Africa will have the largest youth population in the world.[21] Consequently, one of our biggest challenges will be creating economic opportunities for this youth bulge, so it becomes an asset in our growth trajectory, and not a liability that could hamper our progress.

In many ways, I'm privileged and well-positioned to tell the story of African entrepreneurship. Growing up in Ghana, I thought I could understand and change my world through humanitarian activism. I led anti-poverty and environmental campaigns at age 12, and even founded my first non-profit at age 16. Though I remain committed to service, I grew disillusioned with my goal to help Ghana through conventional activism.

In 2007, when I was a college freshman, my roommate Darryl Finkton and I founded a non-profit focused on clean water and sanitation called Cleanacwa. For our first project, we spearheaded the provision of water and sanitation infrastructure in Agyementi, a village in Ghana with an *E. Coli*-infested spring source that resulted in high diarrhoea incidence and high infant mortality rates. During our project in Agyementi, I asked one of the community members 'What is the greatest need in your community?' Expecting him to say a hospital or a school, I was stunned by his response: 'Yɛ pɛ ajuma,' he said. *We want jobs.*

Partly inspired by this man in Agyementi, I founded Golden Palm Investments (GPI) in 2007 with the equivalent of $100, and then subsequently raised $50,000 in seed capital from investors. Under the umbrella of GPI, we invested in agriculture in southern Ghana, employed over 30 people, and provided technology such as tractors and high-yield seeds to local farmers. By the end of 2008, GPI's investments in Ghana had doubled the capital invested. But 2008, being an election year, saw a sharp widening of the fiscal deficit and plummeting depreciation of the currency: our returns halved overnight in US dollars. Ten years later, GPI has backed businesses operating all over the African continent. We initially invested in diverse businesses including a real estate development company, a baby food business and a fish feed business, but in the past five years we have focused exclusively on technology start-ups ranging from a mobile survey start-up, a FinTech company to a precision agriculture autonomous systems company, and many others. Collectively, our portfolio companies have raised over $500 million in venture financing. Many have been successful, and a few have been failures.

In 2017, I decided to focus our efforts on healthcare as I believe it is one of the most compelling opportunities from both a business and a social impact perspective. I partnered with Dr. Chinny Ogunro (who is profiled in this book) to build Africa Health Holdings, a technology-enabled healthcare platform that acquires and manages hospitals, clinics and other healthcare assets across Africa. We are adopting emerging technologies such as telemedicine and artificial intelligence that will lower the cost and increase the quality of healthcare delivery in Africa, as well as managing these healthcare facilities more efficiently at scale. Dealing with volatile macro-economic conditions, human capital challenges, and an infrastructure deficit, being an entrepreneur on the African continent for over a decade has been a journey in strategy, operations, finance, leadership and everything in between.

While entrepreneurship offers one of many important tools in addressing our socio-economic challenges on the continent, I recognise that the glorification of entrepreneurship and the romanticised view of every poor person as a potential entrepreneur is a recipe for failure. Entrepreneurship will play a key role in building a sustainable economic future for the region, but it cannot solve intractable challenges of governance and infrastructure. It is important that we do not fall for the ruse some policymakers and government officials are guilty of, which is abdicating their responsibility to solve our economic challenges by outsourcing solutions to "entrepreneurship". It is an abstract illusion which creates a false sense of hope.

Making Futures: Young Entrepreneurs in a Dynamic Africa is not just a collection of stories of a changing Africa through the eyes of some of the youngest and most promising African entrepreneurs; it is the telling of the story of an emerging entrepreneurial ecosystem in Africa, and how young entrepreneurs are building enterprises at scale in a digital age. My goal is to equip readers with intimate knowledge of the markets and growth across the region, and to show how young entrepreneurs are identifying problems as opportunities and making futures in a continent that is poised for economic growth and opportunity.

THE ASPIRING MOGULS

ON FLIGHTS, AT AIRPORTS, AND AT CONFERENCES, MY
favourite pop quiz questions are: a) How many children did my
grandfather have? and b) How many companies in Africa generate
over $1 billion in annual revenues? What are your guesses? Without
googling, write your answers down. For both questions, most people
guess 20 to 30. My late grandfather, who was a polygamous chief
in Nandom, a district in the Upper West region of Ghana, had 86
children. According to McKinsey, Africa is currently home to 700
companies with an annual revenue greater than $500 million, and
400 of those companies generate over $1 billion, and these companies
are achieving greater growth rates and profitability than their global
peers. [22] African consumers and African businesses together spend
over $4 trillion annually and this number is estimated to rise to
almost $6 trillion by 2025.[23]

While these statistics sound impressive, they are overwhelmed
by the reality of our demographics, which cries for more inclusive
growth. Africa's youth is expected to double to over 830 million by
2050. With as many as 11 million African youth entering the job
force every year, and the formal sector only creating 3.7 million
jobs, there is great pressure on African governments to solve this
annual youth employment deficit of 7 million jobs, and growing.[24] An
estimated 67% of African youth are unemployed or underemployed,
with women disproportionally impacted.[25] As a result, the future of

employment in Africa is increasingly dependent on its entrepreneurs who are expected to be the primary drivers of the much-needed creation of jobs on the continent. Partly due to the digital age, which has lowered the costs of starting and running a business, we have seen an emergence of larger classes of young business entrepreneurs. This is a global phenomenon, but with greater importance for the African continent, given our unique challenges with job creation and our growing youth bulge. The lack of formal employment opportunities across many African countries has contributed to igniting these young entrepreneurs who see many of our problems as opportunities, and who exhibit what my friend and author of *The Bright Continent,* Dayo Olopade calls *kanju*, which she defines as 'a specific creativity born from African difficulty.'[26] These entrepreneurs are building fast-growing businesses in food manufacturing, hospitality, solar energy, healthcare, engineering, technology, media and other sectors.

A global report on entrepreneurship revealed that the African continent leads the world in terms of early-stage entrepreneurial activities, with Zambia and Nigeria at the forefront. In addition, African entrepreneurs were ranked as the most confident to launch a start-up, with those in Malawi being twice as likely to launch a new business as entrepreneurs in the UK.[27] Malawi is one of the least developed countries in the world, with substantial challenges in health, infrastructure, education and governance. I visited Malawi and met many young entrepreneurs in Lilongwe, who, despite their country's difficulties, were all filled with optimism. One such entrepreneur, Ahmed Sunka, a Mandela YALI fellow and the CEO of Rab Processors Limited, the leading agro-processing company in Malawi, believes his country has the potential to feed the Southern African sub-region and beyond.

The African continent also has a much higher proportion of female entrepreneurs as compared to any other region, with countries like Nigeria and Zambia (both 40.7%) leading the pack, compared to the

United States (10.4%), the UK (5.5%), Norway (3.6%) and France (3.1%) who lag behind when it comes to female entrepreneurship.[28] The MasterCard Index of Women's Entrepreneurship survey also showed similar results and noted that 'female entrepreneurs in developing countries are driven by grit and determination, along with a desire to provide for their families.'[29] While most African entrepreneurs are involved in the informal sector, where 80% of the working population of Africa is employed, a growing number of formal businesses have sprouted across the continent over the past decade.[30]

By 2016, 19 Sub-Saharan African countries were securing growth rates of 5% or more annually, there was poverty reduction in 15 countries, democracy was spreading across the continent, 33 countries had qualified for debt relief, and the number of major conflicts in the region had significantly declined.[31] Many African countries are increasingly trying to promote entrepreneurship as a matter of public policy. Countries such as Mauritius, Rwanda and Botswana have shown that it is possible to improve competitiveness swiftly and successfully. In 2008, Rwanda was ranked as the 150th nation in the world in the ease of doing business, but, in a space of 10 years, the country has managed to improve its business climate and as of 2019, ranks as 29th in the world.[32]

What is unique about this new transformation on the African continent is that the traditional players such as telecoms, banks, and retailers are not driving the change. Rather, a new wave of business models is emerging, crafted by young entrepreneurs tackling specific market breakdowns and frictions head on. These visionaries are leveraging digital tools, collaborating with the public and private sector, large and small, to tackle specific problems and form a need-based ecosystem to capture value that has previously been constrained or unable to be realised.

In this section, we will meet some of Africa's aspiring moguls:

four imaginative business entrepreneurs building enterprises in agribusiness, healthcare, advertising, and financial services. These entrepreneurs have all faced challenges in the pursuit of their dreams, but have shown remarkable tenacity, persistence, and relentless drive to overcome the many obstacles that litter the path to success for a young entrepreneur daring to pave his or her own way. Like their counterparts in other parts of the world, some of these entrepreneurs have leveraged digital tools to support their various businesses across multiple sectors in ways that simply could not have been imagined a decade ago.

Hamstrung by a dearth of infrastructure, volatile macro-economic conditions, and limited resources, it can be a difficult journey to build and sustain a business enterprise in many countries on the African continent. These are competitive markets. One of the businesses I researched (and invested in), Zamsolar, an off-grid solar company, after raising half a million dollars in financing sent this note to investors: 'The Zambian Kwacha has been in a free-fall since the start of the year, pushing our costs up. Meanwhile, rising competition from non-profits have forced our prices down. Our gross margin has been squeezed to the point that profitability would be unlikely this year or next. Thus, we find ourselves without cash, a management team, or a viable business model.' Zamsolar subsequently liquidated.

Business in Africa is not for the faint of heart, so buckle up. Let's start our journey with one of my favourite countries on the continent, and home to BRCK (the company co-founded by technologist Juliana Rotich that makes water-proof, solar powered 3G Wi-Fi boxes), iHub (the innovation hub that Mark Zuckerberg famously visited), M-Pesa (the world's leading mobile money service) and some of the world's most beautiful safaris.

1

ERIC MUTHOMI

CREATES VALUE FROM BANANAS

AS I TOUCHED DOWN IN JOMO KENYATTA INTERNATIONAL Airport in Nairobi, I wiped my eyes, which had grown red from hours of reading. I had dived through a crash course on Kenya's history and culture, and had covered pre-colonial history dating back to the Neolithic period, all the way to Nairobi's tech scene, and the 2007 post-election violence.[33] I was excited to be in Nairobi, a sprawling metropolis home to over 6.5 million inhabitants and 60% of the country's GDP.[34] Nairobi has a confident, cosmopolitan swag that straddles both local and global cultures. You can enjoy some *nyama choma* and Tusker beer, Brazilian *picanha a ponto para mal* or authentic Indian chicken *vindaloo*, and end the night having a Manhattan cocktail and smoking some *shisha,* while overlooking the city at night from Sankara Hotel's rooftop bar. Kenya is the biggest and the most advanced economy in East and Central Africa with over $60 billion in annual output.[35] From Safaricom to Equity Bank, Kenya is home to some of the most successful corporations on the continent. I was excited to meet its young entrepreneurs. I had asked friends and some reputable contacts to send me lists of the most promising young business entrepreneurs in Kenya. One name stood out across multiple lists: Eric Muthomi.

Africa currently imports one third of the food, beverages and processed goods it consumes.[36] Of the fruits and vegetables that are produced on the continent, over 50% go to waste.[37] The most recent data publicly available showed that out of total aid of $150 billion to African countries, $25 billion was allocated to food aid.[38] We should be focused on solving the waste problem, instead of soliciting food aid, which creates new markets for corn farmers in Idaho. Further, an estimated 38% of children in Sub-Saharan Africa are stunted because their diet doesn't have enough fruits, vegetables, and meat.[39] I've always known that we don't produce enough to feed ourselves despite having 60% of the world's available arable land.[40] What stunned me was to learn that in some places, the problem is not that we don't produce enough, it's that we produce too much. That was the case in Meru, Eric Muthomi's hometown, located in eastern Kenya.

Eric's award-winning company, Stawi Foods and Fruits, is a food processing company that pioneered the processing of bananas into multipurpose banana flour in Kenya. The company has also diversified into the production of other nutritious porridge flours. Eric, through Stawi, is contributing to sustainable and higher incomes for almost 1,000 farmers and creating value out of tons of bananas that would have otherwise gone to waste.[41]

When Eric was a little boy, his father joined a small manufacturing business in its infancy. Over the next 15 years, the company grew to join the league of some of the largest businesses in Kenya. Today, it is a multimillion-dollar business with its footprints all over Africa. Eric was inspired by its growth story. Though both Eric's parents are salaried workers – his mother is a teacher – they encouraged their children to pursue entrepreneurial ventures in addition to their professional pursuits, and Eric and his siblings modelled this behaviour. Growing up, Eric's parents would save religiously and invest all their savings into real estate. They inspired him to become an entrepreneur, and supported his risk-taking initiatives, including loaning him his first seed capital.

Before Stawi took off, Eric had already started several business ventures and experienced a fair share of failures. 'I remember the first business I started was selling compact discs. My mom had a shop just nearby, so I would get the compact discs at a wholesale price and then we'd sell them at a higher price. After that, I started another company, an online advertising business... That didn't go well so I left that business after just three months. Then I got into a business that used to make commercial handicrafts such as sandals, beads, and paintings. I teamed up with a guy who was very good at making them. This was in 2007 and I was still in university. That business picked up very well because we exported to Uganda and South Africa. We had a client in South Africa that was buying quite a sizeable number of sandals from us. But I left that business because we had some issues with the payment. Export payment was a challenge; we did two consignments and never got paid so I burnt my fingers. Then in 2009, I started a construction company which still exists. We got licensed to do small road construction and road maintenance projects. We've done a few jobs in rural Kenya and in Embu.'

I smiled and bonded with Eric over the similarities in our entrepreneurial journeys. In the same way Eric had identified arbitrage opportunities with CDs, I had also discovered an opportunity while devouring beef kebabs in Ouagadougou: they were delicious and cheaper than prices in Accra. Upon investigation, I learned that cows in Burkina Faso were trading at a significant discount to the price of cows in Ghana. So, I traded cows and called the operation "cowbitrage." I also related to Eric's stories of failure. Through Golden Palm Investments (GPI), I started an aquaculture business in 2008 and we invested $100,000 in tilapia production. I was so embarrassed when the tilapia we harvested was so small that the market traders coined a moniker for it – "schoolboys" – because only school children would buy tilapia that small. Eric's stories hit home.

Like Eric, many of the young entrepreneurs I met are serial entrepreneurs. They typically started their entrepreneurial journey early in their lives. Eric has a diverse entrepreneurial journey ranging from the sale of computer accessories, to online marketing, to handicrafts and even to road construction. While he was studying law in university, he was simultaneously pursuing these entrepreneurial ventures and learning key lessons from his mistakes and failures.

Eric started nursing a strong interest in food processing, driven by some observations he had made. First, he believed that there will always be constant and growing demand for food as the population expands because it is the most basic universal need. He read a report by Ernst & Young which estimated that fast-moving consumer goods (FMCG) would grow to be the largest consumer vertical in Africa. The FMCG market in Africa is already estimated to be worth $175 billion. He also noticed the growth trajectory of several FMCG companies in Kenya – mainly companies involved in the production of sugar, vegetable oil and beer. From modest beginnings, these companies were able to achieve significant market scale in a few years.

Eric reasoned that Kenya would be an ideal location for a food processing venture because most of the raw materials needed are available in the country. In addition, food security remained a challenge in the country due to post-harvest losses. Eric was convinced that a food processing company could help solve this problem. The Kenyan government and other international development agencies also recognised the need and value of agro-processing and were providing support for agribusiness start-ups. Eric figured he could launch his business and take advantage of the financial and technical support being offered to agro-processors. He decided to start with bananas because Kenya is one of the largest producers and consumers of bananas in the world. Kenya has over 400,000 banana farmers with their farms as their only source of income.[42] A significant amount of the bananas these farmers produce go to waste during the peak season.

Like other parts of the continent, food waste in Kenya occurs at the post-harvest stage.[43] This is driven by bottlenecks in transporting produce from rural farms to market centres in towns and cities. Many of the roads connecting the farms to the market centres are in deplorable conditions. There are also not enough storage facilities such as cold rooms to store produce, or proper packaging material to preserve it. This results in large scale rotting of produce on farms and heavy losses for the farmer. So, a rock star farmer could have a bumper harvest and be forced to sell her produce at a throwaway price. For Eric, this tragedy was personal; he had witnessed many relatives in Meru who were banana farmers lose their surplus produce to rot. Today, technology-enabled logistics start-ups like Twiga Foods and Lori Systems in Kenya and Jetstream in Ghana are trying to solve this problem by sourcing quality produce from farmers in bulk and exporting or delivering them to vendors in urban areas, aggregating demand using a digital marketplace.

These solutions were not available in 2010, so Eric wondered: 'What can I do with all this produce?' He buried himself into research on options for processing bananas. After several Google clicks, he discovered that bananas can be refined into many products including wine and flour. The flour can be used for preparing porridge; baking or making pasta; it can be processed into chips; or it can be mixed with maize flour to prepare a popular East African dish, *ugali*. Eric further researched food processing techniques, market sizing, and the licensing requirements.

However, Eric knew that not everything global would apply in a local context, so he sought to validate his online research. His findings were confirmed by an official in the agribusiness department of the Ministry of Agriculture in Nairobi. This government official was helpful to Eric and encouraged him to consider additional opportunities for processing and export, such as dried mango.

Banana processing was unchartered territory for Eric. It was quite new to Kenya, too. Eric was undeterred, he was motivated to be a pioneer. To build capacity, he researched opportunities and enrolled in an incubator program run by a government institute in Nairobi with a mandate to do research and incubate start-ups. For 6 months, he was trained on how to process bananas into banana flour. He produced prototypes, then went through the testing, validation, safety and certification phase from the Kenya Bureau of Standards.

When Eric graduated from the 6-month training program in the latter part of 2011, Stawi was born. He was 24 years old. With his savings and a loan of $3,000 from his parents, he travelled to Mitunguu village – about 40km from Meru – and rented a small facility to start production. He contacted banana farmers, explained his business concept and contracted them to supply him with bananas. Stawi began with a group of 50 farmers. Eric didn't have the capital to hire a big team, so he used SMS to manage the farmers and send them information, in lieu of hiring agents to go into the field.

Eric also scouted the internet for funding opportunities, discovered the Nature Challenge Africa competition and participated with the hope of winning the cash prize to invest in his business. The competition, sponsored by the Worldwide Fund for Nature (WWF) in conjunction with NETFUND, is geared towards promoting businesses that make use of Africa's natural resources in their activity.[44] He took home the first prize. He also won support from the Enablis business plan competition, which he also discovered online.[45] From these two contests, he raised an additional $17,000 which gave him additional start-up capital.

Processing the bananas into banana flour involves washing and peeling them, slicing them with a knife and washing them again with water. The bananas are then sun-dried till they are hardened, and then they are milled. Eric engaged some people from the village to assist with this process and outsourced the milling to a small mill nearby since he didn't own a milling machine.

Since Stawi was a new company, it was a great challenge convincing shopping centres to stock their shelves with his product. Eric used social media, especially Facebook and Twitter, to market the product, reach consumers and to conduct consumer research. With Facebook, he was able to reach his target demographics using the platform's advanced targeting advertising tools. With all this data in hand, and together with a new salesperson he hired, Eric succeeded in signing up with Nakumatt, East Africa's now defunct supermarket, but at the time the largest retailer in the region. This was followed shortly after with a deal with Uchumi Supermarket, another large retailer.

After operating from the village farm for almost two years, Eric moved back to Nairobi. He leased a piece of land and set up a processing unit with a new milling machine from a $9,000 loan. Using Alibaba, Chinese entrepreneur Jack Ma's e-commerce platform, Eric contacted sellers in China and was able to source the machines at a significant discount to local prices. The new milling machine enabled him to add two new products to his product line – Nurture Junior for babies and Nurture Family precooked porridge flour for adults. Why the additions? While the banana flour attracted export clients from the United States and Hungary, it had limited domestic appeal. Eric realised that with a fertility rate of 4.4 at the time, which was 76% higher than the global average, Kenya was experiencing a baby boom.[46] He had done a lot of online and social media research on consumer preferences and discovered that mothers would spend a significant portion of their incremental income on better nutrition for their children. He also learned that a significant percentage of a child's cognitive development occurs by age three, a process that is linked to nutrition. This inspired him to move into the baby category where he sought to produce highly nutritious, affordable, baby porridge that is both convenient to prepare and familiar to the local taste.

Still on the lookout for more financing opportunities, in 2012 he participated in three competitions for agro-processing businesses. One of these competitions was presented under the auspices of Kenya's Ministry of Industrialisation and its purpose was to promote innovative business ideas. That competition was keenly contested, involving over 3,000 young contestants with start-ups. Eric emerged the overall winner. Once again, he invested the financial proceeds into Stawi. Eric raised a total of about $25,000 from winning all three competitions and invested most of the funds in purchasing new machines.

In Stawi's new production facility, the company produces 50 tons of flour a month if it runs 8-hour shift days. As Stawi increases its working hours to a 24/7 shift, this will increase the factory's output to at least 150 tons. The capacity of the milling machine was greater than Stawi's monthly sales at the time of purchase, but Eric strategically made the investment anyway in anticipation of future growth. In addition, he also bought a mixer which has the capacity to mix 50 tons of flour a month.

Due to Stawi's limited financial strength and unique production cycles, Eric had to adopt an efficient and frugal approach to human resources. He kept a lean staff and varied the employment arrangements with each of them. In addition to his work as CEO, he also served as the marketing manager assisted by two salespeople. He hired a sales team of independent contractors to reduce his labour costs. Eric also outsourced administrative functions such as accounting, auditing and legal services. This approach enabled him to maintain a lean model and control costs early on. Most of his employees are young women from the community. When Eric was looking for a sales force management system, he received proposals in the thousands of dollars. Since he couldn't afford an expensive IT system, Eric uses WhatsApp to create various internal groups and teams for communication. For example, to track the movement of sales and marketing agents and ensure that they are working productively, Eric can ask them for their WhatsApp locations in real time.

So, what makes Stawi products different? 'I'm trying to bring in innovation, but I can't really say I'm there yet. But we're trying to look for ways we can innovate, even if it's in terms of the distribution of our strategic and unique products that we're offering: the pricing, the packaging and the target market.' Eric has sought to differentiate his products in three ways based on online surveys and customer feedback on Facebook. The first is regarding the nutritional content of the products. He focuses on making his flours healthy by fortifying them with vitamins and minerals, and making them free of fat, soya, and gluten. The iron and folic acid content makes the flour valuable for expectant mothers. Vitamin A and iron also increase erythropoietin and haemoglobin concentrations in children, which have been found to be neuroprotective. These additives help children grow and develop. He has researched so much on child nutrition that he jokes that he has a diploma in paediatrics.

Beyond the nutritional value, the second factor that sets Stawi apart is the uniqueness of its packaging. Knowing the overriding effect of design and presentation, Eric made significant investments in this feature of his product. Stawi flours come in a pouch with a re-sealable zip lock so that after pouring out the required quantity, the consumer can close the zip lock, thereby maintaining the freshness of the product. Eric did a lot of online research on packaging and sourced designs from all over the world including the UAE and China.

The third differentiating factor for Eric is affordability. One of Stawi's main competitors is Nestlé, but where Nestlé's baby food product Cerelac costs 600 shillings ($6), Stawi's product retails for

100 shillings ($1). Nestlé has had a controversial history of selling its products in Africa. In 2018, the company was accused of 'violating ethical marketing codes and manipulating customers with misleading nutritional claims about its baby milk formulas.' It was cited for using sucrose in infant milk formulas in South Africa while marketing its Hong Kong formulas as being sucrose-free 'for baby's good health.'[47]

Like many Kenyans, Eric leverages mobile money, M-Pesa, to receive payments from small customers and to make payments to suppliers of transportation and factory consumables. Launched in 2007 by Safaricom, the country's largest mobile-network operator, M-Pesa is now used by over 17 million Kenyans and over 25% of the country's GDP flows through it. It is the most successful mobile money scheme in the world.[48] Eric explained that 'M-Pesa allows us to send and receive money to our suppliers and customers and enjoy the convenience of never having to visit in person.' In a city like Nairobi with notorious traffic, that is a game changer and a boost to productivity.

Eric believes the vision for Stawi is still in motion and continues to expand. He is unapologetic about his goal to displace Nestlé from the continent and to build the most innovative healthy food company in Africa. He has been recognised for his efforts in Kenya and abroad. The government, through the Ministry of Industrialisation, gave him the JITIHADA award.[49] Forbes Africa also listed him in the Forbes Africa Top 30 entrepreneurs.[50] CNN has also featured him as one of the young African entrepreneurs with promise.[51] These awards and accolades inspire him to reach greater heights. However, after climbing the stage to receive recognition for attaining these milestones, when he walks back to his factory, some challenges continually stare him in the face. Obtaining financing to grow the business is still a huge hurdle, for instance. Eric bemoaned the high interest rates charged by banks and the lack of interest from traditional venture capital funds for small-scale businesses like

Stawi. Microfinance focuses on small businesses looking to raise a few hundred dollars, and larger impact investors typically focus on businesses with larger revenues. This leaves small growing businesses like Stawi with no real institutional funding response to the needs of this "missing middle."

Stawi is not yet where Eric aspires it to be. Stawi, derived from the Kiswahili word "ustawi" which means prosperity or success, is still on its way in its bid to create prosperity for the farmers, shareholders, employees, and suppliers. So far, Stawi has impacted over 150 farmers who have increased their incomes by about 30%. 'The big picture is to see us distributing across the country so that if you're in Nairobi, Mombasa or Kisumu, you'll find our products. Eventually, we can export into the East African region and have trade agreements with nations. In terms of finances, [our goal is to surpass] $1 million in turnover. Because I see the potential is there, even by serving the local market... I'd like us to have moved to an industrial area where we'll be doing our own production because I see Stawi like a small Nestlé and we are headed there. I ask myself why should we import things that you can make here? The food that Nestlé is making, such as Cerelac, can all be manufactured here in Kenya, and it would provide income for our farmers. I would like to see a situation where we can create a cereal company from Kenya that can spread across the continent as is happening with companies such as Equity Bank and Safaricom, that have really done well in Kenya. We are looking at a point where we may get investors on board, just to grow the company and then eventually get listed on the stock exchange.'

Eric believes digital tools create unique opportunities for aspiring entrepreneurs in Africa today: 'For one, I would tell [aspiring entrepreneurs] to try and start wherever they are without saying that they lack the capital or networks to do their business. Those are things that come as one moves along, but you need to get started, even if it's in a very small or micro way. Use the internet to brainstorm the idea, do a bit of planning and then just launch. See what works, if it doesn't work, try to improve on it. I think it's very important for entrepreneurs in Africa or in Kenya to recognise that they are in a unique moment in history because of the internet. Everything I've done at Stawi, from research to marketing to funding has been enabled by the internet. If you have access to the internet, you have no excuse.'

At the end of the interview, Eric gave me some free samples of Stawi porridge, slipped on his white coat with the Stawi logo etched on the pocket and stepped back into the factory, monitoring the milling, and mixing of sorghum and wheat and other cereals, while scanning his Android smartphone, managing his sales team via WhatsApp, and monitoring his marketing campaign on Facebook and Twitter.

I followed his progress, and the following year, I invested in Stawi and joined its board. In the three years following the interview, the company on average doubled revenues every single year, reaching 30 million shillings ($300,000). To take advantage of local government incentives, Eric is planning to relocate the manufacturing plant to Meru, where he intends to build a larger factory at a cost of $1 million. Pursuant to his Pan-African vision, Eric has also set up Stawi joint venture entities with fellow young entrepreneurs Adom Jude Arthur in Ghana and PJ Okocha in Nigeria, with plans to expand to West Africa.

2

PATRICIA NZOLANTIMA

BUILDS AN ADVERTISING GIANT

WITH OVER 80 MILLION PEOPLE, THE DEMOCRATIC REPUBLIC of Congo (DRC) or Congo-Kinshasa as it is sometimes called, to distinguish it from its neighbour Congo-Brazzaville, is one of the most populous countries on the continent.[52] Formerly known as Zaire, many people remember DRC for its devastating wars in the 1990s, which resulted in the deaths of over 5 million people.[53] Congo is a damning indictment on colonial and neo-colonial savagery. At the infamous Berlin conference of 1884, the European colonial powers divided Africa among themselves, and allocated the Congo Basin region (modern-day DRC) to King Leopold II, the King of Belgium, as his private property. This became known as Congo Free State. King Leopold's rule over Congo Free State was marked with so much brutality and barbarism that even his fellow racist European colonialists had to oppose him. Congo Free State had forced labour camps, with private militias severing off the hands of Congolese forced laborers who didn't meet their quota for the rubber plantations. The historian Adam Hochschild estimates that over 10 million Congolese lost their lives during this period. To put this number in perspective, the number of Congalese lives estimated to have been lost under King Leopold is more than double the lives lost during the transatlantic slave trade, and is on par with the Holocaust.[54] While there has been a lot of debate among historians over whether the atrocities in the Congo Free State technically qualify as genocide, there is no question, as Hochschild notes, that it was 'one of the most appalling slaughters known to have been brought about by human agency.'[55]

In 1908, in response to Leopold's atrocities, the Belgian state annexed Congo. In 1960, DRC won its independence from Belgium with Patrice Lumumba as Prime Minister and Joseph Kasavubu as President. Lumumba was brutally murdered in 1961 with Belgian and American complicity. In 1965, Army chief Joseph Mobutu seized power in a coup d'état and renamed the country Zaire and himself as Mobutu Sese Seko.[56]

The DRC is still recovering from the conflicts of the 1990s which created a prolonged economic and social depression. After the 1994 Rwandan genocide, more than 2 million Hutus sought refuge in eastern Congo. In 1996, armed forces from Rwanda and Uganda invaded the eastern DRC with the purported intention to eliminate the threat from perpetrators of the genocide. They were supported by Congolese opposition leader Laurent Kabila and his rebel army. Eventually, they defeated dictator Mobutu. Kabila became president in May 1997 and expelled Rwandan and Ugandan armed forces. Kabila was supported militarily by Angola and Zimbabwe, sparking what has been referred to as Africa's World War, involving six African countries and resulting in the loss of an estimated 2.5 million lives.[57]

The economy has had a bit of a rollercoaster experience: 'After sharply increasing to almost 9% in the 2013-2014 period, the GDP growth rate (excluding inflation) decelerated to 6.9% in 2015, then to 2.4% in 2016, its lowest point since 2001. This slump [was] mainly due to declining prices and a shrinking global demand for raw materials such as copper and cobalt exported by the country, which account for 80% of its export revenue. This economic shock led to a deterioration in external accounts and a downturn in the country's exchange rate in 2016, as well as a 31% drop in the exchange rate of the Congolese franc against the dollar, which fuelled runaway inflation of almost 24%.'[58] In 2018, real GDP growth was an estimated 4.0%, up from 3.7% in 2017 driven by stronger commodity prices and an increase in foreign reserves. In 2018, the central bank lowered its key interest rate from 20% to 14% in response to the improved economy. Inflation fell to 27.7% in 2018 from 41.5% in 2017. GDP growth is projected to reach 4.5% in 2019 and 4.6% in 2020.[59] Even though the country has made progress in reducing its poverty rate from 71% to 64% between 2005 and 2012, the DRC still ranks among the poorest countries in the world, ranked 176th out of 189 countries on the 2018 Human Development Index calculated by the UN.[60]

Congo's poverty stands in cruel contrast to its immense riches. Arguably one of the richest countries in the world in terms of natural resources, DRC has 70% of the world's supply of coltan, a third of its cobalt, more than 30% of the global supply of diamonds and 10% of global copper reserves. DRC is estimated to have over $24 trillion of untapped reserves.[61] That's almost 8 times the GDP of the entire African continent!

Congo is also world-famous for its music. Congolese soukous, which blends ethnic musicology with rumba and merengue, has spread all over the continent. The late Papa Wemba, the legendary sapeur, has become a household name across Africa and around the world. I've been fascinated by Papa Wemba and the sapeurs, groups of young men dressed in expensive flashy clothes: colourful bowties, suspenders, matching socks and shiny shoes. I made sure I packed my most colourful clothes on my way to Kinshasa, with a green bowtie and matching socks. On my first night out, I ran into some sapeurs and was thrilled when they complimented my outfit.

Kinshasa itself is a force of a city, Africa's third largest after Cairo
and Lagos, and home to an estimated 11 million people. Situated
on the Congo River, across from Brazzaville, the city is a resilient
tower, filled with incredible energy, powered by passionate young
people looking to leapfrog into the future.

On the second day, I asked a friend in Kinshasa, 'If there's one
person in Congo I must see who, should it be?' She replied, 'The
same person that Hillary Clinton and Joe Biden came to see here –
Patricia Nzolantima!' I was intrigued and couldn't wait to meet the
woman that American leaders ensure they meet whenever they visit
DRC. I called her up and she invited me to visit her home for lunch
and then a tour of her office. Her story was fascinating.

Patricia is the first entrepreneur I met who founded her business
based on divine inspiration. On 19th May 2007, Patricia claims that
God appeared to her in a dream and told her, 'Go into marketing
and I'll elevate you.' She said she obeyed and launched CommunicArt
Agency, a marketing communications company. Through faith and
hard work, CommunicArt grew to become a leader in the marketing
communications industry in Congo. Two years later, they merged
with South African advertising agency EXP to become EXP-
Comunicart, one of the leading marketing communication agencies
in Africa, working with major consumer brands such as Nestlé.

Patricia's family and clan are full of entrepreneurs. She is a
Mukongo, part of the Kongo (or Bakongo) people, a Bantu ethnic
group in Central Africa, numbering over 10 million people.[62] They
were among the first to protest slavery in letters to the King of
Portugal in the early 1500s. According to Patricia, most of the
big-name entrepreneurs and businesspeople in Congo hail from
the Kongos. She believes they are uniquely filled with a spirit of
entrepreneurialism. The first people to build a bank and a tower in
Congo are allegedly all Kongos. She told me a fable that explains the
origins of the entrepreneurial spirit of the Kongo people.

'There is a fable about our ancestor who was about to die and so he called all his children together. He told them that he had hidden a treasure on his farmland, so they should dig the land for it after he dies... He died, and his five children began the search for the treasure. To find their father's legacy, they had to dig the land. They dug all over the farmland but didn't find it. As they ploughed the land, they ended up cultivating crops on it and realised that they can generate a greater income through farming than any treasure can give.' In effect, the man had pushed his children to be hard workers. So, among the Kongos, farmland is valued and well utilised. They even have a popular saying, 'Never sell your land because if you use it well, the land will help you get all the other things you want.' Throughout my travels on the continent, I discovered that stories and stereotypes abound about different ethnic groups famed for their entrepreneurial skills. For example, in Ghana the Kwahus are famous for being talented traders and in Nigeria, the Igbos are hailed for their business acumen.

Patricia was born when her father was a 20-year-old university student, so she spent most of her formative years with her grandparents. She considers her grandfather one of the most influential people in her life because he introduced her to entrepreneurship and Christianity. Her grandfather was a staunch Christian; Patricia says her great-grandfather was the first Christian to translate the Bible into their mother language, Bakongo. Learning from their grandfather, four in five members of her clan are all entrepreneurs (it is important to note, however, that the Kongo people are a matrilineal society).

Patricia, like many of the entrepreneurs I met, started her entrepreneurial journey very early. Growing up, one of her pastimes was cooking, especially for her family. A family friend invited her to help prepare pancake, cakes and other pastries for an event. After seeing how good she was at cooking, the woman encouraged her to consider going into partnership to prepare and sell pancakes. Being an independent minded young woman who did not like to rely on other people for her sustenance, she saw it as a money-making opportunity and so jumped at the chance. Soon, she had a thriving business. Her grandfather had taught her to always save part of her income for the future, so, Patricia saved all her profits from her business activities in a piggy bank under her bed. She hoped to save enough to start a bigger business and her savings reached $600. One day, one of her aunties was facing severe financial troubles, and Patricia was able to loan her auntie $350.

Patricia studied public international law at the Protestant University of Congo but decided she did not want to be a lawyer and instead, pursued marketing. After graduation, she worked for two years as an assistant at a small marketing firm in Kinshasa. Then in 2002, international marketing communications agency, McCann Erickson opened an office in DRC and she joined their team as a Client Service Manager. After three years, she moved to South African marketing agency giant, EXP. She was with EXP for two years as a Business Unit Manager shuttling between Senegal and South Africa before returning home to Congo. It was on her return that she had the dream in which she says God spoke to her to start her own marketing communications agency. Her former employers, EXP, were not interested in having an office in Congo because the country was going through political unrest at the time.

In 2007, Patricia started CommunicArt Agency using her room as her first office. Starting a business anywhere in the world requires a leap of faith and a lot of hard work, but particularly so in DRC, a country ranked as 182 out of 190 countries in the World Bank's 2018 Doing Business Report – among the 10 worst countries to do business in the world.[63] With no real office and furniture, Patricia decided to go big or go home, and bid for a marketing contract from Nestlé valued at $120,000 that would require wall advertising in the open markets of Kinshasa, as well as sampling of their products. This contract would be significant, both from a financial perspective and from the stamp of credibility that an affiliation with Nestlé would confer on her start-up. Patricia had sleepless nights over her bid because she was scared that she would not be taken seriously. The Nestlé boss, based in Nairobi, was coming to visit Congo and she was scheduled to meet with him and his team. Her biggest headache was how she would explain her ability to execute a contract of that size without having a real office.

When she picked up the Nestlé team from the airport in the afternoon, they decided that their first stop must be an open market where she was proposing to organise marketing activations for Nestlé. Patricia had innovative ideas for marketing Nestlé's products by having consumers sample and experience the products in the markets. The Nestlé team loved her ideas. Patricia thought they would proceed to her office from the market, but they decided to go to their hotel for dinner instead. As she accompanied them, they discussed the details of the project and asked her for a budget to start the activation. The meeting they were supposed to have in her office was then shifted to the following morning. That night was a long one for her as she tossed and turned in bed, wondering whether her "home office" would cause them to cancel the contract. She prayed to God that night to help her out of her predicament.

Morning came, and the meeting did not happen as planned. The Nestlé team had decided to return early in the morning to Nairobi to attend to urgent business but signed the contract and wrote a cheque as an advance payment for Patricia to start the project. Her greatest fear had been eliminated. Patricia insists that, 'When God gives you the vision, He will also give you the provision.' Later, she was able to leverage her relationship with Nestlé and signed on P&G, Unilever and other major brands as clients. CommunicArt differentiated itself by focusing on bringing brands to life through live experiences. They specialised on developing events where consumers could personally experience the brand because they believed that the most powerful advertising is word-of-mouth.

Two years later, EXP, her former employer, expressed an interest in opening an office in Congo and decided to partner with her to create EXP-Communicart Agency. Over time, EXP-Communicart has grown to become one of the biggest marketing agencies in Congo. They have pioneered innovations in marketing activations in Congo. Today, they employ about 40 full-time staff, have more than 100 commission-based sales people in the field and operate two offices in Congo.

In 2012, Patricia was selected as one of 62 young African leaders who participated in President Obama's Young African Leaders Initiative. It was a three-week professional development program hosted by the U.S. government, made up of a summit with high level speakers from the public and private sector. Each participant was also attached to an organisation to be mentored.[64] Patricia was attached to a marketing firm, Wealth Branding, and it offered her a great networking and learning opportunity.

Patricia had broader business and social interests and created a holding company called Bizzoly Holdings to control her stake in EXP-Communicart, as well as develop new businesses focused on empowering women. She launched the publication of a lifestyle and educational magazine called *International Working Lady Magazine.* The magazine's focus is to showcase African women who are excelling in combining family life and professional success and to empower women to not leave the workforce. It also seeks to catalogue "ordinary women accomplishing extraordinary things." Their initial publication was in French and the magazine is a bimonthly publication. An English version has now been added and they distribute 10,000 copies per publication.

With a communications agency and a magazine, you would think Patricia has her hands full. But the recent wave of technology and globalisation would inspire another business idea. One of Patricia's mentors advised her: 'Whenever you visit another country, ask yourself what is in this country that I don't have in my country'. So, when she visited the United States in 2012, she looked around for inspiration and came across Uber. Founded in 2009, Uber is a global taxi technology company and a pioneer in the sharing economy. It connects riders to drivers through a mobile phone app. Riders send an online request for a car, with GPS technology noting their pickup location, and a driver is sent to pick them up, with upfront pricing. Uber is found in 632 cities in 84 countries worldwide.[65] In 2018, Uber generated annual net revenues of almost $11 billion, and had raised over $20 billion, making it one of the most valuable start-ups in the world, at a valuation of $70 billion. In May 2019, Uber went public in an IPO on the New York Stock Exchange at a valuation of $82 billion.[66] Patricia decided to take the Uber ride sharing concept to Congo, but with a twist. As part of her life-long mission to empower women, she launched an Uber copy-cat called "Ubiz Cabs" that recruits women exclusively as the drivers of the cabs. Apart from economically empowering the female drivers, Ubiz Cabs is also a safer option for female passengers. There have been several reports of violence against women who use Uber, taxi cabs and other transportation.[67]

Patricia launched the company in January 2018, and already has a 50-car fleet working 24 hours a day, 7 days a week. Each car is decked out with Wi-Fi, phone chargers, a tablet, radio and water bottles. The business was generating $150,000 in monthly gross revenues as of October 2018. Ubiz Cabs has launched partnerships with international organisations and corporations such as the World Bank, U.N. Women, Kempinski Hotel and others. In modelling itself after Uber, the company added a food delivery business called UbizEats. Working with corporations on Ubiz Cabs, Patricia realised that there was a growing demand for private charter air travel, so she launched UbizJet as an online platform to facilitate jet-sharing.

Patricia believes in the power of the African woman entrepreneur. 'In Congo every [female] entrepreneur is surrounded by 99% of people who don't believe in them and only 1% who believe in them. As a result, [these female entrepreneurs] rarely get the financial support they need.' In partnership with UBA Bank, Patricia has launched a Working Ladies Prepaid Visa card, which is a rechargeable e-wallet that allows the consumers to participate in banking transactions without having a bank account. She has also set up a microcredit program known as the "Women of the Future" and has disbursed micro-loans to over 1,500 women. The program also focuses on capacity building for women entrepreneurs. In 2016, Patricia, under Bizzoly Holdings launched a Women's Economic Empowerment Hub in Kinshasa. The Hub is a building with 1,200 square metres of space with a training centre, a co-working space that can accommodate 100 women, a call centre, four meeting rooms, a radio station, a TV station, a restaurant, a business centre and a hair salon. The Hub even has a swimming pool and open spaces for events. As of 2019, Bizzoly Holdings and all its subsidiaries generate over $10 million in annual sales.

On my last day in Kinshasa, I was running late to the airport, so Patricia decided to come with me. When we got to the airport, her celebrity status helped me skip the lines and make my flight in time before the gate was closed. Patricia hugged me and said 'God bless you for your work. Come back soon my friend.'

3

YUSUF RANDERA-REES

INCUBATES MICRO-ENTREPRENEURS

OFFICIALLY THE SOUTHERNMOST COUNTRY IN AFRICA, SOUTH Africa has the second largest economy, after Nigeria, commanding a GDP of $300 billion, but more than double Nigeria's GDP per capita (South Africa has a GDP per capita of $5,275 compared to Nigeria's $2,176).[68] South Africa is the fifth most populous country in Africa, with a population of 57.7 million people as of 2018.[69] It is a pluralistic and multi-ethnic society, with its constitution recognising 11 official languages.

South Africa has made great strides in improving the lives of its citizens since its transition to democracy in 1994. Based on the international poverty line of $1.90 per day, poverty fell from 33.8% in 1996 to 18.8% by 2015.[70] Factors driving this included social safety nets, the expansion of credit, and growth in formal housing. A succession of governments led by the ANC have invested in programs to improve the lives of black South Africans and fight the inequality gap, including expanding electrification to townships, investments in housing, and allocation of government contracts for black entrepreneurs. These programs have had a real impact on the lives of people and have been significant drivers of job growth.[71]

However, South Africa is still plagued with staggering economic inequalities, and its inequality is racialised. Research by Stellenbosch University revealed that a tenth of South Africa's population, mostly white, controls more than 90% of the wealth. Roughly half the country lives in poverty (based on the national poverty level), with official unemployment at 27%, and rising to 67% among the youth in the townships.[72] South Africa's President, Cyril Ramaphosa, inherits a challenge to transform the South African economy, which has been experiencing anaemic growth in the last decade, into an engine of much needed jobs, and shared economic prosperity.

I met Yusuf Randera-Rees in Johannesburg. Joburg, or Jozi – easily one of Africa's most developed cities in terms of infrastructure, and an economic powerhouse home to the biggest and most liquid stock exchange on the continent – is also a pivotal space for art, music and urban renewal. Yusuf took me around Maboneng, located on the eastern part of Jozi's central business district. Maboneng's urban renewal reminded me of Williamsburg in Brooklyn, New York. Previously full of dilapidated and abandoned buildings, Maboneng is now a thriving ecosystem of newly designed apartments, galleries, shops, cafés, museums, art installations and offices. It features the famous Arts on Main, where you can sample freshly made South African food (using organic local produce) and buy artwork designed by local artists. Yusuf introduced me to Jonathan Liebmann, the CEO of Propertuity, and the man leading the team behind the revitalisation of Maboneng. From re-purposed containers, to graffiti art, to walls turned into blackboards with "Before I die, I want to….", inviting public discourse, Jonathan's team has turned this part of Jozi into a bastion of creative energy and optimism. However, like Williamsburg, Maboneng has attracted criticism for its promotion of gentrification. Some critics have accused Propertuity of 'making the area too expensive for the poor already living there' who are predominantly black South Africans and African immigrants. In

April 2019, Propertuity collapsed and liquidated all its properties in Maboneng.[73]

Yusuf was full of energy, with long hair, and an infectious smile. He grew up in a mixed-race family in Johannesburg. His father, Fazel Randera, is an Indian South African, and was the only Indian medical student in the Transvaal Province. He left South Africa at the age of seventeen as a political activist and lived in the United Kingdom in exile. He met his wife and Yusuf's mother, Helen Rees, a medical doctor and human rights activist, during his medical school training, and they lived in London for eighteen years. While in London, he was an active member of the South African exiled community in London. The rest of his family was still in South Africa, and he harboured a desire to return to his homeland. A news report on television one day compelled him to move. 'He saw in the news protests in Lenasia, an Indian township just before Soweto. The cops attacked one of the students who were protesting. One of the students was my cousin, who was probably about twelve at the time. My dad told my mum, "We have to go; we can't have my family there with all this happening to them and I just sit in London." My mum agreed.'

It was a tough decision to make. They were living comfortable lives in London. Though Yusuf's father had been a victim of racism in London, it paled in comparison to apartheid South Africa. In fact, the laws of South Africa at the time would not recognise their union. The Prohibition of Mixed Marriages Act and the Immorality Acts of South Africa banned interracial marriages and sexual relations. Despite these challenges, Yusuf's family left London in 1984 for South Africa to support his father's family and to contribute to the greater cause of equality and social justice.

Back in South Africa, his mother found a job in Alexandra clinic, which provided the only source of healthcare in a township of half a million people. His father's first job was in the township of Soweto, overseeing all the maternity wards. The move to South Africa was challenging for the family. 'When I got to my dad's family in Lenasia, I realised I was the only kid who looked like me... everyone else was Indian... I remember painful memories... I played soccer with a bunch of white kids and my dad was coming to pick me up, and the kids used a racist slur to describe him.'

Yusuf and his sister were lighter skinned in complexion compared to his brother. He observed how his brother would receive different treatment when they moved together, and how that was hurtful to him at a young age. 'There was a time when we moved into a working class all-white neighbourhood. This was around the time the racial barriers were falling. There was an all-white-only park across the road, and I went there with my brother. My brother had very dark skin so when the lady in charge saw him, she said I could go in, but my brother could not. I was probably about six and my brother was three or four. So, we went back home, and I told my mum, "There's no way we can go to that place".'

Yusuf's Catholic school was the first to respond to the fall in racial barriers by accepting students from all races. He related one of his experiences when Nelson Mandela visited the school: 'Madiba sent a lot of his grandkids there. One day, when I was in 7th grade, we were playing soccer during PE and suddenly, Madiba came on the field. He just dropped by and sat with us for like 40 minutes just talking to us; just like that.' Mandela, Yusuf's hero, was no stranger to his family. Yusuf's father had gained prominence for his medical work in Soweto and his contributions to the anti-apartheid movement. When Mandela was released from prison, he was appointed his personal doctor, and accompanied him on his travels. He later served as a Commissioner on South Africa's Truth and Reconciliation Commission.

Growing up, Yusuf had early exposure to computers and technology. He took computer classes in school, and had a computer at home, which he used mostly for playing games. As soon as South

Africa was plugged to the world wide web, he was also connected. When he reached college age, Yusuf wanted to attend university in the United States, and was particularly interested in Harvard and Yale. His mother wanted him to go to Oxford instead and was worried that her son would get trapped in the American culture, lose his sense of identity and not return home. Despite her opposition, Yusuf ended up applying on the last day applications were being accepted and received offers from both Yale and Harvard. He decided to attend Harvard.

At Harvard, he was initially overwhelmed with a feeling of inferiority. However, after adjusting to life at the Ivy League, he realised that some of the people he grew up with in South Africa were just as intelligent and talented as some of his classmates at Harvard. At Harvard, he focused more on experiential learning by joining several extra-curricular activities. He was part of the team that organised the Unite Against AIDS Summit with then Harvard classmate, and now Harvard professor, Brandon M. Terry. The duo were able to recruit leading anti-apartheid activist and Nobel Peace Prize laureate Desmond Tutu as Chair of the Summit, much to the surprise of their other colleagues on the organising team. This event was his first involvement in a project with a social impact on the global stage. When I attended Harvard, long after Yusuf and Brandon had graduated, the event was still widely known on campus as one of the most impactful events organised by a Harvard undergraduate.

Yusuf graduated with an Honours degree in Economics in 2005. In his final year at Harvard, he applied for the prestigious Rhodes Scholarship at Oxford University, hoping to join his friend Brandon Terry who was headed to Oxford to study Political Theory. Unfortunately, he did not get the scholarship, but secured a job with investment banking house Credit Suisse, and worked in Alternative Investments in New York and later Zurich as an analyst. While at Credit Suisse, Yusuf would come to work early and work diligently and efficiently to complete all his daily tasks by 2pm so he would have free time to pursue his various other interests. Those interests blossomed into two non-profit organisations: one that partnered with UNAIDS, and another that received support from the International Finance Corporation.

Then, Yusuf came up with a brilliant idea to create a network of young leaders who are interested in using business to catalyse social change in African countries. Together with a friend, they tried, unsuccessfully, to raise a $50 million investment fund to invest in Black Economic Empowerment (BEE) transactions, the racially selective affirmative action program launched by the South African government to redress the inequalities of apartheid. They, however, secured meetings with some of the leading investors in the world like Eric Mindich of Eton Park, and Jack Myers of Harvard Management Company, which runs Harvard's $39 billion-dollar endowment.

Yusuf was still interested in attending Oxford University, so he applied again for the Rhodes Scholarship and succeeded on his second attempt at convincing the panel and was finally accepted as a Rhodes Scholar. It was during his time at Oxford that Yusuf developed the blueprint for Awethu and met his future partner in the project. While trying to start different business ventures, Yusuf and two former Harvard classmates, Kwame Osseo-Asare and Christopher Hill, travelled to Ghana and Nigeria looking for opportunities. The experiences from those travels drilled a realisation: 'There's no money problem, or opportunity problem in Africa, only a people problem. And if you can solve the people issue, that's how you solve most of the problems on the continent.' Yusuf recalls once they were standing at a corner in Lagos, looked around and listed twenty different ways they could make money in Lagos.

Yusuf believes that there is untapped talent across the African continent that is under-developed and under-utilised. The challenge he sees is the commitment to identify it, develop it to the maximum and release it to seize opportunities and solve problems. This insight about the untapped talent of Africans, coupled with his passion for creating a more equitable and more just South Africa, led to the birth of Awethu. As a student at Oxford, with his co-founder Ryan Pakter, start-up capital of R60,000 (equivalent of $600 at the time), and the backing of his mentor, Archbishop Desmond Tutu, Awethu was born.

Awethu, which means "people" in Zulu, is a business incubator that works with micro-businesses in South Africa, supporting entrepreneurs, mostly from the very poorest townships. They have a rigorous application procedure for entrepreneurs. A flair for entrepreneurship is a fundamental requirement demonstrated in possessing qualities such as solution orientation, perseverance, ambition and a learning attitude. Selected applicants go through a series of cognitive and psychometric tests. The results of the tests for one of the applicants validated Yusuf's belief in the opportunity hidden in untapped talent on the continent. Nketsi was a cab driver operating in a slum in Johannesburg when he applied to join the program. The results of his cognitive test revealed that he was in the top 1% of cognitive ability globally. Yusuf was therefore not surprised that four months after they trained him and gave him start-up capital to start an online IT retail company, he had already booked revenue in excess of $15,000, and employed two additional staff members.

The program is designed to benefit all applicants, even those who don't pass. For example, applicants who fail certain sections of the tests are eligible for training and learning programs. Applicants who pass are moved to the next stage where they receive basic entrepreneurship training. After the training, they are required to raise a minimum of $10 in 1 week to start a business. Yusuf highlighted a success story of a woman from a township who raised $35 and was able to start a business selling handbags imported from China. By reinvesting her proceeds into buying more inventory, she was eventually able to generate annual profits of over $1,500.

The most successful candidates are supported with additional start-up capital, a stipend, office space, coaching and mentorship, technology and administrative support. They also have an added opportunity to pursue a course in advanced entrepreneurship training at Wits Business School. Awethu takes a 50% equity stake in these companies. By its fourth year, Awethu had proven that its program can successfully incubate poor, under-resourced South Africans with business acumen to build profitable businesses at scale.

Awethu won the Echoing Green Social Entrepreneurship Fellowship and attracted a lot of attention and publicity globally. Backed by Discovery Holdings, the South Africa Government Jobs Fund and the Small Enterprise Finance Agency, Awethu raised a $10 million fund to invest in micro-entrepreneurs in South Africa. Awethu invested $5,000 in each of 2,000 micro-entrepreneurs in South Africa. The fund has been successful in financial terms, generating annualised returns of 84%. It has also generated meaningful social impact, resulting in the micro-entrepreneurs tripling their earnings on average, and helping create thousands of jobs.

However, Yusuf realised that to achieve the scale needed to impact the millions of talented Africans in need of the services of his incubator, his model would have to change. He knew he would have to digitise his model. Yusuf took all the learning and experience from working with thousands of micro-entrepreneurs in South Africa and partnered with ABSA (formerly Barclays Africa) on a suite of mobile-based applications for aspiring entrepreneurs. The Awethu Project Launch Pad helps entrepreneurs start with their business ideas. The Awethu Project App provides tools and information to help with finances, marketing and running a business. Recognising the importance of networks, the Awethu Connect program facilitates e-networking with like-minded entrepreneurs. It was launched in June 2017 and already has over 25,000 users, reaching 13 times more users in less than a year than Awethu's in person program achieved in 8 years, demonstrating the power, reach and scale of digital. It won the MTN App Award.

Upon reflecting on Awethu's business model and impact, Yusuf recognised two key challenges and opportunities for impact. First, he saw that there was very little growth capital available for SMEs. The only available capital was bank loans, which often isn't appropriate and risks saddling the business with debt. Secondly, Yusuf was concerned about the racial inequalities in business: he wanted to invest in more businesses owned by black entrepreneurs who have the training and support to grow the business. Yusuf and his team asked the question: how do you provide $100,000 to SMEs as growth equity (instead of debt), but scale this a thousand times?

One of the key challenges for asset managers or funds that want to invest in SMEs at that level ($100,000) is getting the unit economics to make sense. Most funds charge a management fee of 2% of assets, and then earn a performance fee, which is typically 20% of any investment gains. So, a fund with $10 million in assets under management would charge its investors $200,000 a year in management fees and will earn 20% of any investment gains generated over the lifetime of the fund. If the fund grew to $20 million in assets, the fund manager could earn 20% of the investment gains of $10 million, which is $2 million. The challenge with investing in SMEs is that for a typical $10 million fund with 10 core investments, the team can focus on managing those investments, which are manageable in size. At $100,000 per investment, a $10 million fund would need to make 100 investments, which will be very difficult to manage because whether it's a $100,000 or $1 million investment, it still requires the same amount of work and diligence.

To solve this problem, Yusuf and his team have created an online portal that manages the entire process from sourcing deals to managing portfolio companies that allows for effective scale. In addition, they train black entrepreneurs and provide them with the support and capital to engage in entrepreneurship by acquiring existing businesses or assets. They have effectively created a micro-cap private equity fund focused on BEE transactions. They have raised $30 million for this fund and have invested in 24 companies already. The fund is already up 65% in its second year of operation and Yusuf has backed black entrepreneur-owners in 86% of all eligible companies in the fund's portfolio. Yusuf has figured out a sustainable, profitable way to invest in micro-entrepreneurs at scale through Awethu, and in doing so has disrupted the traditional private equity models.

4

CHINNY OGUNRO

DESIGNS AFRICA'S HEALTHCARE FUTURE

I INTERVIEWED OUR FINAL ASPIRING MOGUL, CHINNY OGUNRO in Lagos, Nigeria. I've always believed our progress as a continent will be driven by the success of our biggest economy and most populous country. With an estimated population of close to 200 million people, Nigeria is the seventh most populous country and has one of the largest populations of youth in the world.[74] It is the 21st largest economy globally with a GDP of $376 billion, down from its peak of $568 billion in 2014.[75] Goldman Sachs has added the country to its "Next Eleven" list of economies projected to become the biggest in the world.[76] Nigeria is also a leading centre of African art, culture, music and innovation. The country boasts cultural icons including Wole Soyinka, Chinua Achebe, Fela Kuti and Chimamanda Ngozi Adichie.

Nigeria is a complicated country with over 500 ethnic groups, with 40-45% Christian (mostly residing in the south), the other half Muslim (mostly residing in the north) and 5-10% who identify with indigenous religious practices.[77] Nigeria has made the news too many times due to its experience of terrorism at the hands of the Boko Haram group, which the Global Terrorism Index calls "the world's deadliest terror group."[78] Since the current insurgency started in 2009, the terrorist group has killed over 20,000 people and displaced 2.3 million people from their homes.[79]

Lagos, far removed from the Northeast where Boko Haram resides, is a bastion of unbridled entrepreneurial energy, pulsating with vigour. They say if you can make it in Las Gidi, you can make it anywhere.[80] In spite of the many challenges (lack of infrastructure, incessant power outages), Lagosians are optimistic and everyone, from the cab driver at the airport to the barber cutting your hair has a side hustle. Lagos is Africa's fastest growing city; the United Nations estimates that its population grows by 77 new inhabitants *every hour.*[81] In her TED talk, my friend, OluTimehin Adegbeye, sums up Lagos: 'Like any major city, [Lagos] is a lot of things, many of which are highly contradictory. Our public transportation doesn't quite work, so we have these privately owned bright yellow buses that regularly cause accidents. Luxury car showrooms line badly maintained and often flooded roads. Street evangelism is only slightly less ubiquitous than street harassment. Sex workers sometimes have two degrees, a bank job, and a prominent role in church.'[82]

I love Lagos and have invested in many technology companies that operate there: Supermart (the largest grocery shopping e-commerce site), Andela (an education technology start-up), mPharma (a health tech company), Cars45 (Nigeria's largest online marketplace for selling cars), Tizeti (solar-powered wireless internet provider), Fibre. ng (online apartment rentals in Lagos), SOLO (a digital content and smartphone company) and Reliance HMO (a digital health insurance company).

There's one more thing you must know about Nigeria. Nigerian food is amazing. From pounded yam to egusi to pepper soup, Nigerian cuisine is an eclectic basket of mouth-watering spicy dishes. Yemisi Aribisala penned a whole book, *Longthroat Memoirs: Sex, Soups and Nigerian Taste Buds,* dedicated to the poetics, erotics and delicious intricacies of Nigerian cuisine. There is however one exception: Nigerian jollof. Admittedly, I am Ghanaian, and Ghana and Nigeria have been engaged in a heated debate on social media as to which country's jollof is superior, but that doesn't bias me at all. Nigerian jollof – according to legend – was an epic failure of one Nigerian chef several hundreds of years ago who was attempting to make Ghanaian jollof. In short, visit Nigeria, but, by all costs, avoid the jollof!

Chinenyenwa Ogunro ('Chinny') was born in a town called Obosi in Anambra State, Nigeria. She grew up speaking Igbo before she learned how to speak English. She jokes that everyone in her lineage comes from Obosi. 'My mother is literally from one side of the village, and my father is from the other side.' Her family lived in Obosi until she was eight years old. 'In Nigeria, life was good... we lived relatively comfortably... my grandparents had their house, my parents had their house, my dad worked in banking and my mum was a paediatrician.' Chinny's parents left Nigeria in 1992 amidst military rule to seek a better life for their family in the United States.

Between 1980 and 2010, the World Bank estimates that African migrants in the world doubled to reach 30.6 million.[83] This brain drain has been particularly acute among health professionals. Between 2005 and 2015, the outflow of African-educated doctors to the US increased by over 27%.[84] There are an estimated 8,000 Nigerian doctors in the United States and only 35,000 doctors in Nigeria, putting its doctor-to-population ratio at 0.3 per 1,000.[85]

Nigerians as a migrant group have been successful in the United States. A 2018 report showed that Nigerians are the most educated ethnic group in the United States. 37% of all Nigerians in America hold bachelor's degrees, 17% have master's degrees and 4% have a doctorate degree. To put these numbers in perspective, 19% of the white population in the U.S. have bachelor's degrees, 8% have master's degrees and 1% have doctorates.[86]

Chinny's family moved to Silver Spring, Maryland, where many Nigerians lived. She recalls humble beginnings in the US when she and her siblings (two older sisters and a younger brother) had to sleep on mattresses on the floor in their modest one-bedroom apartment. Her mother worked as a security guard while taking her board exams to qualify as a doctor in the United States.

Once her mother qualified and could work as a doctor, life changed for them. They moved to New Jersey and then to Long Island, where the family got a nice house in Dix Hills, an area the New York Times describes as having 'large lots and good schools.'[87] Moving to Dix Hills was the first time Chinny noticed her blackness. 'It was the first time I really understood that being black was different... and not really a good difference.' Her schoolteachers would oppose the selection of honours classes for her and her siblings even though they were academically gifted, and her mother would often have to intervene. Chinny was also involved in a lot of athletics in school. Back in middle school, she discovered that she was faster than anyone else in gym class and became a runner. Being an athlete became a defining part of her identity and her experience. It taught her discipline and hard work.

Chinny's parents were liberal and progressive but emphasised academics in their household. Following her two older siblings – one a surgeon, the other an oncologist, Chinny also pursued the track of academic excellence and student leadership. Chinny remembers when some of her classmates in high school would make statements suggesting the bar was lower for her because she is black. She was baffled. 'I had one of the highest scores in the country... how is that a lower bar?'

With near flawless grades, Chinny gained admission into her dream school – Stanford University. At Stanford, she participated in track and field and immersed herself in her academics. She won a scholarship for athletics in her junior year, which she grew to resent, because she had to 'earn her keep' by pushing the limits on her athletic performance. Chinny entered Stanford as a pre-med student majoring in Human Biology, but she changed mid-way to International Relations and Economics with a triple minor in Human Biology, Communications and Japanese. She studied Japanese because of her passion for anime.

At Stanford, her love and desire for healthcare developed fully. Every woman in her lineage is a medical professional, from her mother and most of her aunts, to her sisters. However, Chinny realised that she wasn't passionate about *practicing* medicine; she was more interested in healthcare policy and the *business* of medicine. She had a mentor who had a PhD in mathematics and business at Stanford who kept encouraging her to get a PhD in mathematics. He kept telling her 'Get a PhD in mathematics and you can make millions of dollars at a hedge fund.' 'But I really care about healthcare,' she'd retort. He responded, 'Don't worry about healthcare, make millions at the hedge fund and then you can invest in all the healthcare you want, but first get a PhD in math.'

Chinny didn't care about working on Wall Street so they compromised on a PhD in business focused on healthcare and in 2009 she started Harvard Business School's PhD program in operations and technology management and strategy, combining two units of the business school and focusing her research on healthcare operations in developing countries. After excelling academically all her life and doing well at Stanford and Cornell where she did her master's degree in healthcare management, Chinny expected the PhD program to proceed similarly. She confessed that she struggled with the intensity and academic rigour of the program. She also felt particularised at times, being the only black person in the program. 'Imposter syndrome is real.'

Chinny and I overlapped at Harvard. I was a senior at the College at the time, and her boyfriend, now husband, Kayode Ogunro, was in his second year of the MBA program at HBS. Chinny faced a lot of pushback when she dated and eventually married Kayode, who is Nigerian but of a different ethnicity; he is Yoruba. Though her parents and family were very supportive, she was chastised and shamed by some fellow Igbos for marrying outside the ethnic group. 'It should not matter that you're Igbo, or Hausa or Yoruba. We are all Nigerians.'

Chinny acknowledged that among her fellow Igbos there has always been a very strong sense of ethnic allegiance, which she didn't understand fully at first. When she was in 5th grade, she wrote a paper on the Biafra war that shocked her. Biafra was Nigeria's civil war that lasted from 1967 to 1970. The fatalities from Biafra have been hotly contested with estimates ranging from 500,000 to north of 6 million.[88] Writing the paper was the first time Chinny had even heard about Biafra. Growing up, she said her parents never talked about the war and its aftermath. She later found out that her uncle had been a general in the army and fought in the war. She recalled that he had severe mental illness and attributed it to post traumatic stress disorder, likely stemming from his experience during the war. Chinny grew up identifying as Igbo first, often introducing herself as 'I'm an Igbo from Obosi.' However, her experiences in America morphed her identity to 'I'm Nigerian in America' and finally to 'I'm African.'

At HBS, Chinny's PhD dissertation was titled *Network Administrative Organisations: Improving the Performance of Health Care Networks in a Developing Country Context*. As part of her research on hospital networks, Chinny spent almost a year studying healthcare operations in India and this shaped her views on solving healthcare challenges in Nigeria. 'My own personal theory of change and entrepreneurial outlook was formed through the work I did in India, at the hospitals there, standing through a couple of hundred surgeries and looking at every nook and cranny of different hospitals.'

For Chinny, India felt familiar. 'I thought to myself, this place looks like Nigeria except the people are different.' From urban traffic to overcrowding to signs of gaping inequality, Bangalore and Mumbai could easily have been Lagos. Chinny spent time immersed in the operations of Narayana Health, a network of hospitals spanning 23 hospitals, seven heart centres and 19 primary care facilities all over India with over 6,000 operational beds across the network. Narayana is focused on delivering high-quality, affordable healthcare services to the masses by leveraging economies of scale, skilled doctors and an efficient business model. For example, Chinny recalls a wheelchair that was like a plastic lounge chair with wheels. The staff told her 'We don't need more than that... the fancy American wheelchair costs $3,000. This plastic alternative cost less than 1% of that and functions just as well.' As Chinny was spending time in India, she was travelling to Nigeria and doing research on the healthcare system in Lagos, taking comparative notes and noticing many areas where Nigeria could borrow models from India.

Chinny took some time off her PhD to work in Nigeria. She spent two years working for Nigeria's Ministry of Health. That experience gave Chinny a deep dive into how healthcare works across Nigeria, government budgetary allocations for healthcare, donor financing and the challenges with public health in general. After her stint with the government, she worked for a Gates Foundation-funded non-profit that worked on a number of initiatives including supporting the Nigerian government agencies at both the federal and state level in their efforts to eliminate malaria and the mother-to-child transmission of HIV; working with healthcare facilities to generate credible data for evidence-based decision making and planning; and working with service providers to strengthen their operations and improve healthcare outcomes. Chinny recognised certain challenges with this approach. 'Donor partners are investing billions of dollars every year in African healthcare, but they are focusing on verticals e.g. TB or HIV, but the problem is that if you approach it from a vertical then you have hospitals that are great at only providing TB or maternal or HIV service, but if the patient has typhoid or some other condition that isn't funded in the vertical, then they are not prepared and they will likely receive sub-optimal care.'

It was clear to Chinny that a more comprehensive approach was needed. This led her to create Carepoint Healthcare, which aimed to build a network of hospitals starting in Nigeria focusing on a comprehensive approach to improve quality, build efficiencies and optimise at scale to provide high quality healthcare at an affordable price for Nigerians.

I started speaking to Chinny in-depth about her strategy for Carepoint in 2015 because of my own interest in healthcare. The more Chinny and I discussed our respective strategies and ideas for healthcare in West Africa, the more we realised we shared a similar vision and complementary experiences and skill sets. We decided to merge our efforts and create Africa Health Holdings (AHH) in 2017. AHH is an African healthcare company focused on delivering high quality healthcare at an affordable price for the African consumer. AHH's vision is simple: 'Building Africa's healthcare future.' At AHH, Chinny believes that Africa's healthcare future will be delivered by a technology-enabled network approach to healthcare facilities. The African continent has significant deficiencies in its healthcare system; it is home to 15% of global population yet produces 26% of global disease burden and only 3% of global healthcare workers. AHH has built a team of thirty technologists, healthcare operators and investment professionals across Lagos, Accra and New York. It has invested $10 million in healthcare in West Africa and currently owns and manages 24 healthcare facilities in Ghana and Nigeria, with plans to invest $100 million over the next seven years and scale to 300 facilities across the continent.

Chinny's approach is centred on three pillars: Mergers &

Acquisitions (M&A), an Operations strategy, and a Business Development approach. Capital constraints and lack of financing for development have resulted in many one-person run facilities that have limited ability to deliver high-quality care. In addition, many of the healthcare facilities are owned by doctors who are very old and looking to retire with no clear succession plan. The M&A process rests on proprietary relationships Chinny and her team have with hundreds of owners of healthcare facilities. They sell the vision of AHH to prospective sellers and buy a control stake (more than 50% of the shares) in the business or a wholesale acquisition (100% of the shares).

Often these facilities are mismanaged, with crumbling infrastructure, poorly trained staff, an absence of standard operating procedures or protocols, little to no technology, and limited capital for improvement. Chinny embarks on an extensive operations overhaul which includes the installation of an electronic medical record system, integration with mPharma (a cost-saving technology company that is featured in the Techies section), physical renovation of the infrastructure, HR auditing that involves the training of existing staff to meet high quality standards and hiring new members of the team, and a rigorous overhaul of operations from patient check-in to discharge, ensuring that every part of the process in any of AHH's facilities match global best standards. To prove this, AHH puts all its facilities under international accreditation review.

With a newly renovated, operationally improved facility, AHH's business development model is focused on affordable prices that a wider segment of the population can afford. Especially in Nigeria, Chinny is not just focused on the wealthy classes that can afford quality healthcare. She believes quality healthcare is a right that everyone deserves, and she strives to provide it at scale and still run her operations profitably by focusing on efficiencies (in line with what she observed in India). Chinny organises a lot of free screenings and health informational talks and other activities to sensitise the surrounding public about AHH's services. She also often prices services in line with or cheaper than AHH's competitors.

Chinny's pricing approach is based on her research. She estimates that over 90% of the Nigerian population cannot afford to spend more than 1,000 naira ($2.77) per day on healthcare. While there are future opportunities for insurance, currently only 7% of the total population is covered by insurance. The growth of health insurance will also provide a boost to future growth, but Chinny believes that will be captured by facilities which can provide the highest quality care at the most affordable price.

Chinny also focuses on leveraging relevant technologies to improve healthcare delivery. For example, in December 2018, AHH launched a telemedicine "eHealth" service. The eHealth service provides virtual video consultations with physicians, dermatologists, mental health counsellors and psychologists, neurologists, gynaecologists and paediatricians, who are available every day from 8am to midnight. Imagine you are at home with a four-year-old and your child becomes sick at 9pm. Instead of going through the inconvenience of trying to find out which hospital is open, you can virtually consult with one of eHealth's paediatricians. They will then send a lab technician on a motorcycle who will come to your house and take all the necessary bloodwork and tests. When the test results are available, you get an SMS informing you of the results and sharing the doctor's prescription. eHealth then sends a pharmacist on a motorcycle to deliver the drugs to you. All this from the convenience of your home (or office or wherever you may be).

For Chinny, moving back to Nigeria to build a healthcare business has been full of challenges. One of her biggest challenges has been power. 'I wish I was Dangote so that I could build my own power plant. Power is one of the biggest impediments to businesses in Nigeria. We have tried to leverage solar power to reduce costs and we are working with some energy partners to help us improve our energy efficiency, but it is difficult.' Nigeria currently has about 12,522 Mega Watts (MW) of electricity generating capacity, out of which only about 25% is available.[89] Compare this supply to Nigeria's estimated demand of 41,133 MW in 2018, forecasted to grow to 88,282 MW by 2020 and you will understand Chinny's concerns.

Another huge challenge for Chinny has been human capital. 'The one thing that India has that we struggle with is a large population of highly trained medical professionals and staff... We don't have that luxury here.' To work around the human capital challenges, Chinny took a page out of Harvard professor Atul Gawande's book *Checklist Manifesto*. Gawande's research has shown that well-designed check lists can improve outcomes, whether being used in surgeries or by airline pilots. Chinny applied this check list idea to all the operations of the hospital, down to how to register a patient. By breaking each task into a series of checklists, it became easier to minimise human errors and to guarantee some level of quality assurance. 'A lot of entrepreneurs worry about investing so much money training their staff and losing the investment if the staff leaves... For me, it's unthinkable: a poorly trained staff member in a hospital? That's a disaster waiting to happen.' Chinny recognises that the greatest bottleneck to AHH's scale is going to be the dearth of medical professionals. To mitigate against that risk, she's designing network optimisation strategies similar to those in Narayana to get the most out of senior medical professionals across multiple hospitals in the AHH network. And she's also looking at the diaspora. By the year 2000, over 65,000 African-born physicians and 70,000 African-born professional nurses were working overseas.[90] If she can convince a fraction of them to move back, part of the problem will be solved.

Chinny also highlighted another challenge she has faced doing business in Nigeria: gender discrimination. 'Whenever I travel with my husband, I am brushed off to the side and officials only want to engage with him and not me... sometimes in meetings in Lagos, I pretend like my [male] COO is the boss and counterparties will take him more seriously... there was even a fellowship I had applied for where it was an all-male panel and I was told point blank that even though on paper I may be the most qualified, it may not be the right time for a woman to win it... it's frustrating.'

Chinny's complaints are not unique. Throughout my travels and research for this book, many female entrepreneurs had similar stories. Several consistent themes emerged in interviews with female entrepreneurs about the barriers they face: social acceptability; family responsibilities; poor access to market information; old boy networks; limited access to technology; gaps between policy and its implementation; and access to finance, which remains one of the biggest challenges. When Mina Evans, a clothing entrepreneur with a growing and cash-flow-generating business needed expansion capital, the local banks would not lend to her until she produced land as collateral. Other lenders were charging 120% and more in annual interest rates.

Yet, when it comes to female entrepreneurship, African women are leading. Globally, 30% of women in the non-agriculture labour force are self-employed in the informal sector. In Africa, this figure is 63%. Sub-Saharan Africa has the highest rate of female entrepreneurship across the globe, with more women starting businesses in Africa than anywhere else in the world. 41% of women in Nigeria are entrepreneurs compared to 10% in the US and 5.7% in the UK. And women entrepreneurs outnumber men in Ghana, Nigeria and Zambia. Gender equality is not just a moral and social issue; it's also a critical economic issue. Research from McKinsey estimates that advancing women's equality could potentially add $12 trillion to the global economy. And it is reported that in emerging markets, women reinvest 90 cents of every additional dollar of income in their families' education, health and nutrition, compared to 40 cents for men. [91]

For Chinny, despite all the challenges, she is in Nigeria to stay. 'One of me is much more impactful here than one of me in America ever could be... I strongly and passionately believe that having a healthy population is the means through which you can position yourself to even benefit from something like a demographic dividend... My entire life is dedicated to making sure that everyone from Ghana to Nigeria to Rwanda to Kenya and all the countries in between have affordable, quality healthcare. I believe in Africa; I believe in African people and I believe in the betterment of black people across the world. I have dreams that if one country on the continent can become Wakanda, if we just have one African country that makes it, the state of black people all over the world will change.'

THE SOCIOPRENEURS

THE RECOVERY OF COMMODITY PRICES IN 2018 SPARKED renewed interest, excitement and optimism about African markets.[92] In 2018, Ghana and Nigeria were among the best performing stock markets globally.[93] Ghana was the fastest-growing economy in the world, growing at 8.3%, followed closely by Ethiopia at 8.2%.[94] Apart from the economic tide, political changes sweeping across the continent also heralded great optimism: the ousting of President Robert Mugabe, who had ruled Zimbabwe for 37 years, and the resignation of Prime Minister Hailemariam Desalegn of Ethiopia and his replacement by Abiy Ahmed.[95] However, political and economic excitement sometimes masks the grim realities on the ground: the persistent and widespread poverty, the dearth of infrastructure, the gaping and widening deficit in healthcare, the lack of clean water and adequate sanitation, the high levels of illiteracy and low quality of education, and many other poor development indicators.

According to a joint report by the World Bank and UNICEF, nearly half of all children in sub-Saharan Africa are living in extreme poverty (defined as surviving on less than $1.90 a day).[96] There is some progress to celebrate: the poverty rate in Africa fell from 56% in 1990 to 41% in 2015. However, because of population growth, *more people* are poor, with an estimated 413 million poor in 2015 compared to 280 million in 1990.[97] While there has been some advancement, especially in non-monetary dimensions of poverty, challenges remain. For example, adult literacy rates have increased by four percentage points, the literacy gender gap has reduced, and the prevalence of chronic malnutrition among under five-year-old children has reduced from 49% to 45%. Despite improvement in school enrolment numbers, the quality of education often leaves much to be desired, and over 40% of adults are still illiterate. Citizens in resource-rich countries have worse outcomes in human welfare indicators, suggesting that economic wealth does not always result in shared economic prosperity. The future, in this regard, looks less hopeful. Projections by the Bill & Melinda Gates Foundation suggest that by 2050, 90% of all the people in the world living in extreme poverty will be living in Africa; half of them living in Nigeria and the Democratic Republic of Congo alone.[98]

A 2013 IMF Working Paper acknowledged that economic growth rates do not necessarily result in social progress.[99] In examining the correlation between economic growth in sub-Saharan Africa and social indicators, researchers Martinez and Mlachila concluded that, 'For the most part there is little correlation between growth and social indicators in general… while in principle growth should increase the amount of available resources to undertake social progress, the success hinges on a complex interaction of a number of institutional and policy factors.'[100] Inequality also remains a stubborn challenge, with seven of the ten most unequal countries in the world in Africa, most of them in southern Africa. It must be noted that, excluding those countries and adjusting for GDP levels, inequality in Africa is comparable to the rest of the world.[101]

We have been shocked by the heart-breaking photos of many African youth losing their lives migrating to Europe. There are many reasons for the migration including but not limited to the search for greater economic opportunities, armed conflicts, natural disasters, persecution based on sexual identity, and a lack of opportunity in many of their home countries. Research from the International

Labour Organisation show that youth in Africa demonstrate a higher willingness to move permanently to another country than in other parts of the world: 38% in sub-Saharan Africa and 35% in Northern Africa (compared to 20% globally). In Sierra Leone, the percentage of youth willing to migrate is as high as 77%.[102] This is a tragedy and a missed opportunity because the youth are Africa's greatest asset. Africa's youth population is rapidly growing and is expected to reach over 830 million by 2050. Of Africa's nearly 420 million youth aged 15 – 35, only one in six is in wage employment, with two-thirds unemployed or vulnerably employed. Almost 12 million youth enter the labour force in Africa every year to meet only 3 million jobs.[103] Many young people on the continent see migrating to other countries as a means of improving their economic prospects. Such was the case for Francisca Awah Mbuli, a 2018 Obama Foundation Africa Leader and a survivor of sex trafficking, who grew up in Cameroon, graduated with honours from university, had gainful employment and yet could barely cover her expenses. The demand for low-cost labour in the global north (and the Middle East) and a growing transnational network of trafficking criminal organisations results in migrants like Francisca and others falling prey to these networks and being exploited for labour or sex. Francisca started an organisation called Survivors Network, staffed by survivors, to economically empower vulnerable young women and to fight human trafficking.

A lot of these social and economic challenges cannot easily be solved by market-based solutions, or products designed solely for profit maximisation. They require a different type of entrepreneur, what we now call a "social entrepreneur". In the *Stanford Social Innovation Review*, Martin Roger and Sally Osberg argue that the key difference between entrepreneurship and social entrepreneurship is that the entrepreneur focuses on profit, 'the social entrepreneur, however, neither anticipates nor organises to create substantial financial profit for his or her investors – philanthropic and government organisations for the most part – or for himself or herself. Instead, the social entrepreneur aims for value in the form of large-scale, transformational benefit that accrues either to a significant segment of society or to society at large.' This does not mean that these companies founded by social entrepreneurs cannot make money; many social enterprises are for-profit organisations. For example, Helvetic Solar, a company founded by a young Patrick Ngowi based in Tanzania, is focused on renewable energy and reducing dependency on fossil fuels, yet the business generates over $10 million in revenues and enjoys significant profit margins. Instead, 'What distinguishes social entrepreneurship is the primacy of social benefit, what Duke University professor Greg Dees in his seminal work on the field characterises as the pursuit of "mission-related impact".'[104]

In this section, we will meet four extraordinary social entrepreneurs who are focused on "mission-related impact" and are building organisations and ventures that are tackling a wide range of socio-economic issues from sanitation through education, to job creation and even governance.

5

DAVID SENGEH

INNOVATES FROM WAR

OUR FIRST SOCIAL ENTREPRENEUR COMES FROM SIERRA LEONE, a small, beautiful country in West Africa with a population of a little over six million people. The Portuguese explorer Pedro de Sintra named the country "Serra Lyoa" (Lion Mountains) for the impressive mountains he saw while sailing the west coast in the 15th century.[105] English sailors in the 16th century called it "Sierra Leoa" and the name evolved to "Sierra Leone" by the 17th century.[106] Sierra Leone has a special significance in the transatlantic slave trade as it was the departure point for thousands of West Africa captives. The capital Freetown was formed as a settlement for repatriated and freed slaves in 1787. After the British Parliament outlawed the slave trade in 1807, the British government took over the settlement in 1808, and repatriated over 50,000 liberated slaves who hailed from all over West Africa. These new settlers lacked any common language or culture, so the English government implemented a "unification" policy of creating an English-speaking Anglican community. Eventually, the country fought for, and gained independence from the British in 1961.[107]

Sierra Leone has a youthful and growing population of over 6 million people with 20 ethnic groups. The Temne and the Mende people are the largest ethnic groups, comprising almost 70% of the population. Sierra Leone is also a multi-religious society, with the majority of the population being Muslims (79%), 21% Christian, and the rest other religions.[108] About 60% of the population is under the age of 25 and continues to struggle with high levels of unemployment, which was one of the major causes of the infamous 1991-2001 civil war and still remains a threat to stability today. It is estimated that 60% of youth unemployment rate is attributed to high levels of illiteracy and unskilled labour, a lack of private sector jobs and low pay.[109] Over half of the population live below the poverty line.[110]

Sierra Leone is endowed with substantial mineral resources. It is particularly rich in diamonds, and infamous for its "blood diamonds"; conflict over the diamond fields resulted in more than a decade of civil war and destruction that internally displaced over 2 million people - almost half of the population at the time - and destroyed most institutions before ending in 2002.[111] In Freetown in 2013, I met some of the former rebels, who had murdered many people during the civil war. After a reconciliation process, including the Truth and Reconciliation Commission hearings, they are now living in the community, with the family members and friends of some of the people they killed. I was stunned and struck by the capacity of Sierra Leoneans to forgive and move on.

As the country tried to rebuild from the devastating war, it was set back in part by the deadly outbreak of Ebola in 2014, which killed over 4,000 people, coupled with the commodity slump.[112] In 2017, increased iron ore exports together with the end of the Ebola epidemic supported a resumption of economic growth. The country's GDP is estimated to have grown from -20.5% in 2015 to 5.4% in 2017.[113] In 2017, the country suffered a devastating mudslide disaster in Freetown that killed hundreds of people, and awakened memories of other national traumas.[114]

I fell in love with the beauty of Sierra Leone and was inspired by the innocent optimism of its young people. The country is home to beautiful towering mountains, and scenic islands, including Banana Island and Bunce Island, which can be toured by boat. Banana Island is particularly renowned for its diving and snorkelling. Being a coastal country, Sierra Leone had amazing seafood with freshly grilled barracuda, grouper, snapper, lobster and prawns available on the beaches. Like many of its West African neighbours, Sierra Leone had delicious Star beer and palm wine. And it has borne a rockstar – David Moinina Sengeh.

David is easily one of the most brilliant and multi-talented individuals I have ever met. A mentee of U.S. President Barack Obama and Bill Gates, David is a genius polymath, a biomechanical engineer, an artificial intelligence (AI) research scientist, a TED Fellow, a creative designer and an Afrobeats artist. With his hair in locks, his face always in a smile, and impeccably dressed in clothing of his own design, David exudes confidence, hope and promise. I have known David for fourteen years, and met with him many times in Freetown, Boston, Nairobi, Johannesburg, and Arusha to capture his incredible journey from Bo in Sierra Leone to Harvard and MIT, and then back to the continent, creating innovative organisations and products that have caught the attention of the world.

David reflected fondly on his childhood: 'It was a childhood defined by a lot of playfulness. There wasn't any evening where I wasn't out on the field. There wasn't any evening where I wasn't going from house to house with some of my friends to eat their food, wait for them to go pray at the mosque, come to my house, eat with me, go to the football field and play together, shower and then maybe everybody goes to do their homework. This was our daily routine. And when I returned from school, I'd hang out because I didn't want to do any work. At sundown, you had to go and water the gardens, you had to do your own part. It didn't really matter who you were, you always had something to do, you had a responsibility as a kid.

Everybody at home had a responsibility, whether it was to sweep, wash dishes, or water the garden, you did something. So, it was really centred around playfulness, meeting new people and being responsible for some task at home. That wasn't overwhelming, you knew that it was tiny, and you had to do it and once you did it you were free to do whatever else you wanted to do'.

David had an interesting connection to technology as a young boy. His father wanted him to learn how to type and so bought him a typewriter at home and he would practice often with it. He had his first experience with computers while in junior secondary school. He signed up for a computer class and learnt about Microsoft Word and Microsoft DOS. These typing lessons became helpful later in his life.

As a young boy, David showed interest in his father's work. His father was programs manager and head of operations at UNICEF Sierra Leone. Young David read every UNICEF annual report he could lay his fingers on. At that early age he got to know about the UNICEF multi-indicators and was scandalised by how poorly his country and other African countries were doing in terms of child development and standards of living. When he read the reports, he'd engage his father on them and debate every policy that had been introduced.

In 1991, the civil war broke out in Sierra Leone. David lived in Bo with his family at the time. Bo is Sierra Leone's second largest city and is in the central part of the southern province.[115] The war started in the north, so it was quite far from them - initially. He recollects how they listened to news on the BBC about how the war was unfolding up north. In those times, he felt safe because the war was taking place far away. However, there were times when they harboured the fear that it could spread down south to the entire country. Their greatest fears caught up with them as their town was attacked and left them running for their lives. His family was divided in the process and for weeks, he didn't know the whereabouts of some of his family members. He saw children who had been turned into rebels perpetrating inhumane activities and it troubled him deeply. After the war erupted, their home became a shelter for children of family members and friends. The size of his family ballooned from five children and two adults to as many as 50 people.

One of the atrocities that became associated with Sierra Leone's decade-long civil war was the amputation of limbs. Like King Leopold's militias in Congo, the rebels hacked off the legs, arms and hands of civilians and soldiers who fought against them. This was part of their strategy to put fear in the hearts of civilians and their opponents. It was also an economic strategy to protect access to the diamonds of Sierra Leone. They believed that by cutting off the hands or arms of their opponents, they disabled them from mining diamonds to support the government in the war. Over 8,000 Sierra Leoneans had their hands, arms or legs amputated.[116] A walk through the towns and cities of Sierra Leone will not end without seeing some of these double and single amputees. David recalls one of the moments when they were attacked and how it formed his resolve to be an agent of change: 'My family and I ran for safety during one of those attacks when I was about twelve. I resolved that I would do all that I could so that my own children would not go through the same experiences that we had. They would be part of a Sierra Leone where war and amputation were no longer a strategy for gaining power.'

As 12-year old David was fleeing for his life, other children had been inducted as child soldiers. The civil war in Sierra Leone converted an estimated 11,000 children into child soldiers. They also recruited young girls, who were subjected to rape, gang rape and other forms of sexual violence.[117] These experiences scarred David and emboldened him to build a different future for his country.

He initially wanted to be a doctor like his uncle: 'I shadowed my uncle who was a medical doctor in the theatre every time I could. I saw lots of operations and thought I could be a doctor. I wanted to do more, and I knew that he had studied in Germany. I knew that if I did medicine in Sierra Leone, I would have to go overseas to specialise, otherwise, you will remain a general practitioner and I didn't want to be a general practitioner. I wanted to be a surgeon specialist. I wanted to be in a position where I could work with kids and all that stuff. I knew I had to travel overseas to achieve all of that, and the only way I could leave was through a scholarship and the only way to get a scholarship is to do well in the national examinations. I knew that was the path. And so, I put myself in the position to do well in the national exam and was lucky enough to do okay and once it happened, I went to UWC in Norway through the scholarship.'

With a Red Cross Scholarship in tow, he left the shores of Sierra Leone for the first time for the United World College in Norway where he had his high school education. At this time, the only fields of study he was familiar with were medicine, civil engineering, mechanical engineering and electrical engineering. He knew nothing about biomedical engineering until some universities came to visit the UWC campus and spoke about biomedical engineering and piqued his interest. Immediately, he saw a connection between biomedical engineering and some of the challenges his uncle faced during some of his operations. Many of the tools his uncle needed were not functional. There were several procedures he could not perform simply because the technology was not available. As David thought about all this, he saw the ocean of opportunities that lay before him if he pursued biomedical engineering.

After settling on this path, he opted for Harvard University's School of Engineering and Applied Sciences. 'The more I started learning about it, the more I didn't want to be in just an engineering school. I wanted more. I wanted to be in a place where I could do whatever I wanted to do. I studied engineering at Harvard and sure it may not have been the strongest engineering program in the world, but it is the best engineering program for anyone who wants to do more than just engineering.' The deal was sealed when Harvard also offered him a full scholarship that covered tuition and his living expenses.

Before he even matriculated at Harvard, David and his roommate at UWC, Jake Kap, were inspired to make a difference in the world. They were passionate about 'doing things that mattered in the world and we didn't just want it for the name... it was the idea that we wanted to bring problems to a minimum... the idea was to do a set of projects that reduced the burden of humanity in some shape or form.' They thus formed an organisation called GMin, short for "Global Minimum."

Before relocating to Massachusetts, David returned to Sierra Leone and visited his father's hometown for the first time, staying with his uncle. David observed that the most common malaria prevention strategy was the use of mosquito nets but not everyone had a mosquito net. At Harvard, in one of his classes on global health, he was tasked to write a paper on a proposed solution to a health problem and he decided to write on malaria prevention in Sierra Leone. His proposed strategy was to widely and more effectively distribute mosquito nets to ensure full coverage in a household. After the paper, he leveraged social media and emails to build a network of friends and supporters to back his ambitious project in the distribution and use of mosquito nets in a region of Sierra Leone. He was able to build a global digital network of supporters from as far away as Denmark and Pakistan. David's innovation was to measure coverage with respect to all sleeping areas including the floor versus the traditional method of just counting the number of beds in the house. By calculating coverage in this manner, David was helping to ensure that everyone was accounted for, including people who slept on the floor.

David told me of the conversation he and his team had with

stakeholders before, during and after the distribution. Right from the get-go, they realised that it had to be done in collaboration with the Red Cross, district health management teams, the leadership of the village and other opinion leaders in the village. There was also a much wider conversation with people in town hall meetings to explain the project. That open and transparent conversation enabled them to garner support and critical information. To pull the community along and take the conversation to them, they organised other social activities such as a football competition and a dance, all of which had malaria themes.

When the distribution was completed, the Red Cross and other local volunteers were tasked to follow up at three-month intervals to ensure that the people were sleeping under the nets. They achieved full coverage distributing to 27,000 people in a chiefdom and had 90% adoption in three years. The Red Cross had done a similar project and had achieved only 40% adoption. Their process was later incorporated in the government's national distribution strategy. Further, because of the invaluable data they obtained, when the Sierra Leonean government wanted to implement nationwide full coverage in 2010, they involved GMin as part of the project.

David's next game-changing project was inspired by another experience in Sierra Leone. In one of his engineering classes at Harvard, the students were tasked to design lighting solutions for the London Olympic Games. David's thoughts were more focused on solutions for problems facing his country and continent and not the Olympics. 'The ordinary Sierra Leonean wasn't going to be affected much by the London Olympic Games.'

During that period in Sierra Leone, his sister had undergone a risky caesarean section under horrendous hospital conditions. Throughout the operation, there was a power outage and no light, so his mother had to hold a candle for the entire period of the surgery. The poor lighting led to accidental cuts on the baby's back and forehead. This angered and spurred him to find a solution to the energy crisis. He teamed up with some of his classmates and decided to focus on generating energy solutions for off-grid regions in Africa – instead of the London Olympic Games. They discovered that Professor Peter Girguis in Harvard's Department of Organismic and Evolutionary Biology was conducting research in this area, so they tapped into his expertise and pioneering work in microbial fuel cell (MFC) energy sources. The project won the World Bank Lighting Africa 2008 Development Marketplace Competition, winning $200,000 in grant funding and the team was selected to implement the project in Namibia.[118] It was further tested by one of his co-founders in Tanzania, who later raised $1 million in grants from the Gates Foundation and other funders.

These innovative ideas to combat malaria and lack of energy alone are impressive. But what really sets David apart is his pioneering work on prosthetics, inspired by conversations with Sierra Leonean friends of his who were amputees. They complained bitterly about their experience of using prosthetics. It was difficult for some amputees to get the appropriate prosthetics to use. It took three weeks to a year for some to get the right prosthetics and even where they could get access, it meant they often travelled long distances across cities and countries. Another challenge many amputees faced was the intense discomfort they experienced wearing the prosthetics, because they didn't fit well. They experienced pain and developed blisters. It was also financially prohibitive for many amputees, with prices as high as $6,000 for a prosthetic limb. This created challenges especially for children, who would outgrow their prosthetics. Listening to some of these stories broke his heart. 'How do you design products that [solve these challenges] for amputees?'

In college, he dreamt of a prosthetic bank with custom-made, comfortable and affordable prosthetics. 'It should be possible for children to walk in, change their prosthesis, be fitted with new ones and walk away happy. Some of these prosthetics can be recycled or repaired.' Unfortunately, David did not have an opportunity at Harvard to work on this project. However, four years later, when he was pursuing PhD opportunities, a friend told him about the freedom to work on any project of choice at MIT's world-renowned Media Lab. As he investigated the possibility of pursuing the prosthetics project at MIT, David discovered that this issue wasn't just a Sierra Leonean problem, it was a global problem. There are over 10 million amputees globally and many of them face similar problems as the over 10,000 amputees in Sierra Leone.[119]

When David first suggested this idea of a custom-made prosthetic for amputees for his PhD at MIT, his mentor, a double amputee himself, was initially sceptical. This did not deter him from researching further into the possibility of his idea. Eventually, he developed a custom-made prosthetic leg. It is a product of biology, mechanical engineering and electronics and makes use of advances in imaging, modelling and manufacturing. David has pioneered a new system for creating prosthetic sockets by using MRI to map the shape, computer-assisted design to predict strains and 3D printing to allow for different materials to be used in different places. The result is more comfortable sockets that can be produced more cheaply and quickly with the potential to reach more amputees globally. David's prosthetic innovation won the 2014 Lemelson-MIT National Collegiate Student Prize Competition, a nationwide search for the best young innovators. It has been featured on TED, CNN and many other media outlets. David has been testing the product and working with several victims of the 2013 Boston Marathon bombings as well as with veterans from the Iraq and Afghanistan wars.[120]

Perhaps David's greatest contribution to the African continent, however, has been the Innovate Programs he has launched under the auspices of GMin to inspire young innovators to solve problems they encounter. At MIT, David had a lot of freedom to create anything, to be a critical thinker, to experiment, to build prototypes, to collaborate, to engage, to solve problems. He realised that many young people on the continent do not have access to such opportunities. So, he created the Innovate Program to empower young people to think, learn and solve local problems. He wanted that creative and innovative approach to be embedded in their thinking, the activities they engage in and the products they make.

After contacting some friends in his network, he raised some seed money and launched the program initially as a national challenge in Sierra Leone. The plan was for applicants to form teams, identify a local problem and come up with an innovative and effective solution. GMin, in turn, would give them the resources they need and guide them through the process of creating a solution. They gave them feedback on the feasibility of their project, how innovative their solutions were and granted them access to a network of mentors.

In the first year, 300 students expressed interest, 72 completed applications, and 10 finalists emerged. The projects these high school students embarked on ranged from pig farms and bamboo coffins, to radio stations. Following its success in Sierra Leone, GMin expanded the program to Kenya and South Africa. In the first two years, over 1,000 children have applied to be part of the competition. The program now has two offices in Sierra Leone and Kenya and sends teams every year to the Robotics Olympics in Washington D.C. The team from Sierra Leone recently placed in the top 50 globally. Alumni from the program have matriculated at Africa Leadership Academy, Harvard University, Africa Leadership University and many other top tier institutions; some have even won Echoing Green fellowships. They have obtained over $1 million dollars in funding.

One of the greatest success stories that has emanated from the Innovation Program is the discovery of Kelvin Doe. A child prodigy, at 13 years old Kelvin created a radio station out of waste materials, and electrified his community. People in his community sent announcements, covered football matches and played music through his station. His story now has over 1 million views on YouTube. David made it possible for him to visit the MIT Media Lab through the MIT International Development Initiative Program. Kelvin became the youngest lecturer to give a talk in MIT history.[121]

David believes that 'if we want to have a generation of people who can think creatively and solve problems and thus add value, they don't just come from the sky, you have to create activities and tools and processes through which they can learn. They form themselves, but you have to give them the medium through which they can develop, through which they can learn, through which they can grow.' Digital tools and technology have created tremendous opportunities to allow young people to create things.

In 2018, David called me with exciting news. The newly elected President of Sierra Leone, His Excellency, Julius Maada Bio extended an offer to David to join his team as the first ever Chief Innovation Officer for Sierra Leone, heading a newly created Directorate of Science, Technology and Innovation (DSTI) in the Office of the President. As David explained it, 'the 21st century is the age of big data, innovation and rapid technological advancement. This brings new forms of opportunities, risks and challenges for every government around the world. For Sierra Leone to compete in the global economy, its leaders and the government require support, insight and policy advice related to innovation.'

While I have been encouraged by the examples of innovation spearheaded by young entrepreneurs across the continent, there are limits to the impact and scalability of these private sector initiatives. The reality for many African countries is that governments are the dominant economic and political force and has the scale and reach to have the biggest impact. We cannot innovate our way out of bad governance. For David, who had recently become a father, he felt a moral responsibility to play a role in transforming Sierra Leone so that his daughters can experience a more prosperous and developed country than the one their father grew up in.

David accepted President Bio's offer and is now leading DSTI with a simple vision: to help transform Sierra Leone into a prosperous nation through science, technology and innovation. David has built a team of scientists, technologists, researchers and artists in DSTI. 'We are problem solvers first. We believe that technology and innovation must be used to solve problems that impact the broader society.' He also has a goal to make Sierra Lone an innovation and entrepreneurship hub for the sub region. David has organised DSTI's work along four core pillars. The first pillar is to support real-time decision-making for public officials through state-of-the-art analytical methods and visualisation. The second pillar is to develop data systems, solutions and designs that support cross sector collaboration and planning with government ministries, departments and agencies. The third pillar is to provide citizens with digital services and solutions that enhance their engagement with government. The fourth and final pillar is to support the innovation culture and create a network of researchers, data scientists, innovators and entrepreneurs in Sierra Leone.

DSTI has already embarked on several ambitious projects in support of these pillars. They have created a dashboard to monitor and assess the government's flagship quality free education program, collecting data in real-time. DSTI is also collaborating with the Ministry of Finance, the National Revenue Authority, banks and other public and sector entities to systematically map out the financial and revenue ecosystems of government. This will help government plug leakages in its revenue collection and to build a more robust public finance system. DSTI is also digitising the immigration process for Sierra Leone. They have also created a GoSL Appointment System that allows government officials to book and manage appointments across government seamlessly using SMS and an app-based solution.

David is optimistic about Sierra Leone's prospects and the continent's future. He believes strongly that young people need to participate in government to transform it and leverage it for maximum societal impact. 'If not us, Sangu, then who?'

6

ANDREW MUPUYA

PIONEERS PAPER BAGS

OUR NEXT SOCIOPRENEUR TAKES US TO UGANDA, A COUNTRY of 42 million people and a GDP of $26 billion. Many people globally remember Uganda for its fight against a brutal 20-year insurgency in the north led by the Lord's Resistance Army under the leadership of the infamous Joseph Kony, who became a globally recognised figure after the Kony 2012 film by Invisible Children went viral.[122] Demonstrating the power (and potential danger) of the global digital world in which we live, in less than a week of its release, the film had been viewed over 100 million times, making it the most viral video of all time.[123] The film has received a lot of criticism. Some of my Ugandan friends were angry that the film perpetuated a stereotype of an African country as a war-torn region, and for exaggerating the scale of the insurgency, which had been diminished at the time of the film's release.[124]

Uganda's 77-year-old president, Yoweri Museveni, has been Head of State since January 1986 and is one of the longest serving presidents on the African continent. In 2017, an age-limit on presidential candidates was removed by Uganda's Parliament that would technically allow Mr. Museveni to rule until 2034.[125] Museveni is a controversial figure. While many condemn him for holding on to power, he is widely credited with bringing relative political stability and economic prosperity to the country following years of civil wars and repression under former dictators Milton Obote and Idi Amin.[126] The National Resistance Movement (NRM) led by President Museveni introduced a number of economic reforms which resulted in a long period of strong economic growth and impressive gains in poverty reduction. Over the 30 years since Museveni assumed power in 1986, life expectancy rose from 47 years to 60 years; the national poverty rate declined from 56% in 1992 to 21%; and primary school enrolment rose from 73% in 1986 to 99%. From 1987 until 2010, Uganda's economy averaged 7% GDP growth, though growth later slowed to 4.5%. In 2015, GDP grew at 5.19%, decelerating to 4.69% in 2016 and 4.04% in 2017, before accelerating to 5.5% in 2018.[127] Uganda's GDP is projected to average 6.3% over the medium term.[128] Under Museveni, Uganda has also accomplished some of the most progressive advances in fighting the HIV/AIDS scourge, going from a prevalence rate of 30% in the 80's to 7% in 2017.[129] I interviewed President Museveni on stage at the Africa Global Business Forum in Dubai in November of 2017. He had great ideas on building a Pan-African economy and promoting intra-Africa trade, but side-stepped my questions on empowering the next generation of political leaders in Uganda.

This question of leadership change became a lightning rod in Uganda in 2018 with the Bobi Wine controversy. Born in the slums of Kampala as Robert Kyagulanyi, Bobi Wine is a 37-year-old activist and Uganda's most famous musician. In 2017, he entered politics and was elected as a Member of Parliament. Bobi Wine is leveraging his celebrity status to disrupt Uganda's politics. He became an international cause célèbre in August 2018 when he was detained and assaulted by Ugandan police after campaigning for another independent candidate. His driver was killed during the incident.

His detention resulted in a global outcry and local demonstrations. Eventually he was released and allowed to seek medical treatment in the US. Even though he claims he will not be running for President in 2021, Bobi Wine is the uncrowned king of Uganda's youth-led opposition movement against Museveni.[130]

When I think of my experiences in Uganda, I think of the many entrepreneurs I met there who were filled with optimism for the future. I think of the rapid development in real estate and infrastructure – a highway connecting Kampala to Kigali and Mombasa was recently constructed. I also think of some of the wildlife which includes the famous silverback gorillas, and many rare birds (Uganda has over 10 national parks).[131] I carved out time during my visit to Uganda to experience some of its world-famous wildlife. Uganda was also a lot of fun. Of all the cities across Africa that I visited, Kampala was without question the most fun city: Ugandans party like there's no tomorrow!

I was in Kampala to meet a young entrepreneur and environmental activist called Andrew Mupuya. I was wearing a brown and orange embroidered kaftan and felt overdressed when Andrew showed up in blue denim jeans, slippers, and a simple black sweater. 'You must be Sangu. Welcome to Uganda.' When I asked him to tell me his life story, the first thing he said was: 'I hate plastic!' 'Why?' I enquired. Straight-faced and aggrieved, he responded 'It killed our goat!' He then explained how his hatred for polythene bags began the day his family's only asset, a goat, choked on a polythene bag and died. He was six years old at the time. A decade later, in 2008, he launched a company to help end the use of polythene bags by manufacturing a substitute – paper bags. At the time, his family faced severe economic hardship, so his foray into paper bag production, the first in Uganda, also alleviated the financial pressures at home. Through his passion for the environment, inspired by the dead goat, and his shrewd business acumen, Andrew Mupuya has become Uganda's paper bag pioneer.

Andrew was born in Mbale in the Eastern region of Uganda to very poor parents, who couldn't afford basic needs such as a pair of shorts. He grew up and attended school in the village until it was time to take his O-Level examinations. As early as six years old, he was already fed up with the dire poverty in his house. His first entrepreneurial idea crystallised after he observed the farmers in his village harvesting their maize and noticed the waste and inefficiencies. He would walk through the farms and collect the leftover maize, wash, roast and sell them by the roadside and in the markets. He bought his first pair of used shorts through this micro venture.

At another time, Andrew carried out some tasks for an aunt and earned 100 shillings (the equivalent of US $0.03). His eyes lit with excitement as he recounted how overjoyed he was after earning that amount. He invested his 100 shillings in a stick of sugarcane which he took to school with the intention of selling it. Before he arrived in school, he had peeled, washed and cut it in three pieces. Young Andrew succeeded in selling each of the three pieces to his friends for 50 shillings each. He made a profit of 50 shillings which he re-invested into more sugar cane sticks... and kept going on. 'When the money came to a good amount, I bought a shirt for myself. So, I had to work through hard times. There were risks and I was taking on risks by going into those maize farms barefooted. At times I cut my foot. My parents would ask me, "how did this happen?" And I wasn't honest with them,' he recounted.

When he was young, he recalls a moment when his parents were in tears due to financial difficulties. Andrew was nine years old at the time and had some savings from his little side hustles. He loaned his savings to his parents, and felt very proud that he could support them, despite his young age. Where many members of his family and community prayed every day waiting for a miracle from God, Andrew learned at an early age that he had some agency and needed to do everything he could to try to make a difference in his life. 'You can't just cry to God to help you. If a lion is coming towards you, do you stand and say God help me? No, you run and ask for his help at the same time hoping that by running, God might bring a tree in your sight or give you extra speed or something. You have to help yourself for God to help you.'

Spending most of his formative years in the village limited his learning since there weren't many resources at the village school. He took a daring decision to move from his village to Kampala, Uganda's capital. By 2008, he was 16 years old and the financial hardships in his family had worsened because his parents had both lost their jobs and were unemployed. He applied for and won a partial scholarship to attend a school that was better resourced than his village school. His parents were not supportive of his move to Kampala, but he moved anyway. Apart from a brother who was also hustling in the city, he knew no one there.

A few months after his arrival in the capital city, he had an idea. It was triggered by the Ugandan government's announcement of a policy to end the use of plastic bags, introducing a ban was to end their production, sales and importation.[132] From small convenience stores, to pharmacies and multinational supermarkets, most purchases are carried in plastic bags. This means millions of plastic bags are taken home by Ugandans every year. They are a great environmental hazard due to the poor waste management culture in Uganda. When plastic bags are not well disposed of, the wind easily blows them away littering the environment. Most of them find their way into open gutters and block the sewerage systems.

Plastics are a global environmental nightmare. Plastic is now ubiquitous and part of our lives. Global production is estimated at 330 million tons a year, a sharp rise from the 2 million tons a year in the 1950s. This number is estimated to rise to 1 *billion* tons by 2050. Plastic is used to make our bottles, electronics, paint, pipes and packaging materials. Scientists have been discovering microplastics and fibres in our honey, sugar, beer, water, food, and marine life. In one study, plastics contamination was found in more than 90% of bottled water samples.[133]

It is difficult to get rid of plastics because they take an average of 450 years to decompose. A lot of plastic waste ends up in the oceans and scientists estimate that the plastic in the ocean will match the weight of fish by 2050.[134] The head of the United Nations Environment Programme called this the "ocean Armageddon." Ocean plastic is estimated to kill millions of marine animals every year from zooplankton to whales.[135]

These environmental reasons compelled the Ugandan government to take the bold decision to ban the use of plastic bags, following the lines of neighbouring countries Rwanda and Kenya. The obvious substitute was paper bags. That was Andrew's light-bulb moment. He saw a unique opportunity to destroy his two enemies – polythene and poverty - with one stone, or many paper bags.

The ban created high demand for paper bags overnight. Businesses had to substitute the weekly demand for 90 tons of plastic bags with paper bags. The major player in the paper bag market was a manufacturer from neighbouring Kenya, but its imports couldn't meet all the local demand. It became obvious to Andrew that there was more than enough room for a competitive local manufacturer. However, he noted that even though the ban was announced, it was poorly enforced. The government had made the announcement without any proper transition plans to move the nation from the use of plastic bags to paper bags.

Andrew decided to conduct market research. Unlike Eric Muthomi, who relied on digital tools to conduct his market research, Andrew took an 'old school' approach. He visited convenience stores, grocery shops, pharmacies, supermarkets, and even little kiosks and small retail outlets to talk to their owners and managers and assess the level of interest in substituting plastic bags with paper bags. He walked away from these market research studies with a renewed confidence that strong demand existed. A few of the retailers even requested a prototype.

Andrew had validated the demand for paper bags, but he had a major problem: he had no idea how to make or manufacture paper bags. In a different era, that would have ended his dreams and aspirations. However, in a digital age, Andrew had access to online learning tools. Uganda was one of the first countries in the region to gain full internet connectivity. At the time of his market research in 2008, internet penetration was 6.4% (compared to 31% in 2017), with an estimated 2 million users throughout Uganda. Orange Uganda had also just entered the market and was the first to popularise mobile internet services. Andrew did not have a personal computer or a smartphone, let alone internet access, but there were many computer cafés in Kampala. So, he went to a computer café and spent time researching how paper bags are made. He eventually found a video from India which he nicknamed 'How to Produce Paper Bag 101.'

Andrew further honed his business skills at a Junior Achievement chapter in his school, Kololo Secondary School. Junior Achievement is one of the largest NGOs serving young people globally. The organisation creates experiential learning opportunities for the youth in financial literacy, work readiness and entrepreneurship.[136] Andrew's school chapter had several Junior Achievement teams and he was part of one of the teams that created a company known as Quapack. He was the finance manager of this company. There were over 200 students involved in collecting plastic bottles and selling them to be recycled. Andrew's teacher, Timothy Mugerwa, encouraged him and helped him draft a business plan. Andrew calculated that he needed starting capital of 36,000 Ugandan Shillings ($14) to launch his paper bag company. So, with the help of his classmates, he collected 70 kilograms of used plastic bottles to raise the capital. But he was only able to raise 28,000 Ugandan Shillings ($11). His fellow students thought he had lost his mind. He borrowed the remaining 8,000 Ugandan Shillings ($3) from Mr. Mugerwa. With the 36,000 Ugandan shillings in hand, Andrew bought the raw materials and started making paper bags. He recalls that he sold a ream worth of paper bag every 3 weeks and from each ream, he earned 20,000 Shillings ($7) in profit. Thus, Youth Entrepreneurial Link Investments (YELI) was born, the first indigenous Ugandan company to make paper bags. While $7 of profit every three weeks may not seem like a lot of money, annualised it is $121, which represented 22% of GDP per capita at the time – quite the impressive feat for a 16-year-old student!

Andrew pleaded with the head of his school for permission to use the school premises as his first "factory." He got his first orders from local food and commodity suppliers. From the profit of 20,000 shillings ($7) on his first order, he paid his first angel investor, his teacher, and ploughed the remaining profit into the business. He had an order at the early stages of the business to supply a supermarket with 10,000 bags in 24 hours. He was unable to meet this demand because of low capacity, even though he worked hard through sleepless nights.

With demand increasing beyond his personal capacity, he employed and trained some of the same fellow students who thought he was "crazy" to participate in his paper business venture. With time, he engaged 30 other high school students on a part-time basis. He later even roped his parents into the business by opening a distribution outlet for his mother. The cost of employing them was not too prohibitive for the business. Most of the students came from poor backgrounds just like him. They were so poor they couldn't even afford lunch. Andrew enticed them to work for YELI by buying lunch for them and paying them a commission on bags produced.

Meanwhile, Andrew continued to attend classes, study privately and prepare for examinations. In his second year of operation, he completed his A-Level examinations and passed, much to the shock of some of his colleagues and teachers. He had no intention to end his education there despite the great potential of his business. He enrolled in Makerere University to pursue a Bachelor of Commerce degree.

Today, YELI employs 22 people directly. Andrew has provided livelihood to several families, including a 50-year-old father of 8 and an orphan who was 19 years when he employed him. He has also created jobs for the several suppliers he works with in the production and distribution of paper bags. He has gone multinational with over 70 clients in Uganda, Rwanda and other countries in East Africa. His customers include pharmacies, restaurants, supermarkets, retail shops, local hospitals and major local flour manufacturers.

We visited his "factory" – a simple one room operation, about 60 square metres, with his desk, a brown wooden desk in the corner, his plaques and awards on one end, a pile of folders on the other, and paper bags all over the floor. The surrounding neighbourhood had all dirt roads, covered in dust and plastic waste, even though there was a giant sign that read: *Toyiwa Wano Bisasiro, Bwokwatibwa 200,000*, which Andrew explained meant 'Public Notice: No "Dumping, Fine 200,000". The neighbourhood was quite busy, with many kiosks with 'Airtel' signage engaged in commerce, and cars and motorbikes carrying passengers and goods alike, jostling to get past the Ankole cattle (also known as the Cattle of Kings), with their majestic massive horns, aware of their royalty and indifferent to the blaring horns of vehicles.

Despite its modest operation, Andrew has ambitious goals for the company, with a target to produce over 90,000 bags a week and achieve $1 million in gross revenues. YELI is further spreading its model by leveraging the internet and digital tools to train other Africans on how to setup and make paper bag companies. So far, over 500 people from Uganda, Nigeria and Kenya have benefitted from his digital training programs. The training has enabled 16 smaller paper bag companies to be established.

Ironically, the government policy that brought in Andrew's Eureka moment was not well implemented. The government introduced legislation banning the use of plastic bags under 30 microns and imposed a tax rate of 120% on thick bags but didn't enforce it. Polythene was still in use till 2015 when the National Environmental Management Authority (NEMA) stepped in to enforce the legislation.[137]

Andrew therefore still had to deal with competition from polythene bags. He used a two-pronged strategy of price and education to fight the competition. For some of his first-time clients, he sold the product to them at a price lower than the cost price. It meant that he made losses, but he was willing to make that sacrifice to win customers over. The second strategy has been to educate prospective clients and the general public on the disadvantages of plastic bags and make the case for a "green economy".

Another challenge he constantly faces is the negative attitude towards young entrepreneurs. He got a call from a prospective client in Rwanda. This man flew to Uganda to meet with him but didn't believe that the young man in front of him was *the* Andrew Mupuya. He had read about YELI on the internet and spoken with him on the phone but had expected to see an older and bigger person. He genuinely believed he was talking with the wrong person. He also recalls a time when he went to a local shop to buy paper and the woman at the shop ignored him, so he walked away from the shop. The attendants ageism cost the shop over $35,000 worth of business.

Like Eric Muthomi, Andrew focused on grants and business plan competitions in order to secure capital for growth. In 2011, he participated in a business plan competition called Youth Entrepreneurship Facility (YEF). YEF supports African youth to turn their energy and ideas into businesses, create work opportunities and increase their income. It is the brainchild of the Africa Commission in partnership with the Youth Employment Network and the International Labour Organisation.[138] He received $1,000 in prize money, which he used to invest in his business.

Perhaps the most impactful award for Andrew was winning the Grand Prize of the second annual Anzisha Prize in 2012. Sponsored by the African Leadership Academy and the MasterCard Foundation, the Anzisha Prize is the premier award for Africa's young entrepreneurial leaders under the age of 22, awarding $100,000 in prize money to the winners. I served as a judge in 2016 and I was impressed by the breadth of accomplishments of these teenage entrepreneurs across the continent and the diversity of innovative start-ups – from a moringa tea start-up in Cameroon to a bio-fertiliser start-up in Madagascar. Andrew was in the competition with 270 African youth from 23 countries. He was selected amongst the 13 finalists who participated in a week-long entrepreneurship workshop at the African Leadership Academy campus in South Africa. He won the Grand Prize and took home $30,000.[139]

In 2012, he competed with 4,000 members of Junior Achievement and received the Ferd Award for Social Entrepreneurship. 'I was simply striving to go forward. I wasn't looking for these awards', he said to me. The eco-friendly nature and job creation opportunities of YELI made him the winner of the 2012 edition.[140] Jarle Tommerbakke, Senior Advisor, JA-YE Europe, said of Andrew: 'You have shown a great strategic insight, and the fact that you spread your idea for others to use and then capitalise on the market created, to the benefit of local communities and the environment says a lot about the social impact created. You are a true entrepreneur with a great mindset and a big intellectual capital. Focus on your growth strategy and keep your mindset of sharing the idea!'[141]

In 2013, Andrew also won the Youth Entrepreneurship Challenge Award for Innovation. The award is given to an innovative and entrepreneurial young person and is organised by Inspire Africa.[142] Forbes listed him amongst the Top 30 Under 30 Entrepreneurs in Africa, a group of outstanding entrepreneurs and innovators under the age of 30. In the Forbes publication, they are described as representing the 'entrepreneurial, innovative and intellectual best of their generation.'[143]

The green economy is creating many business opportunities for young entrepreneurs. In neighbouring Tanzania, I met Patrick Ngowi, the CEO of Helvetic Solar, who had grown his solar business from scratch to over $10 million in annual revenues. As of April 2019, Andrew Mupuya was setting up a factory to shift from manual production to expand production to 1 million bags per week and to employ 1,000 people. He envisions a polythene and poverty-free Uganda. With YELI he hopes to make his country clean, to create jobs and to empower thousands of young people.

7

SARAN KABAN JONES

WATERS A NATION

MY NEXT ENTREPRENEUR COMES FROM LIBERIA, A SMALL country of under 5 million people with a troubled history.[144] In Ghana, I had grown up with first-hand awareness of human rights abuses. My father had founded the African Commission of Health and Human Rights Promoters in the late '80s and I grew up in the '90s with refugees from Liberia who had fled the brutal civil war which claimed over 250,000 lives.[145] I remember torture victims that we would host in our house, like Throble Suah, who had been beaten mercilessly for writing against Charles Taylor. Our home served as a refuge for these survivors of violence. At a young age, I was moved by their courage in the face of such tragedy. The Buduburam refugee settlement in Ghana for example hosted over 38,000 Liberian refugees during the war.[146] Liberians and Ghanaians share a powerful bond.

The Liberia I was visiting in 2016 was different from the Liberia of the '90s. Here was a country that embodied many of the contradictory notions about contemporary Africa which I've been confronted with during my journey. War-torn, but with a fast-growing economy, politically ahead of the curve in some ways (having elected Africa's first female president), but still deeply attached to ethnic identities and politics, Liberia seemed to simultaneously capture the promise and perils of a fledgling post-conflict nation.

Liberia began as a settlement of the American Colonization Society, an organisation which relocated freed slaves from the United States and the Caribbean. Liberia's first president in 1847, Joseph Jenkins Roberts, was a free-born African American from Virginia. He would also serve as its seventh president in 1872. The Americo-Liberians, as they became known, created a ruling oligarchy, which excluded indigenous Liberians from power. These tensions contributed to a military coup overthrowing President William Tolbert in 1980 and marked the beginning of political instability which would reign for several decades. After the brutal civil wars that resulted in the deaths of over 250,000 people, a peace agreement was reached in 2003, which led to democratic elections in 2005, under which Harvard-trained economist and former Minister of Finance, Ellen Johnson Sirleaf was elected as the first female president in Africa. Driven to the presidency mainly by the outsized contributions of Liberian women, President Sirleaf focused on gender issues, implementing one of the continent's most comprehensive rape laws and setting up a fast-track court to deal with gender violence.[147]

"Ma Ellen," as she is popularly called in Liberia won the Nobel Peace Prize in 2011, shortly before she was re-elected for a second term. At the end of 2017, she handed over power to George Weah, the newly elected President of Liberia and a former soccer star, marking the first peaceful democratic transition of power in Liberia in 73 years. Ma Ellen was awarded the $5 million Ibrahim Prize for Achievement in African Leadership, with the prize committee remarking that 'she took over a country that was devastated and broken by 14 years of civil war and was later struck again by the Ebola crisis... Such a journey cannot be without some shortcomings. Today, Liberia continues to face many challenges.'[148] While Ma Ellen is celebrated on the international stage, her legacy at home is mixed. Her fellow Nobel laureate Leymah Gbowee quit as head of Liberia's Truth and Reconciliation Commission and criticised President Sirleaf for corruption and nepotism, after she appointed her sons to key posts in the government.[149]

The Liberian government under Sirleaf's presidency took an interesting bet on digital technologies as a solution to the country's education challenges. After nearly 25,000 students, and 100% of all test-takers, failed the admission test to the University of Liberia, the country was forced to take radical action.[150] In a global first, they outsourced the running of some of its public schools to Bridge International Academies, a private company backed by Bill Gates and Mark Zuckerberg.[151] Described as the "Uber of Education", Bridge uses technology, standardisation and rigorous monitoring, with teachers reading word-for-word from a scripted lesson plan displayed on cheap tablets.[152] While highly controversial – critics have accused Bridge of undermining the teacher-student relationship, charging high fees to poor families, and paying its teachers low wages – initial studies suggested that Bridge schools outperform their public counterparts in Liberia.[153] Are tablets and digital lesson plans the key to solving Liberia's educational woes? I was headed to Monrovia to meet an entrepreneur tackling a problem even more basic than schools.

As my plane descended into Monrovia, I was surprised to see that most of the planes and helicopters bore the baby-blue UN seal, far outnumbering the commercial vehicles on the tarmac. A UN observation post with armed soldiers still watches over the airport, even though the civil war officially ended a decade and a half ago, in 2003. The cab driver who took me to my hotel proclaimed his devotion to Charles Taylor, the convicted war criminal and former president of Liberia. As we drove through the streets of Monrovia, some of which looked brand new, some of which are still scarred by bullet holes from the conflict in which Charles Taylor was ousted, my driver declared, 'If he were allowed to run for president again, he would win in a landslide.' I later reflected on this conversation when Taylor's ex-wife was elected as Vice President of Liberia in the 2017 election, on the ticket of George Weah. When I arrived at my hotel, the bellman gave me an impressive pitch as to why I should invest in Liberia. The war had ground the local economy to a standstill, but as this new era of peace and security appeared to be the new normal for Liberia, many people and businesses began returning to work, creating potential for rapid growth.

One of the biggest factors limiting this growth, however, is the dearth of basic infrastructure. I came to Monrovia to meet Saran Kaban Jones, the founder of FACE Africa, a non-profit organisation that provides clean water, sanitation and hygiene programs in remote communities in Liberia. Popularly known as the Water Lady, Saran has made it her life's work to ensure that every Liberian man, woman, and child has access to clean water.

I met Saran in the lobby of my hotel where she was attending a conference on US-Liberian investments. She was wearing a suit that matched the MacBook on which she was furiously typing. She looked tired, but she had a distinct twinkle in her eyes when she spoke about her work. When she saw me, she quickly put aside her computer and gave me a big hug, welcoming me to Liberia. As she was busy, and I was tired from my trip, we agreed to meet at the hotel the next day, when she would take me on a tour of the city before going back to her house to answer my questions about her work.

The next day, we set off early in her car from the hotel to Westpoint, one of Monrovia's most notorious slums. I've always found slums fascinating. OluTimehin Adegbeye summed it up best in her TED talk: 'After all, what is a slum besides an organic response to acute housing deficits and income inequality? And what is a shanty if not a person making a home for themselves against all odds? Slums are an imperfect housing solution, but they are also prime examples of the innovation, adaptability and resilience at the foundation – and the heart – of every functional city.'[154]

When I told Saran about how I had been impressed by the signs of development and growth in Liberia; the new roads, the new businesses springing up everywhere, the impressive growth in GDP, she insisted that I visit Westpoint, in order to understand the disconnect between these signs of progress, and the lives of Monrovia's poorest citizens. For our safety, Saran arranged for us to be taken around by some former gangsters who had now become activists and community organisers. Although I was familiar with impoverished neighbourhoods in Accra and Lagos, I was shocked by Westpoint. Young girls, who looked no older than 12 or 13 were being pimped in broad daylight, openly recruiting customers outside the make-shift brothels where they worked. A group of boys, no older than the girls, were smoking and shooting up drugs. The streets were littered with garbage and human waste, from the overflowing refuse heaps, causing a heavy stench that clouded the area. Even the rain that had started to fall couldn't wash away the garbage or the smell. I took out my phone to take some pictures, but our guides warned me to put it away, as it would be snatched in seconds. Saran introduced me to Abigail, a child survivor of sex trafficking at Westpoint. When I met her, she was 13 years old and the top student in her 7th grade class. Abigail has a bright smile that lights up the dark clouds of poverty and hopelessness that hangs over Westpoint. Abigail wants to be a community leader and empower other young girls like her mentor Saran did for her.

Visiting Westpoint was, by far, the most difficult part of my entire trip, and served as an important reminder of the gap between rosy economic numbers, and the lives of the poor and marginalised on the ground who are often excluded from the economic growth. As we climbed back into the car to leave Westpoint, I found I had even more questions for Saran. What could possibly motivate her to give up her lucrative and prestigious job working in private equity for the Singapore Economic Development Board to work in Monrovia?

'You know, it never started out that way,' Saran explained. 'When I went to college, I wanted to eventually get involved in foreign service, whether it was for the US or for Liberia, I hadn't figured out at the time because I was going through a major identity crisis: am I American, or am I Liberian? Who am I? What am I? But I knew I wanted to do something internationally because I was really inspired by my father and his work.'

Saran explained to me how her identity as a Liberian, cemented during her childhood partly growing up in the country, motivated this decision to come back and work in Liberia. She described her childhood in Liberia before the war as happy and privileged. Her father was a university professor, her mother was a businesswoman, and she attended St. Michael's Catholic School, one of the best schools in the country. As a child, Saran dreamed of becoming the first female president of Liberia. A precocious and ambitious student who was usually first in her class, Saran won all the spelling bee competitions.

Although she has always considered Liberia home, Saran considers herself a 'global citizen'. She is fluent in English, French, Arabic and Mandingo. Saran's parents were Liberian diplomats and ambassadors, her father originally hailing from Guinea-Conakry, while her late mother is originally from Côte d'Ivoire. When she was eight years old, Saran's family fled Liberia for Côte d'Ivoire right at the outbreak of the Liberian civil war. After two years in Abidjan, her father was appointed Ambassador to Egypt and the family spent four years there, before moving to France and then Cyprus for two years each. Then Saran came to the United States for college, studying at Lesley College in Cambridge, Massachusetts. She later worked at the W.E.B. Du Bois Institute at Harvard University as a Fellowship Coordinator. Then she moved to Singapore in 2005 to work for the

Singapore Economic Development Board (EDB). EDB is the leading government agency responsible for enhancing Singapore's position as a global business centre and growing the Singaporean economy. Saran's role at the EDB was focused on private equity.

In 2005, Saran began sending funds back to Liberia to help one of her brother's friends with his school fees after discovering that his parents couldn't afford it. After two years, he went on to complete high school and enrolled at the University of Liberia. When Saran realised just how much of an impact her few hundred dollars had made, she decided to scale up her efforts and dedicated herself to improving the lives of those less fortunate in Liberia. She was also inspired by Bill Clinton's book, *Giving: How Each of Us Can Change the World,* to do more – something on a larger scale. In early 2008, she launched Fund A Child's Education (FACE) Africa with the goal of providing educational opportunities to children and young adults in Liberia and other war-torn countries.

Saran returned to Liberia for the first time in 2008. Saran described her return as overwhelming: the country's two civil wars had radically altered her childhood home. When she returned, she had to stay with a cousin because her parents' house had been burned down in the conflict. While making the rounds visiting relatives whom she hadn't seen in over a decade, Saran was shocked by the devastation and poverty she saw all around the country. Saran decided that the first task of FACE Africa would be to discover what students and teachers wanted and needed to improve education in Liberia. While interviewing principals and teachers at various schools, Saran discovered that every single school complained about the problems caused by the lack of clean water. Students would leave school to look for water to drink, and then get sick from drinking contaminated water, missing days and sometimes weeks of school.

Saran told me, 'I thought, "Wow, there's something to this water thing!" It's linked to education, to healthcare, even to a country's development and GDP, because if you are putting so much stress on a country's healthcare because of basic water-borne diseases, simple things like diarrhoea and typhoid and cholera, then a country can't really develop without tackling the basic need of water. So, it just kept coming back to water, water, water, and I decided "You know what? I'm going to champion this water cause!"'

Water wasn't just an issue for Liberia – it is a global issue. The United Nations estimates that 2.2 billion people lack access to safely managed drinking water services and 4.2 billion people lack safely managed sanitation services.[155] Yet, while the challenges of clean water and sanitation are clearly global, South-east Asia and Sub-Saharan Africa face some of the worst problems.[156] Water and sanitation have a very broad impact, covering all genders and age groups, and affecting health, economics, education and the central features of life in a community.

Lack of access to clean water and basic sanitation undermines efforts to end extreme poverty and disease in the world's poorest countries where people in rural areas continue to be disproportionately underserved. Together, unclean water and poor sanitation are one of the leading causes of child mortality: diarrhoea causes about three hundred thousand deaths annually of infants under the age of five.[157] In Liberia, less than 10% of the population has access to safely managed drinking water and sanitation services.[158]

As with many challenges in development, women and girls are disproportionately impacted because of their higher exposure rates. Twice as many women as men are responsible for water collection. In addition to higher exposure rates, women in the developing world walk six kilometres each day to collect water, time which could be spent in school or at work. Studies show that more than half of girls who drop out of primary school in Sub-Saharan Africa do so partly because of a lack of separate toilets and lack of access to safe water. The effects of the lack of access to water and sanitation have a macroeconomic impact as well. The World Health Organisation estimates that the loss of productivity to water and sanitation related diseases costs many countries up to 5% of GDP.[159] Moreover, water and sanitation scarcities will be exacerbated through challenges such as climate change and urbanisation.

Even though Saran was pivoting from education to water and sanitation, she decided to keep the name of the organisation 'because the name FACE Africa can apply to anything... let's face Africa, let's face the challenges and I chose Africa because I am not limiting my work to just Liberia, I want to focus on other African countries and expand beyond Liberia [in the future].' This responsiveness has become something of a hallmark for Saran's work with FACE Africa. Initially, Saran attempted to set up several projects across Liberia, but she soon noticed that FACE Africa's resources were spread too thin to have a measurable impact, so she decided to focus on one region of the country and create a sustainable solution to its water crisis before moving on to do the same in another region.

The region Saran chose was the Rivercess county, one of Liberia's most underdeveloped and rural areas. According to Saran, there is not a single paved road in the whole county. 'There are a number of NGOs here in Liberia,' Saran remarked. 'After the war, the country got a lot of aid money and so there are a lot of NGOs working in the country. At my last count, there were over 150 organisations in Liberia that focus on water, sanitation and hygiene projects: 150 for a country of less than 4 million people. But you don't see the impact, even if you travel 10 or 20 miles outside Monrovia. Even here in Monrovia, there's a huge water and sanitation crisis, but outside of Monrovia it's even worse.'

Saran and her team selected Rivercess county for two important reasons: firstly, because the county is so rural and underdeveloped, virtually no other NGOs were working there, and if FACE Africa could get its projects to work there, it would be easier to scale up to other counties; and secondly, because the county's population is relatively small, so the challenge of providing clean water to every resident is more manageable for a new organisation with limited resources. Rivercess is under-populated with 115,000 people. The goal was to use Rivercess as a pilot for the greater goal of ensuring that every single person in Liberia has access to safe drinking water.

The first step of the "County by County" initiative was, with the help of county officials and local partners, to conduct a complete countywide assessment of the county's current water and sanitation resources and projected needs. Based on the study that Saran and her team conducted, they estimated a need to install 250 water points in Rivercess. They initially thought the project would cost 1.2 to 1.5 million dollars, and gave themselves a timeline of 5 years, contingent on raising the required funding and increase the capacity of the organisation on the ground. They also realised that by working with local partners to implement the projects, they could scale up faster. As Saran declared, 'We can solve this water crisis...it's not rocket science.'

A part of FACE Africa's model requires spending a considerable amount of time collecting baseline data in beneficiary communities as the analysis of this data is imperative to the planning, design, implementation, monitoring and evaluation of the organisation's interventions in various communities. FACE Africa collects baseline data using participatory methods to ensure that the community has a stake in the success of the project and to reveal any hidden issues that can affect the design and implementation of the interventions.

The baseline data collected includes the background of the community, population, socio-cultural practices, past interventions, infrastructure, existing socio-political structures and their various roles, hygiene practices, economic activities, water and sanitation facilities, leadership structures and communication channels, norms and taboos, common diseases, perceptions about their community and gender roles.

FACE Africa uses participatory learning approach (PLA) tools to collect the data[160], and analyses the results together with the entire community at community meetings to ensure that the has an ownership stake in the entire process and as a result would be more likely to stay committed to the decisions derived from the analyses. For each community, FACE Africa facilitates the formation of a Water and Sanitation Committee to oversee the operation and maintenance of water, sanitation and hygiene activities. As part of the organisation's model, women make up 50% of the committee structure. Community members are trained by technical engineers; they participate in the construction and installation of any hardware as well as maintenance. FACE Africa commits to monitoring projects for up to 10 years after implementation and has maintained a 100% functionality rate of all its projects since inception.

Saran says the FACE Africa model 'requires us to roll up our sleeves and get our hands dirty.' She emphasises the local elements of their approach – the projects utilises local materials, local labour, and ownership is transferred to the communities upon completion. 'We focus on optimising sustainability of our water projects by forming long-lasting, collaborative relationships with communities. We do not build water systems in isolation. Instead we work with communities to co-create programs that are appropriate for them and the environment in which they live.'

The power of this collaborative, inclusive and participatory approach that empowers local communities became evident during the Ebola outbreak. The World Health Organisation reported cases of Ebola Virus Disease (EVD) in Guinea in 2014 and later that year declared it a public health emergency of international concern. Over the duration of the epidemic, the largest in history, EVD spread to 9 countries: Liberia, Sierra Leone, Italy, Mali, Nigeria, Senegal, Spain, the United Kingdom and the United States. In Liberia, an estimated 10,678 cases resulted in the deaths of 4,810 people, the highest global death count, before the epidemic was finally contained in 2016.[161]

According to Saran, part of the challenge during the epidemic was the lack of trust between local communities and Liberia's national government. As a result, many community members would chase out NGOs, believing that EVD was a ploy by the government to obtain more international aid money. In addition, EVD symptoms were like those of other diseases such as malaria and water-borne illnesses so did not immediately raise concerns. Unlike the national government, FACE Africa had developed trust with communities in Rivercess. They had also developed local socio-political leadership structures to manage the water and sanitation projects, which they were able to leverage to put together advocacy teams and Ebola Committees, training community members to join this response. As a result, Rivercess was spared the devastation that EVD wrecked across many communities in Liberia.

Reflecting on FACE Africa's growth, for Saran, the greatest challenge that she initially faced was raising funds for the organisation. In 2009, the organisation received a $10,000 grant from the Davis Project for Peace, a Vermont-based charity, to implement its first clean water project in Barnesville, Rivercess. Later, they won a grant from Concern Worldwide, an organisation based in Ireland, and another $20,000 grant from the Chase Community Giving program. FACE Africa has focused on social media and online newsletters to raise awareness about its work and generate a buzz. Currently 85% of all the funds they raise comes from online giving. FACE Africa recently participated in a grant challenge online and were able to leverage their social media followers to raise $124,000 in six weeks.

All Saran's persistence has paid off. At the end of 2018, FACE Africa was close to reaching an important milestone. While it took double the time (nine years) and double the capital ($3 million), FACE

Africa was finally on track to achieve its original goal of 100% water coverage in Rivercess county, in the process impacting over 115,000 people and becoming the first NGO in Liberia to achieve this feat. Saran wants her organisation to change the way NGOs do business in Liberia. She explained to me, 'As we are looking to prove this model in Rivercess, we hope to influence policies, and show that if we really take this water situation seriously and commit to it with the right partnerships, and the right level of commitment, we can solve this problem in all of Liberia. So that's the bigger goal that we are trying to accomplish, not just deliver access to water, which is our number one goal, but to also show that this can be achieved by being strategic about where we put resources. The government needs to get involved at this level, because we can't have over a hundred organisations that claim to be implementing water projects, and that have the resources and the funding to do it, but you don't see the impact.'

Saran doesn't want to work on FACE Africa forever. When I asked her where she hoped she'd be if I return to interview her in 20 years, she replied, 'Well, I would hope by then Face Africa doesn't exist, I would hope that we are still not around and digging wells, because that would be a major problem, that would mean we haven't done anything!' I am inspired by Saran's optimism, and that of her fellow Liberians, and the courage they all exhibit in deciding to pick up the pieces after the civil war and rebuild their country.

As I reached the airport to leave Monrovia, I was stuck by contradictory feelings of hope and trepidation. I was buoyed by Saran's work, by the signs of increasing development that were springing up all over Monrovia, but I couldn't shake the memory of what I had seen in Westpoint. Westpoint served as a haunting reminder to me that economic development and GDP growth is meaningless if it marginalises those at the bottom.

8

M'HAMED KOUIDMI

LEVERAGES TECHNOLOGY TO CREATE JOBS

THE NEXT SOCIOPRENEUR TOOK ME TO ALGERIA, AFRICA'S largest and the world's tenth largest country by land mass.[162] I had learned a lot about Algeria before my visit. One of my favourite teachers at the Peddie School in New Jersey, where I attended boarding school, was Anne-Marie Gustavson, a French teacher. I developed a close relationship with her, and she shared stories with me about her late brother, Bishop Pierre Claverie, a French Catholic priest who served as bishop of Oran, Algeria. Bishop Claverie, popularly known as "the bishop of the Muslims" was famous for preaching Muslim-Christian dialogue for years before he was murdered in a bombing at his residence in 1996.[163] Madame Gustavson also told me about some of the horrors of the Algerian War of Independence, which claimed over a million Algerian lives by its end in 1962. After elections were cancelled in 1992, when it was clear that the Islamists were going to win, the country erupted into a brutal civil war, claiming 150,000 lives.[164]

Prior to the colonisation by the French in 1830, Algeria was originally inhabited by Berbers until the Arabs conquered North Africa in the 7th century. The Berbers resisted the Arab conquest and fought to preserve their culture. To this day, the Berbers make up about 30% of Algeria's population. Algeria was later part of the Turkish Ottoman Empire until the French conquest.

With a GDP of $160 billion in a country of 41.5 million people, Algeria is classified by the World Bank as an upper middle income economy.[165] Oil and gas reserves were discovered in the 1950s, and energy exports are the backbone of the economy, with estimated oil reserves of nearly 12 billion barrels.[166] Algeria faced an economic crisis in 2015 when oil prices plunged, given that it depends on energy for 97% of its exports and over 60% of its government revenue.[167] In the last two decades, Algeria has taken significant steps to improving the wellbeing of its people. The government has cleared its debt, invested heavily in infrastructure projects and social projects, and has made great progress in key human development indicators. Life expectancy, for instance, has increased by 16.6 years, and the country has now achieved universal primary education with a 98% primary net enrolment rate in 2018 with gender parity. These results have contributed to Algeria's overall socioeconomic stability.[168]

Challenges, however, remain. The government needs to improve the quality of education given Algeria's lacklustre performance, with its 15 year-olds ranked 71 out of 72 countries in science and mathematics in the 2015 Programme for International Student Assessment (PISA).[169] Poverty also remains widespread, and unemployment is high among the youth.[170] While official unemployment hit 11.2% in 2015, it was 29.9% among the youth.[171] Government corruption and poor quality of public services have further engendered discontent. Almost 75% of the poor in Algeria live in urban areas, relying on informal jobs or subsistence agriculture to survive.[172]

During graduate school at Harvard, I dated an Algerian neuroscientist and STEM cell researcher, Dr. Wardiya Afshar Saber, who introduced me to Algerian cuisine and culture. I learned about novelists like Assia Djebar, became aware of philosopher Frantz

Fanon's time in Algeria, and explored Algerian pop music, raï. Wardiya introduced me to Imad Mesdoua, an Algerian political risk consultant who specialised in the Maghreb region. I asked Imad to help me find the most interesting young entrepreneurs in Algeria, and he insisted: 'You *must* meet M'hamed Kouidmi.'

M'hamed was one of the most interesting entrepreneurs I met during this journey. He is the founder of a social enterprise that helps address youth unemployment, with a focus on helping marginalised communities including women, people living with disabilities and the LGBTQ (lesbian, gay, bisexual, transgender and queer) community. 'These marginalised communities face discrimination in Algeria. For example, we do not have a gender pay-gap problem in Algeria, which is great, however, even though more women than men access higher education, only a third of women who graduate have access to jobs. People living with disabilities and members of the LGBTQ community also face ostracisation and discrimination.'

LGBTQ rights have long been controversial on the African continent. In Algeria, homosexuality was criminalised in 1966 and is punishable by a fine and up to two years imprisonment.[173] Throughout Africa, 38 out of 54 countries have enacted laws that make it illegal to be gay, and in countries like Somalia and South Sudan, homosexuality is punishable by death. A Pew Research Survey revealed that 98% of people in Nigeria believe LGBTQ people should not be accepted by society. In Uganda, that number was 96%; Senegal, 96%, Ghana 96%, Kenya 90%.[174]

Uganda has made headlines for its anti-LGBTQ movement and produces one of the highest numbers of LGBTQ refugees in the world. In 2014, the government attempted to introduce the Anti-Homosexuality Act, which included a provision for punishment by death. Even though it was later declared unconstitutional by the Supreme Court in Uganda, it legitimised widespread homophobic violence, with newspapers and the media publishing identities of LGBTQ people.[175]

There is a sense among many Africans that LGBTQ is "un-African." Queer Nigerian-American photographer Mikael Owunna once protested that 'I felt my existence was an inherent contradiction because of my sexuality. I experienced considerable homophobia in African spaces and was told that being gay was "un-African" – a disease from the West and white people.'[176] Former President Yahya Jammeh of the Gambia, represented this view most violently, in a speech to the United Nations, where he condemned homosexuality as 'very evil, antihuman, as well as anti-Allah.'[177] He also called homosexuals "vermins", saying 'we will fight these vermins called homosexuals or gays the same way we are fighting malaria-causing mosquitoes, if not more aggressively.' He went on to declare that 'LGBT can only stand for leprosy, gonorrhoea, bacteria and tuberculosis – all of which are detrimental to human existence.' [178]

However, other African countries have been pioneers in the fight for LGBTQ rights. For example, South Africa's constitution was the first in the world to protect people from discrimination based on sexual orientation. South Africa was also the first country in Africa to legalise same-sex marriage.[179] Kenya is one of the few East African nations that has provided homes for LGBTQ refugees, 90% of whom flee from neighbouring Uganda.[180]

Many African leaders, and Africans who oppose LGBTQ people, often root their arguments in the two Abrahamic religions (Islam and Christianity) and an apparent African culture. The Catholic Pope himself waded into this controversy, when he reacted to reporters asking about gay priests at the Vatican, with the viral response 'If someone is gay and he searches for the Lord, who am I to judge?'[181] Pope Francis followed this with his declaration in his post-synodal apostolic exhortation *Amoris Laetitia* that 'every person, regardless of sexual orientation, ought to be respected in his or her dignity and treated with consideration.'[182] This sparked great opposition among African clergy, with South African Cardinal Wilfrid Napier tweeting in response 'God help us. Next, we'll have to apologise for teaching that adultery is a sin! Political correctness (PC) is today's major heresy!'[183]

I was nervous about profiling M'hamed and interviewing him in a country where people with different views about religion, sexual orientation and politics are ostracised. We met at a café terrace in Algiers. 'I would not advise you to leave your phone on the table. It might disappear.' M'hamed warned me, as I sheepishly slipped my iPhone back into the deep pockets of my salmon coloured, loose flowing Malian kaftan. Bespectacled, he sported a crescent-shaped earring and had a suitcase in tow.

Born and raised in Algiers in 1988, M'hamed's father died when he was only eight years old. His mother was forced to work three jobs to make ends meet to support her six children. Despite their modest means, M'hamed's mother constantly reminded him that there are many others who are in worse socio-economic conditions and thus, they had a moral obligation to be grateful and to support the less privileged. From age nine, he would attend camps to support the poor in the Sahara. In Algeria, regional disparities meant that there was twice as much poverty among the inhabitants of the Sahara region of the country.[184]

At the age of 14, M'hamed began to suffer an internal conflict about his identity. Around that time, he was doing homework for his French class, and procrastinating by reading the newspaper when he came across an advertisement for an exchange program in the United States. He wanted to apply. He recalled that when he came home and first told his mother that he wanted to apply for this program, she scolded him and told him to be realistic, warning, 'Why would they take you? You are not the son of a minister.' The next day, she felt bad for her outburst and encouraged him to apply.

The interview was being held in a fancy neighbourhood in Algiers, a place he had never visited. M'hamed remembers that everyone attended with their parents, but he came alone because his mother had to work. He recalls a Tunisian employee of the American embassy who openly remarked, 'He is not a good student, he will fail academically in the United States.' However, two women on the panel, who cried after hearing his life story, fought for him and he ended up being one of the 25 Algerians chosen to study in the United States on scholarship.

M'hamed recalls his time in America with great fondness. 'It was spiritually, politically and culturally awakening.' He shared, 'I had doubts about my [Muslim] faith because it presented challenges to my identity, but I realised in the United States that so did the Torah and the Bible.' M'hamed also struggled with his identity. 'I dated the most gorgeous blondes in high school. I struggled with my faith. I ultimately realised that while I may not believe or fully follow all the rules, I am a Muslim at my core.' He was heavily involved with promoting interfaith dialogue in the local community and today the Walnut Hills United Methodist Church in Des Moines, Iowa, honours his legacy by awarding the M'hamed Kouidmi Bridge Building Award every year.

It was in America that M'hamed had access to the internet. He remembers, laughing, at how he struggled to use Apple computers, and his initial misunderstanding of the rules of plagiarism. He would copy and paste material from Wikipedia in his essays and would be failed for "plagiarism" – a term that was foreign to him. 'I did not know I was doing something wrong.' M'hamed saw a huge potential in ICT and put a lot of effort into learning how to use all the Microsoft suite of software, and how to use the internet effectively. However, he also learned how dangerous the world wide web could be for children. He recalls how he faced abuse from an adult when he was on Myspace, and how easy it was to access pornography and illicit materials on the web. The internet was new and overwhelming to him.

At age 18, M'hamed returned to Algeria, with an early conviction in the power of technology, and a renewed sense of self, having come to terms with his identity. He decided to share his evolution with some of his family and friends on New Year's Eve, and recalls being shocked and overwhelmed by the reaction. 'I was hugged and kissed.' Nevertheless, M'hamed still faces discrimination and challenges for being vocal and different in Algeria. He recalls a moment when some of his colleagues refused to vote for him as president of the Rotary club. When he persisted and eventually won the election, half the membership left the club in protest. 'No one fought for me. It still hurts to this day,' he admits.

M'hamed has tried to empower youth in Algeria to embrace their identity, including the LGBTQ community, who face discrimination and at times, violence. 'We are a religious country. Sodomy equals hell. It will never be publicly accepted. Never.' However, he noted that there are more homosexual activities occurring than is publicly acknowledged, with a cultural nuance on what is considered homosexual. 'As long as you are on top, you are not gay, only the man at the bottom is a "faggot" ...there is no homosexual in Algeria, there is only the man and the faggot.' M'hamed also revealed that sexual abuse of young boys is more prevalent than one would imagine in a conservative society like Algeria's. He was a survivor of sexual violence when he was only ten years old. Acknowledging the difficulties with fighting for LGBTQ rights in Algeria, M'hamed insists, 'My work focuses on building a more inclusive Algeria. I just want to help the Algerian youth, including the LGBTQ community to be more accepting of themselves. Culturally, we are very accepting. We have singers who cross dress and sing about man-love. It's very complex.'

M'hamed explained that in a country where homosexuality is taboo, the internet creates a virtual community for LGBTQ people to support themselves in an anonymous environment. 'Through social media, the LGBTQ community has been able to discover that some famous people like TV anchors, journalists and actors in Algeria were gay. Realising that there are other people who are doing amazing things in their lives and are successful on a professional level [despite their sexual orientation], has been inspiring for the community.' M'hamed noted that there is a community of LGBTQ people on Facebook who are using online videos with hidden faces to promote understanding of LGBTQ people. Their work has been meaningful in creating support for members of their community; however, it has also risked a backlash. 'The internet has been a tool for helping many members of the LGBTQ community to gain confidence in terms of their sexuality, but it has also opened their eyes clearly on the reality on the ground. We cannot forget that the society is not the 100 people that surrounds us, society is the 40 million people in Algeria. When I read the quotes, comments, articles and videos about the LGBTQ community in Algeria and see the comments from people, full of hatred with very scary threats, it forces me to realise that life of many members of the LGBTQ community is at risk. I remember stories of gay men who had been killed in their house and a lesbian girl who was beaten up on the street, and reading the comments online and realising the dangers many LGBTQ Algerians face. However, there is growing acceptance among the younger generation, which makes me hopeful.'

Moving back to Algeria from the United States, M'hamed was forced to do one year of baccalaureate since Algeria did not recognise his American high school diploma. He then moved to Egypt to do research on conflict resolution, participating in a program in International Politics and Conflict Management from the United States Institute of Peace. M'hamed also pursued a diploma in social entrepreneurship, and a diploma in SME management from Institut International de Communication et de Marketing. He then spent a year working on youth empowerment programs with Injaz, the MENA branch of Junior Achievement. Then, as a technical adviser to the German development agency, GIZ in 2012, M'hamed facilitated a training and acceleration program for social entrepreneurs. While the project was initially conceived as an entertainment event, it evolved into helping young people garner access to decent work and intensive training programs. M'hamed also helped build and implement the Algerian government's strategy on local sustainable economic development. M'hamed then worked with the United Nations Industrial Development Organisation on cluster development in creative industries. Turned off by the bureaucracy of the UN, M'hamed decided to shift his focus to leveraging business to eradicate poverty and founded Business Wise, a social enterprise focused on helping young people in Algeria to find jobs, with a focus on marginalised communities.

M'hamed believes despite the challenges, there is a lot of opportunity for young people in Algeria. 'We have free education, free healthcare, free social housing programs, and free funding.' He contrasts the current state of affairs with the 90's: 'I grew up with tanks in the street, going downtown and seeing the [decapitated] head of my mayor, the 90's changed all of us. Algiers used to be a city of a thousand bars in the 60s and 70s with movie theatres, casinos, it was a party city like Ibiza and then terrorism changed all of this. But in the past 10 years, we have changed a lot. We went from billions of dollars in debt to helping bail out many countries and assisting Niger and other countries with counter-terrorism. We avoided the Arab Spring when it was happening because of our deep aversion to conflict after half a century of bloodshed, but we risk it all if we do not empower the youth and create opportunities for them. People are tired of being taken for fools. You are starting to see some of this discontent with the recent protests which toppled our President. It took everyone by surprise. There is a new Arab Spring, the smiling revolution. It's happening in Algeria and in Sudan.'

As M'hamed thought about which models to employ for Business Wise, he had an opportunity to attend the Mobile World Congress for free through a friend. At the time, he was only thinking about offline models for training the youth. Everyone he met at MWC was speaking about digital and the power of digital. At this event, he met Mark Zuckerberg, the founder of Facebook, Jan Koum, the co-founder of WhatsApp, and many other technology luminaries. 'I'm meeting all this people and learning about all these new applications of technology and it suddenly hits me that we don't do anything about all this in Algeria, it feels like we aren't even living in the same world or speaking the same language. This was when I realised our only hope to catch up with the rest of the world was by leveraging technology.'

So, when he returned to Algiers, M'hamed immersed himself in learning everything about how he could leverage digital technologies to advance education, to enable greater employment opportunities, and to solve problems. With Business Wise, he launched Mahara'ty, an employment accelerator that helps Algerian youth get employment by offering soft and technical workplace skills and mentoring for career development. However, like Yusuf in South Africa, M'hamed realised that an offline model would be very limited in its ability to scale and reach all the Algerian youth that needed their services. M'hamed knew they had to go digital. 'We are working with 30 students per classroom, but how do we reach thousands of people across the country? The only way is through technology.'

M'hamed and his team have built an online adaptive learning tool to train people with the technical and soft skills and knowledge they need to help them get an entry level job. The tool currently operates in French (with an Arabic version under development) and uses artificial intelligence and machine learning to determine the learning needs of people. It features 65 e-courses focused on soft skills, behaviour at work, job search techniques and entrepreneurship. The tool will propose learning journeys for a user based on an assessment and unlimited access to the e-courses. The online tool was piloted with three hundred users for free, but M'hamed launched a paid version in early 2019 where it costs $7/month for a basic version and $12/month for a premium version. A premium version gets the user in-house training, certification of learning journeys and a career adviser to help with CVs and job interview coaching. However, based on early user feedback, they realised that they could not go completely digital and are now employing a hybrid model blending both online and offline learning. The platform is called Ensõ Learning.

In addition, M'hamed and his team also launched an online mentoring program in partnership with a co-working space called The Address. The Address already had a mentoring program called Tawdjih for entrepreneurs, so they built on that program and digitised it. They developed a curriculum for mentors, and reached out to potential mentors using Facebook ads, and LinkedIn and vetted them through online tests. 'We are building a community of mentoring, and I believe in the long run, we might be shaping a new approach to mentoring in Algeria where mentoring can be a very natural part of the recruitment process of a company.' The mentoring program hosts one-hour webinars taught by a mentor every week based on specific topics e.g. the future of work, or an industry or skill.

Mahara'ty has also developed a job board which will be launched in 2020. They realised that many of the human resources departments in Algeria are outdated, and there's a unique opportunity to offer solutions and services to companies to modernise their HR processes. They initially create an app for companies who are looking to hire people, a "Tinder" for jobs of sorts. Both employers and job seekers can swipe left or right on a profile of the job/company and the applicant, and where there is a match, the app grants access to LinkedIn profiles and resumes, and even helps to book a meeting for an interview. They have also developed online portals for job applicants where they can host their CVs, examples of past work products, etc. and that can be accessible with a QR code. Applicants can simply share the QR code with people they meet, or potential employers.

However, they decided to also use artificial intelligence in the job board to create predictive matching. There is a lack of big data available for Algeria, so his team is using data from Egypt and Lebanon as proxies. The tool they have developed analyses a company's culture, brand, values and the skills needed for a role. On the job seeker's side, it analyses cultural background, educational level and values based on the user's life online – social media and publicly available online data – and creates an e-reputation score of the candidate. For the candidate, the tool suggests ways they can improve their candidacy e.g. if a candidate's LinkedIn page is missing recommendations, it will suggest that the candidate reach out to past employers or peers for recommendations. It also allows candidates to upload CV videos or video pitches. The job board is currently free for companies, but they charge a success fee of 10% of annual gross salary for every successful recruitment.

M'hamed has had to be innovative with fundraising. Part of the platform he has developed has been funded by income from Business Wise's consulting revenues, which were ~$200,000 in 2018. In addition, he has received grants from a few NGOs and development agencies, including a grant from the Middle East Partnership Initiative of $133,000 and another grant of €100,000 from a Dutch NGO called Hivos and the Dutch government. It has been difficult for him to raise investor capital for a social enterprise because there are not a lot of private investors in Algeria. He came up with an interesting model where he got some corporations to provide investment capital to his team and in exchange, they offered them complimentary use of the product for a year for example. It did not work out, so instead he now works with firms like Ericcson and Le Grand to leverage their CSR budgets to train youth in sales and ICT, so the companies can hire from this pool of better trained potential workers. 'We take the youth, train them and help place them with the companies. This pivot helped us reach profitability.' M'hamed has grown the team to about nine full time employees, and ten part-time consultants.

M'hamed is now thinking of ways he can scale his efforts Pan-African. For example, he is exploring collaborations with Josiah Eyison of iSpace Hub in Accra and Teresa Mbagaya of Omidyar Network in Nairobi. 'I've been talking with some of them on how we could do more about governance in North Africa, we've been talking with Josiah on how he can help me with business coaching and how to extend the business to West Africa. We've been talking with Teresa about access to investment, I'm amazed, because you know one other thing I told these guys is that yes, I'm Algerian, I'm deeply African but then I don't have that feeling in Algeria, when you talk to people here, we don't feel we are African and that is something that I find very sad. So, these people are the kind of people that for the past year or few months have been making me feel I'm part of this greater African story.'

M'hamed raises an interesting issue that's tied to identity politics in the Maghreb. Throughout my travels in North Africa, I observed this "gulf" as if North Africa was not a part of continental Africa. Kamel Daoud, an Algerian journalist, captured this in a powerful NY Times op-ed in which he observed: 'In their anti-Western discourse, Algeria's bien-pensants think they protect black people by denouncing the prevailing racism [in Europe]. Yet they would never visit the dreary refugee camps, much less live with blacks, let blacks marry their daughters or shake hands with blacks on a hot day. Secular Algerians often refer to sub-Saharan people as "Africans", as if the Maghreb were on a different continent. Religious fundamentalists are no less racist: during a soccer match between Algeria and Mali in November 2014, the Islamist daily Echourouk published a photograph of some of the Malian club's black fans under the caption, "No greetings, no welcome. AIDS behind you, Ebola ahead of you".[185]

M'hamed feels strongly that he is a part of the Pan-African story, and believes that greater connectivity among African countries, powered by digital technologies, will erase many of the barriers that separate North Africa from Sub-Saharan Africa. One of his proudest moments was when New African Magazine named him as one of the top 100 African Influencers. As he shared with me 'I want to be known as the guy who built a technological platform to help solve the unemployment challenges not just in Algeria, but across Africa.'

THE CREATIVES

CAROLOS LOPES, A BISSAU-GUINEAN DEVELOPMENT ECONOMIST and author, beautifully captured the breadth of Africa's creative economy in an op-ed in the Mail & Guardian, in which he highlighted several of Africa's creative talents – from South African opera stars Andiswa Kedama and Pauline Malefane, Niger's guitarist Bombino, Nigeria's afrobeats rockstar Wizkid, Tanzanian fashion designer Anisa Mpungwe, Congolese artist Rhode Makoumbou, Nigerian writer Chimamanda Ngozi Adichie and Sudanese artist Ibrahim el-Salahi.[186] The global creative economy, encompassing the fine arts, publishing, music, dance, theatre, media and architecture, among others, is a major part of the global economy and is estimated to contribute over $2.2 trillion to global GDP, and to create almost 30 million jobs.[187]

Africa is the cradle of humanity, and its art is as old as its cultures. My college professor at Harvard University, Suzanne Blier, an eminent historian of African art and architecture, taught us about the many ways in which Picasso was influenced by African cultures, and how, for example, in his iconic *Les Demoiselles d'Avignon*, Picasso's deep engagement with African cultures was downplayed for a long time in order to deny Africa as the source of creative inspiration for one of the most influential art pieces of the western canon. From Picasso to Beyoncé, Africa has been a source of artistic inspiration. Yet Africa's contribution to the creative economy has been marginal,

estimated at less than 1% of its global trade.[188] This is largely driven
by a lack of investment in the sector.

Globalisation, and the advancements in digital technology has
helped spur a growth in Africa's creative economy. E-commerce has
created enormous opportunities for the creative products, with 50%
of the continent expected to have internet access by 2025, and online
shopping expected to be a $75 billion market.[189] In Nigeria, in spite
of less than one cinema per 1 million people, digital cinematography
has helped turn Nollywood, Nigeria's film industry, into the third
most valuable in the world, behind Hollywood and Bollywood.
Nollywood creates over 2,000 feature-length movies every year sold
as $2 DVDs and streamed online through platforms like irokoTV
and Buni, employing over 300,000 people and generating $500 to
$800 million annually.[190] In Kenya, the mobile music industry is
estimated to grow by $10 million between 2015 and 2020.[191] In
South Africa, "Joziwood", as the film industry in Johannesburg is
dubbed, contributes $200 million to the country's GDP. It made
global headlines when *District 9*, a 2009 sci-fi thriller produced
and directed by a South African was nominated for Best Picture at
the 2010 Academy Awards.[192] The internet is also enabling fashion
designers on the continent to achieve global acclaim. In 2014, after
Beyoncé was spotted wearing a skirt and a jacket from South African
brand Kisua, it sold out in days.' Beyoncé's stylist had discovered the
brand online. Kisua's founder Samuel Mensah stated that 'the internet
is a great leveller. The speed with which you can access markets and
can generate awareness about your brand is unprecedented in the
history of fashion.'[193]

A similar transformation is happening with African music. You're
likely to hear some Fela Kuti records blaring if you swing by my house
on a weekend. Sometimes, I'll even play some Tiwa Savage and sing
along, much to my neighbours' irritation. Of all the different types
of music, nothing lifts my mood more than African music. But what

is African music? What makes "African music" African? Can we justify a category of music as African music? Is it African because the singer is African? If an Irish singer made music in Niamey, would that be African music? If a Mauritanian composed a classical piece, would that be African music? Is the idea of African music itself another form of the essentialising and oversimplifying of the African continent? The ethnomusicologist Alan Merriam as far back as 1959 noted that 'the problem of what constitutes the identifying characteristics of African music is not a simple one...there is little attempt to generalise for the continent as a whole.'[194]

Nobel Prize winning Harvard economist Amartya Sen once remarked that 'music is not just entertainment, but also dialogue. It is not surprising that music has often been at the vanguard of protest movements and in general has tended to give some voice to the voiceless. The destitute and the marginalised can use music as a vehicle of communication and expression, and a well-developed music industry, with firm channels of transmission, can give eloquence to voices that are otherwise muted and muffled. The development of the music industry in Africa can, thus, make many distinct but interrelated contributions to economic development, social change, political cohesion, and cultural progress.'[195]

Aubrey Hruby, senior fellow of the Atlantic Council's Africa Centre and co-author of *The Next Africa: An Emerging Continent Becomes a Global Powerhouse* published an article in Axios titled "The African music industry is gaining global interest." She highlighted the events in 2018 when Universal Music Group, the world's biggest music company, opened an office in Nigeria and acquired a Kenyan record label, and Spotify, the world's largest music streaming service, launched in South Africa.[196] She didn't and couldn't say African music is gaining global interest because African musicians have long achieved global fame and dominance from Hugh Masekela (South Africa), Fela Kuti (Nigeria), Angelique

Kidjo (Benin), Papa Wemba (DRC Congo), Salif Keita (Mali), Yousso N'Dour (Senegal) and Daddy Lumba (Ghana), among countless others. The African music *industry,* however, has been on the rise, enabled by technology and supported by the growth of a consumer class within the continent itself that supports concerts and live events.

Nigeria has been the undisputed leader in the development of the music industry in Africa. As diverse as our continent is, in almost every single country I visited doing research for this book, I encountered Nigerian music on radio, in the clubs or in people's cars. In Lagos, I met Asa Asika, a young music entrepreneur who was responsible for launching the music career of Davido, one of Nigeria's biggest superstars. Asa believes the key to the global success of Davido and his contemporaries has been authenticity. 'Davido always says I'm never going to sing R&B more than Chris Brown, and I can never rap Miami rap more than Rick Ross, but I will kill myself if Chris Brown or Rick Ross can ever come and sing Skelewu more than me.'

Some of the entrepreneurs in the creative sector are leveraging digital technologies to connect to new markets, innovate new business models, and bring Africa's creativity to the forefront of its economic revolution. Fred Deegbe, for example, a Ghanaian luxury fashion entrepreneur, used Facebook and Instagram to create viral marketing and a movement for his Heel The World (HTW) empowerment bracelets, made of black beads and gold, which became so popular that they attracted the patronage of hip-hop artists in America. Eventually Jameson, the whiskey brand, came calling and partnered with HTW on branded empowerment beads.

Running businesses in the creative economy in many African countries is extremely difficult. One of the creatives I interviewed, Chief Nyamweya, a Kenyan who had co-founded a leading graphics art studio, sent me a note, 'Spoiler alert: Tsunami is no more. We had a lot of passion and enthusiasm. We built an ecosystem for digital artists and an amazing community of animators. But there was no viable business model. The cracks began to show and by the end of 2015, we had to shut down because we were insolvent.' Chief was not alone. Three of the entrepreneurs I interviewed for this section were all forced to shut down their fashion businesses due to mounting losses and high operating costs. Others like Ruby Buah, the CEO of Kua Designs, pivoted from initially just producing African print bags to including jewellery and opening a children's spa, which has contributed to her commercial success in Ghana. In this chapter, we will meet four creatives from Ethiopia, Egypt, Zimbabwe and Kenya, who have figured out ways to build thriving businesses.

9

ABAI SCHULZE

RECONNECTS TO HER ROOTS

OUR FIRST CREATIVE RESIDES IN ADDIS ABABA, ETHIOPIA, Africa's oldest independent country, and second most populous. The country has a rich cultural heritage and is home to the Ethiopian Orthodox Church, one of the oldest Christian churches in the world. Christianity became the official state religion in the 4th century.[197] My brother is married to an Ethiopian doctor, and she and I regularly trade playful jabs at each other, making fun of our respective countries. She never fails to throw low blows in reminding me that Ethiopia has never been colonised. That history is a point of pride for most Ethiopians.

In 1896, the Ethiopian army defeated invading Italian forces at Adwa, and the great power Italy was forced to recognise Ethiopia's independence. Several decades later, the fascist dictator, Mussolini, who was enraged by Italy's humiliating defeat in Adwa, invaded and occupied Ethiopia from 1935 to 1941, before being driven out by Ethiopian resistance forces, supported by British and Commonwealth soldiers.[198] Because of this unique history, during the colonial period, Ethiopia served as a symbol of African independence under its famous Emperor, Haile Selassie. Haile Selassie was one of those great historical figures, along with Kwame Nkrumah and Julius Nyerere, that I looked up to as a young boy growing up in Accra.

My sister-in-law also teases me about how Ghana has no real coffee (she is not a fan of our instant Nescafé) and boasts about Ethiopia's superior coffee. I am not a coffee drinker so I can't personally attest to this, but what I do know is that in Ethiopian culture, coffee is everything. In what CNN calls 'the land of the finest Arabica coffee,' legend has it that coffee was first discovered in the sixth century by an Ethiopian shepherd boy and his goats.[199] Regardless of how true that story is, coffee remains very special and integral to Ethiopian life. Over 12 million people are involved in the cultivation of coffee in Ethiopia. There are many expressions that illustrate the centrality of coffee in Ethiopian culture; a common Ethiopian saying, 'buna dabo naw', literally means 'coffee is our bread.'[200] One of the most important cultural rituals is the coffee ceremony. It typically involves the woman of the house participating in a 2-hour coffee ceremony to welcome visitors into the home or in celebration; it is considered the preeminent social event in many local communities and the venue for discussions of politics, community affairs and gossip.[201] Ethiopia is also home to mouth-watering cuisine, with their local staple injera (a sour tasting "bread" that looks like pancake) eaten with beef, chicken, vegetables and sauces.

As one of the fastest growing economies in in the world in 2019, Ethiopia has come a long way after the country suffered famines from 1984-1985, which resulted in a long civil conflict and a border war with Eritrea. Ethiopia's prime minister, Hailemariam Desalegn resigned from office in February 2018 to help restore peace following three years of anti-government protests, which had resulted in the deaths of hundreds of civilians and the arrests of thousands.[202] The new prime minister, 43-year-old Abiy Ahmed has been making waves with his series of reforms since his assumption of office in April 2018. In October 2018, Ahmed's political party in Parliament

elected Ethiopia's first female president, Sahle-Work Zewde, a week
after he had announced that women had been appointed to half the
cabinet posts. Zewde has given hope to many Ethiopians, inspiring
comparisons to Empress Zeditu who governed the country in the
early part of the 20th century.[203]

The United Nations brokered a peace deal in 2002 that ended the
border war which had claimed 80,000 lives and displaced over 500,00
people. Ethiopia refused to cede the disputed territories. Both sides
militarised the borders and armed each other's rebel groups. Upon
taking office, Prime Minister Ahmed called for peace and offered to
implement the UN peace agreement without preconditions. In July
2018, Prime Minister Ahmed met with President Isaiah Afwerki of
Eritrea, and they signed a historic peace treaty that formally ended
the conflict between their countries.[204]

Prime Minister Ahmed is the first Prime Minister from Ethiopia's
largest ethnic group, the Oromo, who have complained for years
of political marginalisation and were behind the wave of anti-
government protests that led to former Prime Minister Desalegn's
resignation from office. Ahmed has overseen a wave of reforms
including freeing thousands of political prisoners, ordering the
privatisation of many state-owned companies and ending the state
of emergency that was imposed to suppress the protests.[205]

Ethiopia is a landlocked country, bordering Eritrea, Somalia,
Kenya, South Sudan and Sudan, with neighbouring Djibouti serving
as its access to a port. With its massive population of 102 million
people, even though it has been one of the fastest growing economies
in the region, it is also one of the poorest, with a per capita income
of $660. Ethiopia's economy grew at an impressive average 10.5%
a year from 2005 to 2016 (compared to a regional average of 5.4%).
This economic growth has been broad based, resulting in strong
progress in poverty reduction: the number of Ethiopians who live
in extreme poverty fell from 55.3% in 2000 to 33.5% by 2011. In

addition, Ethiopia chalked up some successes in improving its key human development indicators. For example, it was able to reduce its child mortality in half, double the number of people with access to clean water, and quadruple its primary school enrolment numbers. However, Ethiopia still faces many challenges, including a large infrastructure gap (with one of the lowest road densities in Africa), health challenges with maternal mortality and nutrition, and gender disparities in development.[206]

In every country I travelled to, I would mine my network and the internet to find the 10-20 most dynamic entrepreneurs worth interviewing. In Ethiopia, many roads led to Abai Schulze, an entrepreneur with a fascinating personal story. Abai was born in a village known as Wolo in Ethiopia, where she lived with her grandmother. When she was three years old, she moved to Addis Ababa to live with her mother. Her mother worked for an army general in the city, as a maid. Too poor to afford Abai's education, her mother enrolled her in a Catholic orphanage run by an Ethiopian nun, which offered free education.

When Abai was in 3rd grade, the nun passed away and events thereafter changed the course of her life. Before the nun's death, her mother visited her often, pretending to be her aunt so she would still qualify to be in the orphanage. As Abai recalled, 'When she came, she would come as my aunt and I was a little confused as to who she was. Was she my mother or not? I wasn't sure anymore.' After the death of the Ethiopian nun, a foreign nun from Malta became the new head of the orphanage. With this new Maltese nun and her new rules, her mother's frequent visits could result in Abai's dismissal from the orphanage because it would suggest that she had family and thus did not need to be there. As painful as it was, her mother suddenly stopped visiting. So, 'from 3rd grade to 5th grade, I never saw her again.'

At the orphanage, families that wanted to adopt orphans contacted them occasionally. The orphanage produced a video to introduce the orphans and the orphanage to potential host families. One such videos featured Abai and found its way to the United States. She had (and still has) a wide, infectious smile that caught the heart of a family in Texas. This family showed up in Addis and before she knew it, she had been adopted and moved to live with them, unbeknown to her biological mother.

Abai never dreamed of leaving the orphanage and never imagined she would ever live in the United States. She initially found her new family to be very "strange". She didn't understand why her adoptive mother had red hair and was amused by the freckles on her face. Similarly, her new family and everyone she met in Texas thought she was strange as well. She recalls that people she would meet found her to be "exotic" and she felt treated like a doll sometimes. Everyone kept complimenting her on her beautiful smile.

Despite the welcoming environment from her new family, the transition was rough for Abai. She could not speak a word of English so her adoptive parents got her a tutor to help her improve English language proficiency. Initially, she was enrolled in a public school, but was later moved to a private school after 5th grade. She struggled with the transition from the school in Ethiopia to the America system. For example, when she was given a homework assignment that she found to be difficult, Abai would cry over it out of fear of being beaten, which was how she was treated in the Catholic school back in Addis. Gradually, with the help of the tutor, she improved in her academics, and began to show an aptitude for mathematics.

Her new parents, understanding the importance of being connected to your roots, always encouraged her to stay in touch with her friends in Ethiopia. 'They definitely encouraged it very much. They pushed me to read in Amharic and when I was on the phone with different friends, they made efforts to make sure I continued to speak in Amharic. Otherwise, I wasn't allowed to talk to my friends.

Sometimes you get into the language that's most comfortable and you just want to get to the juicy point and talk, but when my dad came into the room I would switch into Amharic. He made me keep journals as well, which are funny to read now. They also bought me different Amharic books. At some point I did lose the language, but when we adopted more kids, I was forced to try to translate which helped me [regain fluency].'

After three years in America, her dad gave her an opportunity to relive her childhood by taking her back to Ethiopia on a visit. She remembers how emotional and dramatic an experience it was for her. She reconnected with her friends who were still at the orphanage. The most emotional part of her visit was when her biological mother showed up and it was déjà vu for her again: she wasn't sure whether it was her mother or her aunt. Her adoptive father had ordered a DNA test which confirmed that she was indeed her biological mother, so he promised to bring Abai back to Ethiopia when she was ready. Abai recalls that visit as emotionally draining.

The next summer, she paid another visit to Ethiopia with her adoptive family. A meeting was arranged for her adoptive family to meet her biological mother, in the house of the army general, where her mother worked. The cultural differences between both families erupted in a clash. Her mother resorted to authoritarian tendencies which her new family resisted strongly. Her mother's employer, the general, also dropped a bombshell when he revealed that Abai's biological father was not dead as her biological mother had made her believe all her life. Her biological father was alive and worked in a hotel in Addis.

Arrangements were then made for her to meet her biological father for the first time. At the first sight of him, it was obvious to everyone that he was her father because she was the spitting image of him, so much so that there was no need to do a DNA test to confirm paternity. He was also noticeably younger than her mother, by about ten years. She also learned that while her mother is Christian, her biological father is Muslim. Since then, she has visited Ethiopia every summer to reconnect with the country, as well as spend time with her biological parents. She also developed relationships with her half-siblings. With all the drama and history, she found it difficult to relate to her biological parents and struggled to engage in a "normal" parent-child relationship. During her summer visits, she always volunteered at orphanages, motivated by her experience growing up in one. These visits kept Abai connected to her native Ethiopia.

When Abai reached her senior year of high school and was applying to colleges, she wanted to leave Texas, so she applied to schools in other states, and gained admission at George Washington University in Washington, D.C. There Abai was surprised to discover a huge Ethiopian community. Washington D.C., often referred to as "a second Addis Ababa", has the largest population of Ethiopians outside Ethiopia, with over 35,000 thousand Ethiopians residing in the city.[207] Her adoptive dad continued to encourage her to learn and practice Amharic. In the summers, she would organise gatherings with her friends from the orphanage in different cities across America. At GW, she pursued Economics and Fine Arts and was very active in extra-curricular activities. She was particularly involved with the African Students Association (ASA) and served as its financial director.

Abai first began thinking about business opportunities in Ethiopia when she volunteered for the USAID's trade and investment department, through which she learned a lot about the Ethiopian business environment. At the time, USAID was working with small local designers in Ethiopia on creating products for the global market. She also interned at The Whitaker Group, a US-based consultancy that focuses on trade and investment in Africa.

Abai's regular visits to Ethiopia always revealed the stark contrast between life in the U.S.A and life in Ethiopia. 'I always wanted to go back to Ethiopia and start a business. I was moved by the poverty and wanted to [help] my country. I spent time with the people in the community and I realised that people honestly needed jobs. We complain about lack of higher quality education in Africa, but I met many people with education but without jobs.' An estimated 50% of the ten million university graduates coming out of Africa are unemployed.[208] Abai started brainstorming.

As she learned more about the economy in Ethiopia, she became intellectually curious about the dearth of manufacturing in the country and was interested in understanding why it succeeded in other emerging economies, but not in Ethiopia. For her undergraduate thesis, she conducted a comparative study of the manufacturing sector in Vietnam and Ethiopia. She believed Ethiopia could emulate Vietnam's policies to expand its manufacturing sector. She initially planned on getting work experience before diving into entrepreneurship. After graduation, she worked for a year at the Office of the President of the Overseas Private Investment Corporation (OPIC), where she deepened her knowledge in trade and investment. She then moved to Ashoka, and her experience and interaction with social enterprises there inspired her to immediately start her venture. Ashoka is a pioneer of social entrepreneurship and is the world's largest network of social entrepreneurs. The organisation supports start-ups in the social sector with professional support, finance and a global network.[209]

'The entrepreneurial experiences of the Ashoka fellows inspired me, and I increasingly felt the risk-reward trade-off between gaining additional, entry-level work experience and launching a business in Ethiopia; tipping towards the latter. I had planned to gain a few years of work experience before earning a graduate degree, but my timeline changed. I decided to move to Addis Ababa to start ZAAF'.

ZAAF is a start-up focused on designing, producing and marketing high quality leather goods crafted by Ethiopian artisans.[210]

Ethiopia is home to the largest population of cattle in Africa, and the tenth largest in the world. The country has over 100 million livestock including 54 million cattle, 25.5 million sheep, 24 million goats, 7 million donkeys, 2 million horses and 1 million camels, contributing 16.5% of GDP and a key source of income for many rural populations. An estimated 13 million households are engaged in livestock farming.[211] The government has been focused on growing leather exports to $500 million. Apart from the vast supply of raw materials for leather goods, Ethiopia, being the second most populous nation in Africa, also offers a large domestic market and relatively cheap labour. Abai concluded that 'the buzz is happening right now in Ethiopia, and I aimed to tap into it as fast as I could.'

While the market for leather shoes was quite saturated in Ethiopia, Abai discovered a niche in high-end leather bags. There were some bag manufacturing companies, but they didn't target the high end of the market and they mostly focused on the domestic market. With this realisation and research in tow, Abai launched ZAAF, which means "tree" in Amharic, in February 2014 at the age of 24 years old, and threw away her plans to get work experience and an MBA. She reasoned that, 'I don't think business school was going to teach me how to run a business in Ethiopia. You don't go by the book when you are running a business here. You just have to jump into it and learn as you go.'

Abai realised that with limited resources and a tight budget, she could not afford a large marketing budget. Instead, she reasoned that she could leverage social media because 'it gives everyone an equal opportunity to tell their story and allows us to communicate to the public with a small marketing budget.' She launched a website and social media handles to market ZAAF and to facilitate online payments. She also aggressively used ads on Google, Twitter and Facebook. All the bags are handmade by Ethiopians and from Ethiopian leather. ZAAF employs over 20 full-time employees, as well as a much larger network of part-time employees, and produces handbags, luggage, laptop cases and other high-end leather products. A typical handbag retails on her website for between $300 and $750.

Abai also recognised that there was a growing trend in ethical fashion that was mostly championed through social media. Capitalising on this opportunity, she launched a store in Addis in 2015, and focused on showing the entire operation of making the bags, being 'radically transparent about our process.'

ZAAF mainly sells its bags online via the ZAAF website and in select stores in Europe and the US. Her company also sells through other e-commerce websites. She has organised pop up events in the United States and some African countries to promote the brand. Ethiopia's upper and middle class, and the expat community in Addis Ababa, have also been patronising her products. ZAAF has found its way to runways at New York Fashion Week, and features in Elle, Lucky and Vogue.

Abai relies heavily on the internet for her business model and she was very frustrated with the poor communications infrastructure in Ethiopia. For a while, the only place she could use fast internet was The Sheraton Hotel, Addis Ababa's iconic luxury hotel built by Ethiopian billionaire Sheikh Mohammed Al Amoudi. 'I'd buy an overpriced Coke to be able to use their internet,' she laughed. 'I can't run an e-commerce business with unreliable internet.'

According to the non-profit Freedom House's index, Ethiopia's internet is among the least free in the world, ranked ahead of only Iran, Syria and China out of 65 countries. It is the worst ranked African country in terms of internet access and freedom of information.[212] Ethiopia's government, in response to the anti-government protests in 2016, often shut down mobile phone and internet connections, and blocked social media like Facebook, WhatsApp and Twitter.[213] Prime Minister Ahmed has since lifted many of the bans after assuming office in April 2018. [214]

Ethiopia is also one of the least connected countries in the world, with an internet penetration rate of only 12% and mobile penetration rate of 43%.[215] Access to the internet is also expensive for most Ethiopians because of the government's monopolistic ownership of the telecom sector, although Prime Minister Ahmed announced plans in June 2018 to privatise state telecommunications company Ethio Telecom.[216] William Davison, Bloomberg's Ethiopia correspondent, complained that 'It cost me 44 birr ($2.05) to watch Al Jazeera's latest 3-minute dispatch on Oromo protests using 4G network on my phone, which is not that much less than the average daily wage of a daily labourer in Ethiopia.'[217] Ethiopians spend an estimated $85 a month for limited internet access, compared to $30 a month in Kenya for superior internet access. internet speeds are also slower, averaging 3 Mbps, compared to the global average of 6.3 Mbps and Kenya's 7.3 Mbps.[218]

These challenges make life difficult for Abai, whose business is dependent on the web. The internet challenges have forced her to spend parts of the year in Europe and the United States to manage the digital and e-commerce parts of the business. 'We use WhatsApp to manage our whole team... every morning we send daily reports, so we are all on the same page, and it allows us to troubleshoot in real time... we also use WhatsApp to communicate with buyers and our partners... it's great because we can send images, voice notes, and videos.' Abai confesses that 'my phone is my tool for everything.' She acknowledges that 'technology is the key to where we are right now... without digital tools, I would need a bigger team and a bigger budget. With limited financial resources, these digital tools allow me to compete in the marketplace.' She also uses technology in the design and creative process, sharing that she uses Illustrator on her Mac, and uses the internet for inspiration: 'I can see what is trending in Milan without having to travel there and meet with designers, and I can be inspired by designs and designers from all over the world.' She is optimistic about Prime Minister Ahmed's initiatives to liberalise and improve the country though she cautions that 'there will be growing pains… and we shouldn't interpret that as failure on his part.'

Abai's success with ZAAF has caught global notice. In November 2015, she emerged as one of three finalists in The Africa Awards for Entrepreneurship for the Outstanding Social Entrepreneur Award category. The award is given to entrepreneurs whose organisations make social impact.[219] Earlier in 2015, she was selected as one of the 1000 African Entrepreneurs who participated in the Tony Elumelu Foundation Entrepreneurship Program.[220] Abai is also a proud recipient of the 2014 UNESCO Tremplin Prize for Entrepreneurship.[221] The Save a Child's Heart organisation presented her with the 2014 Young Leadership Award for her efforts at improving the lives of Ethiopians through ZAAF.

In the next 10 years, Abai hopes to see 'ZAAF as a global brand, an African luxury brand in stores in every city in Africa and across the globe.' She already launched a flagship store in Washington D.C. in December 2018 as part of this global strategy. Abai is passionate about building ZAAF into a brand that will earn respect. 'People must be buying it on its merit and not [due to] pity.'

10

DANA KHATER

EXPORTS EGYPTIAN FASHION

WHILE I'M PROUDLY GHANAIAN, ETHNICALLY I'M PAN-AFRICAN, with my grandparents hailing from Ghana, Egypt and Burkina Faso. My next interview took me to Egypt, the country of my maternal grandmother, Teta. Some of my favourite memories growing up are the sunny days at Teta's house in Labone, Accra where I would kneel in the garden, and carefully prune the tomatoes and peppers she was growing. I remember running around chasing chickens in her backyard till she yelled at me to stop. I would fan the burning coal as she cooked her famous "Hausa" stew, and she would tingle my senses with tales of Cairo. Teta would teach me about my Egyptian heritage, tell stories about Cleopatra and the Pharaohs, and describe the Egyptians who look like me, the Nubians. I would smile dreamily, close my eyes, and try to picture Egypt as Teta described it. Later in my life, I would spend some time in Egypt with my great-grandmother, my cousins, and other family members.

Egypt is famous for its pyramids, archaeological discoveries and its great ancient civilisation. My friend, TED Senior Fellow, Egyptologist and professor at the University of Alabama, Dr. Sarah Parcak, uses satellite imagery and other remote sensing tools to discover hidden treasures in Egypt; her team has spotted over 3,000 ancient settlements, more than a dozen pyramids and over 1,000 lost tombs.[222] Sarah recently told me that 'archaeologists have discovered *only 1%* of ancient Egypt's treasures' and we can expect to see 'Tut-like discoveries in the next decades, and they'll be made using new technologies.'

Egypt is the largest Arab country in the world and a power broker in the Middle East. Egypt's president in the 1950s, Gamal Abdul Nasser, was a pioneer of Arab nationalism and one of the key architects of the non-aligned movement (a group of states that pledged to stay neutral during the Cold War).[223] My grandfather had a portrait of President Gamal Abdul Nasser in his living room and idolised him so much that he named one of his sons Gamal and his youngest son Nasser. Egypt is one of the most populous African countries, with 96 million people.[224] Cairo, its capital city, is Africa's largest urban area with a metropolitan population of 20 million people.[225] Egypt is one of the largest economies on the African continent, with GDP of $330 billion in nominal terms and $1 trillion in purchasing power parity terms.[226] Its economy has struggled since the Arab Spring uprising in early 2011, which led to the overthrow of the Egyptian government, dominated by President Hosni Mubarak since 1981.[227]

Shortly after the Arab Spring, I visited my family in Egypt to attend my cousin's wedding. There was a lot of energy and optimism in anticipation of sweeping changes. While my younger cousins were jubilant over the overthrow of Mubarak, Teta was sceptical, cautioning that 'the devil you know might be better than the angel you don't know.' Her warning may have been prescient. Mohammed Morsi, who won the election in 2012 was deposed in a popular military coup a year later led by his Minister of Defence, Abdel Fattah el-Sisi.[228] In April 2018, Egyptian President Abdel Fattah el-Sisi won a second term in the presidential elections with 97% of the votes, though the elections were marred with reports of violent suppression of dissent and the absence of any credible opposition.[229]

Despite its political struggles, Egypt is becoming a hub for technological innovation in the region, with a growing internet penetration rate of 40% and a mobile subscription rate of 114%.[230] As the New York Times described it, technology is transforming Egypt: 'Egypt has the largest community of Facebook users in the Arab world. It's a huge part of many people's lives, at a time when the public square is dramatically shrinking. Since President Abdel Fattah el-Sisi came to power in 2013, protest has been outlawed and the news media is largely in thrall to the government. So, people turn to social media to talk politics, mock their leaders and hunt for independent news. If President el-Sisi makes a slip-up on television, there will unfailingly be a flurry of mocking memes flying about on Facebook within hours. It can be funny, dark or both — jokes about the country's pitiful human rights record, for instance. It's not just Western [social media apps that are pervasive in Egypt. Local versions of familiar digital platforms have gained popularity]. Anghami is the Arab version of Spotify, Souq.com is the big online retailer (and was bought by Amazon in 2018), and there's a host of apps that tell pious Muslims when to pray or that help them to read the Quran.'[231]

Even though I have a lot of family living there, my go-to person for anything Egypt is Tewfik Cassis. I first met Tewfik fifteen years ago when we were both selected in a global search for "25 Leaders of Tomorrow" and featured in TIME magazine while we were juniors in high school. Since then, we have become good friends. Tewfik attended college down the road from me at MIT, and we were classmates in Business School. When I called Tewfik and told him about my research project, he recommended I speak to Dana Khater, a 23-year-old Egyptian serial entrepreneur and the Co-Founder and CEO of Coterique, an e-commerce fashion platform.

Dana was born in Cairo. When she was six months old, her family relocated to Dubai, where they lived until she was 11 years old. Her parents overloaded her with activities growing up, forcing her to learn how to multitask, and to be organised and efficient. She recalls having a crazy and hectic schedule: 'As a kid, I was always doing one thing or the other; my schedule was always packed. I would be picked up from school at about 3pm by my mum. And there would always be my food on a tray and my clothes in a bag that I could change into because I had swimming practice right after school. After swimming practice, I had ballet. I also did gymnastics, piano; anything under the sun, I did. It was a hectic life.'

Dana's mother was strict about her diet. She banned eating after 7pm at home and didn't allow Dana to drink soda. Dana remembers that when she was as young as five or six years old, her mother would prepare homemade chips as part of her lunch at school. One of her classmates would bring chips from the supermarket, and Dana would swap with her. She jokes that the chips trading experience was probably the start of her grooming to be an entrepreneur. Like many of the entrepreneurs I met, Dana had early exposure to technology. By 6th grade, she had her own laptop with internet access and a Nokia phone. She grew up fluent in the world of technology.

Life in Dubai was a 'fairy-tale life' for Dana, until she encountered tragedy when her father died unexpectedly during a work trip to Egypt. It was a traumatic experience for an 11-year-old and Dana struggled with the loss of her father. His death also meant that her family had to move back to Egypt. Moving back to Cairo was challenging. Dana no longer found fulfilment in sports. She became restless and bored. Her mother encouraged her to find an internship, and from age 13, she participated in internships every school year. Her first internship was at Abercrombie & Kent, one of the leaders in luxury travel in Egypt. At Abercrombie, she assisted the human resources department in screening and selecting new staff and organising training sessions for them. The following year, she secured a marketing internship at Shell, where she was inspired to launch her first company.

Dana Khater loved watching *Sex and the City*. She watched the episode where Carrie and Miranda ate cupcakes and talked about their love life outside Magnolia Bakery in New York City. She became hooked and learned how to make cupcakes. Cupcakes weren't popular in Egypt at the time. During the internship, on her manager's birthday, she baked cupcakes to celebrate at the office, and everyone who tried them, loved them. Her manager saw an opportunity for her to build a business around this and changed her marketing internship into a business incubation one.

It was an inflection point for Dana. 'I think that was very pivotal to have someone mentor you like that and say, even though it is supposed to be a two-month program, I am just going to throw that out and work on you. Let's figure out how to do a business plan, let's figure out marketing. And I was in 10th grade at the time, so I did that during the summer. I opened the business, [and] called it Iced & Sliced. And I worked on that for two years while I was in high school. I'd come back from school to do orders and that was tons of fun.'

Early on, Dana recognised the marketing power of social media. She launched the bakery business with four products, and built a direct sales channel using Facebook, and leveraged the social network as her primary marketing medium. She later added local supermarkets, schools and universities to her distribution channels. She eventually expanded to over 35 different products, and they became so popular, she was selling over 800 units every month.

Up to this point, Dana had been using the kitchen at home as her bakery which became challenging as she scaled, since her family also used the same kitchen to prepare family meals. The business was growing beyond the capacity of a shared family kitchen. She decided to set up a store with a bakery and looked at options to lease, visiting some potential sites. Three days later, Egypt's Arab Spring erupted, bringing an end to her expansion dreams. While Dana thought the instability could help in acquiring land at trough prices, her mother feared the climate was too risky, so they decided she would shut down Ice & Sliced. 'It was not a decision I or my mum are proud of because right after the uprising, tons of cupcake stores opened.' Anytime they drove past a cupcake store, they would feel a sense of regret.

At age 16, Dana graduated from high school and started university. She wanted to study chemical engineering overseas, but her mother was worried about her 16-year-old daughter living in a foreign country by herself. She encouraged her to attend a university in Egypt to start with, and offered that after one year, she could transfer to a foreign university if she did not like her experience. Dana begrudgingly agreed and enrolled at the American University in Cairo (AUC).

Dana has always nursed an interest in fashion and aspired to be a fashion designer. During Fresher's Week at AUC, she walked to a newspaper booth where all the newspapers and newsletters printed by clubs run by students were on display. She asked a student at the booth whether there was a fashion section in the newspaper she could possibly write articles for. This young man just looked at her and laughed. Dana walked away frustrated and annoyed. When she returned home that day, she argued with her mother, making the case that she wouldn't have faced such opposition or mockery in the universities she wanted to attend overseas. Her mum's response was simple: if you don't like it, stop complaining and 'start your own fashion magazine.'

The next day, Dana applied to the university press board and obtained the approval to publish a fashion magazine. It took her a year to get the approval, by which time her agreement with her mother to study in Cairo for a year was over. Her application for a transfer had also been sent to the transfer board of AUC. It meant Dana had to decide whether to transfer overseas and abandon the fashion magazine or remain in Cairo and pursue it. She chose to stay. The next step for her was to put together a team of students to launch the magazine. She sent e-mails to the entire student body inviting interested students to apply and was overwhelmed by the response - over 200 people expressed interest in the space of 48 hours. Leveraging the skills and knowledge she gained during her experiences at Abercrombie & Kent, Shell and Ice & Sliced, Dana created job descriptions, set up a club managerial structure and created a founding team to launch the magazine. By February 2011, *VITRINA*, the first fashion magazine at the American University of Cairo, was on the stands. The focus of the magazine was creating content about fashion from Egypt and the Middle East. She succeeded in securing partnership deals with many of the leading boutiques in Cairo. The boutiques offered some of their products for *VITRINA's* photo shoots. Several corporate sponsors also came on board to support the magazine. *VITRINA* had become a sensational hit: under Dana's leadership as editor-in-chief, the readership base increased more than six-fold after its first year.

One of *VITRINA's* partner boutiques, Ego, reached out to Dana to assist them with revamping their buying process and increasing their sales. Dana jumped on the opportunity. She worked on a major project for them to incorporate a younger clientele by focusing primarily on social media and collaborating with social media influencers. This resulted in sales increasing significantly that season. She also convinced them to implement a technological system to analyse sales reports, understand purchasing patterns and to predict figure buying patterns according to trend and sizing. Dana was leveraging technology to order a significant value of clothing and accessories for the boutique. She became passionate about merging her love for fashion with her love for technology.

One day, amidst Cairo's infamous traffic, Dana thought deeply about how technology could be integrated into Ego's operations to further drive sales. She remembered the success they had leveraging social media to engage with younger clientele and thought of a website that could help reach a broader audience. She shared the idea with Ego's fashion designer, but the designer was too overwhelmed with the day to day challenges of running a fashion house to deal with Dana's technological ideas.

Dana decided to focus on this new idea to merge fashion with technology. This birthed the business concept of *Coterique*. The idea entailed creating an online marketplace for high end international designer products. She would work with boutiques and designers to create and combine styles which were then posted on their website. It was a strategy of creating a site that integrated boutiques around the world. As *Coterique* describes itself, 'Coterique curates emerging independent designers from around the world and cross-styles them in a way that's relevant to the modern buyer. We hold no inventory and instead choose to drop ship our items from the designer's atelier directly to the client'[232]

A few days later, Dana came across an application for an accelerator program, Flat6Labs. Flat6Labs provided start-ups with seed funding of $11,000 (funding has now been increased to $35,000), office-space, training and mentorship, and helps the start-ups to commercialise their ventures and scale up. Some of the start-ups are also eligible for follow-on funding of up to $150,000.[233] Dana excitedly filled out the application and was selected to attend a series of interviews. During the interviews, the Flat6Labs team asked her if she had plans to drop out of school. The implication was that all the serious founders did. For Dana, that was not even a possibility, so the only real option was for her to find a co-founder. She went on a search for a co-founder but struggled to find the right partners. Eventually, the Flat6Labs managers introduced her to two co-founders of another start-up, and they agreed to join her to launch *Coterique*. Her new partners all shared complementary skills. For example, one of them had a lot of business and operations experience, and the other was the "technology guru" who focused on developing the website. Dana brought her knowledge of fashion and the fashion industry on board to round out the team. They were successful in being selected by Flat6Labs as one of the beneficiaries of the accelerator program. They received seed funding, mentorship and office space to start the business.

After they completed participation in the Flat6Labs program, her co-founders dropped a bombshell on her: they had lost interest in fashion. They wanted to start a company in another field, and so they had decided to leave *Coterique*. This came as a shock to Dana. It was a three-person team so with the two partners leaving, she would be left alone to run the business. Should she go ahead with the company? What about the stigma associated with a young person, a woman, running a business? Her co-founders had taken care of the operations and technology aspects of the business, how would she bridge the experience gap? Dana struggled with the decision on a path forward with *Coterique*.

She decided to move forward alone, but the breakup stretched her to her limits and pulled her in all directions. She had to learn quickly about managing the website, figuring out the finances and running the operations of the business. 'But I had to understand the business inside out and I think it made me a better founder in the long run. I think it is very important that women around the world know that they can do stuff and not wait to be told that they can do things. Don't second guess yourself, just go for it. I have always had my mum as a perfect support system. However big or small the factor is, she would say, "Just do it because you have nothing to lose. Just do it." She has always pushed me. I think it is great when you have support like that.'

She recruited the support of some friends to help her manage the business. They had no orders for a month and a half and then they received a first order not from Cairo but all the way from Los Angeles. The next order came from New York City a few days later. From March to May, orders were quite encouraging. But the summer months of June and July were extremely disappointing – *Coterique* didn't receive a single order.

During this time, Dana decided to spend the summer pursuing a program at Sophia University in Tokyo. She also enrolled in an online course on Fashion Design with The Academy of Art in San Francisco. While studying in Japan, she visited incubators, engaged with entrepreneurs, attended tradeshows and visited several boutiques. It was during one of the tradeshows that it dawned on her that 'the real impact in helping the fashion industry to grow wasn't going to happen just by creating a network of boutiques. It was also all about the emerging designers, the ones that were too small to show at Fashion Week or be stocked by giants like Net-a-Porter'.

With this insight, Dana pivoted and scouted for up and coming designers and signed them up to the website. She also engaged in more aggressive social media outreach. The result was very encouraging. Sales grew exponentially, averaging 300% month-over-month during the last quarter of the year. Designs made in Egypt were being ordered by customers in the U.S., U.K., South Korea, Australia and many other far-away places. Dana was inspired to continue to leverage technology to introduce emerging brands to the world. To bridge her knowledge gap in technology and finance, Dana also interned at Microsoft and investment bank EFG-Hermes.

Being digital has also allowed *Coterique* to be provocative in its appeal and outreach in countries that are socially conservative. One homepage of *Coterique* features a model in sexy swimwear, with exposed mid-section, and the slogan 'Winter blues begone, it's never too early to shop swimwear.' Dana readily admits that they would not be able to use such ads in Egypt or the Gulf countries, and often use more conservative images when they organise offline pop-up stores. However, working in the digital space unshackles their creativity from the binds of conservative ideology and allows them to freely appeal to the inner desires of their customers. Even in the heart of conservative Arab lands, 'the provocative still sells.'

Finally graduating in 2015, Dana was ready to dedicate all her time and energies to running *Coterique*. Under her leadership, *Coterique* now works with 75 designers from 12 countries, and boasts clients from 25 cities all over the world. The website offers 500 unique products and most customers spend on average $400 per order. It has not been an easy journey for her. For example, family members keep asking her when she plans on getting a real job, not recognising "fashion" as a real job. She has also struggled with discrimination against young people and against women. For example, until she turned 21, she was legally barred from signing contracts or entering into any legal agreements. She also recalled that many of the owners of boutiques she interacted with were men who didn't take her serious. Her experience isn't unique in the region. Egypt generally ranks low in gender equity compared to the rest of the world, at 136 out of 145 countries globally in the 2015 Global Gender Gap Index, which measures disparities between men and women across countries.[234]

Despite the challenges with youth and women entrepreneurship in her country, Dana is excited by the aftermath of the revolution. 'I do love the aftermath of the revolution on entrepreneurship now. Five years ago, when I was working on the cupcake business, a lot of people were telling me to go get a real job. I still hear that now. I didn't have a single friend who owned a business or wanted to start one. Five years later, I have two friends running their own businesses. It is not a huge percentage but at least I have two friends who own their businesses. There is an entrepreneurship wave that is growing. There are tons of people who just really want to be entrepreneurs. For some reason, big names like Bill Gates, Steve Jobs, and Mark Zuckerberg have their images plastered around everywhere. I think the reason the revolution ties in is this idea of hope. Things have been quite difficult here, but people see a sunshine, a rainbow after all that has happened. There's the hope that it will get better for us.'

11

MARCUS GORA

PROMOTES CONTEMPORARY ARTISTS

MY MEETING WITH THE NEXT CREATIVE, MARCUS GORA, TOOK me to Southern Africa - to Harare, Zimbabwe. Growing up, Zimbabwe had a special place in my imagination. Down the road from my grandparent's house in Labone lived the Zarbos. I was friends with their daughters Mimi, Nicole and Ella. The Zarbos often travelled to Harare for vacation and would return with lots of shopping bags from international brands. Ella and Nicole would tell me about taking high tea and other fancy shenanigans. In my imagination, Zimbabwe was this very cool place that I yearned to visit.

In college, I had a lot of Zimbabwean friends – there was a strong contingency of them at Harvard – and they were all brilliant and shared a soft spot for Ghana. Their founding First Lady, Sally Mugabe, was Ghanaian and for that reason, Ghanaians do not need a visa to travel to Zimbabwe. Many of them often joked that Robert Mugabe, their freedom fighter and liberation hero turned authoritarian leader, "lost his rails" when Sally died in 1992. Several of my college friends are still involved with affairs in Zimbabwe – like Naseemah Mohamed Ogunnaike, a social entrepreneur who is working on art and education projects in Bulawayo and Dalumuzi Mhlanga, who founded a youth leadership non-profit in Harare. Through their eyes, I experienced a different Zimbabwe – one certainly troubled, but full of great hope and aspiration.

Zimbabwe has primarily made the news in the past decade for negative headlines. But to better understand Zimbabwe today, it's important to understand Zimbabwe's historical trajectory. Zimbabwe is a country of great archaeological and historical significance. Archaeologists have discovered remains in Zimbabwe from 500,000 years ago.[235] Present-day Zimbabwe was home to the empire of the Mwene Matapa, covering territory between the Zambezi and Limpopo rivers from the 14th to the 17th century. The Portuguese invaded the Mwena Matapa empire in the late 16th century, eventually deposing the emperor in 1629. They came across the Great Zimbabwe Ruins, the largest collection of ruins in Africa south of the Sahara, and originally thought it was the fabled capital of the Queen of Sheba.[236] The Portuguese colonisers were eventually repelled in 1693 by a coalition of warriors.

Starting in the 1830s, European traders and missionaries including Cecil John Rhodes explored southern Africa. Cecil Rhodes' British South Africa Company obtained a British mandate to colonise Southern Rhodesia in 1889. The native Ndebele organised a rebellion in 1893 against Rhodes that was brutally crushed. Cecil Rhodes was a racist and a violent colonialist, who left a trail of tears and destruction in his wake. He later re-invented himself as a philanthropist, most famously endowing the Rhodes Scholarship, arguably the most eminent scholarship in the world, funding two years of graduate study at Oxford University. I grappled with Rhodes' legacy when I was asked to join the Africa advisory body of the Rhodes Scholarship. Eventually I joined and helped launch the Rhodes Scholarship for West Africa. Even though I still have deep reservations about Rhodes the man, I have deep respect for the Rhodes Trust, which openly acknowledges its troubled history, and is taking active steps to invest in leadership and capacity building across Africa, including through a partnership with the Nelson Mandela Foundation.

In 1922, the British South Africa Company's colonisation of Southern Rhodesia ended, and the white minority voted for self-government. Under this new white minority control, the government implemented the infamous 1930 Land Apportionment Act which restricted Africans from having access to their land and forced them into wage labour. This resulted in intense growth of African opposition to colonialism, resulting in the formation of nationalist groups such as the Zimbabwe African People's Union (ZAPU) and the Zimbabwe African National Union (ZANU) in the 1960s.[237]

In 1964, Ian Smith became prime minister and tried to lobby for independence. When that failed, he unilaterally declared independence under white minority rule, resulting in international condemnation and the application of sanctions against Zimbabwe. Meanwhile, ZANU and ZAPU continued to press forward in their war against white rule, operating out of Zambia and Mozambique. Eventually, in 1979 the British brokered a peace agreement, the Lancaster House Agreement, which resulted in a new independence constitution that guaranteed minority rights. In the elections held the following year, Zanu's leader Robert Mugabe won decisively. In 1987, Mugabe led a change to the constitution and became Executive President of the country.[238]

By 2000, there was a lot of tension in Zimbabwe. Some 4,000 white farmers collectively controlled over a third of all of Zimbabwe's arable land. Many of the black Zimbabweans who had been denied access to land began a violent campaign to seize hundreds of white-owned farms. The ZANU-PF government decided to lend their support to this campaign. In response, many Western donors and institutions such as the World Bank and the IMF cut aid and applied sanctions to Zimbabwe over President Mugabe's land seizure programme and later military involvement in the Democratic Republic of Congo. By 2001, Zimbabwe faced a critical economic crisis, having run out of foreign reserves. This resulted in hyperinflation over the next decade, with Zimbabwe among the highest inflation rates in world history, peaking at a monthly rate of 79.6 billion percent in mid-November 2008. At that point, everyone stopped using the currency which ended the hyperinflation. In 2009, Zimbabwe stopped printing its currency and used currencies from other countries.[239]

Despite Zimbabwe's economic challenges, Mugabe won a seventh term in office in 2013, though the opposition MDC dismissed the polls as fraudulent. Marcus Gora, a gallerist, later gave some interesting insights on why he believes ZANU-PF can generate considerable national support among the populace. 'Zimbabwe is still predominantly rural... the opposition has support in the cities, but in the rural area, there is huge support for ZANU-PF because they gave them land and that's what they need and in the cities the people need jobs... travelling around Zimbabwe I realised we are not voting on the same issues... the opposition's message speaks to an urban constituency and offers little to the [majority] rural voters... there is corruption and many problems with the government, but the international media often fails to capture the nuance of the politics on the ground... it's a lot more complicated.'

In 2015, Zimbabwe switched to the US dollar as the main national currency before switching to a new national currency called bond notes in response to dollar shortages in 2016. In 2017, Mugabe was effectively deposed by the military, and former vice-president Emmerson Mnangagwa became President. In 2018, Mnangagwa won the presidential election for a five-year term.[240] When I visited Harare in November 2018, there was another economic crisis ensuing. The bond notes, which had been pegged one-to-one with the US dollar, was plunging, with some valuing it at four or five to the dollar. There was a lot of panic; prices were rising, fuel was in short supply, and there was great uncertainty.

Amidst the uncertainty, I met Marcus in downtown Harare at First Floor Gallery, the art gallery he co-founded in 2009. The gallery was featuring the work of Troy Makaza, one of its artists, titled *Forever Neverland*. Marcus' co-founder Valerie Kabov described the installation as 'a broad act of defiance and optimism of an artist in the face of yet another cycle of impossibilities and improbabilities in Zimbabwe today. The decadently opulent works in the exhibition speak to both the genuine and imagined wealth the country holds in natural resources, minerals and agriculture, making it almost a definitional land of milk and honey... outside the door is a masquerade of opportunism and the black market, which neatly replicates and makes visible the disparities of the haves and have nots, normally well-hidden by city planning unchanged since colonial times.' Troy's work featured large life-size 3D sculptures made from silicon infused with paint (bold and bright colours) and weaved together using traditional weaving techniques. A young artist, only 24 years old, Troy has already received international recognition, winning the curator's choice award at the Johannesburg Art Fair. Marcus' gallery has a fascinating model. But first, I wanted to understand how Marcus got involved in art in the first place.

Marcus was born in 1983 in a small town called Chinhoyi in central northern Zimbabwe, a town of about 63,000 people. He had a twin sibling who died when they were two years old. Marcus' mother worked on construction sites all over Zimbabwe, so her job created a nomadic lifestyle for the family. 'I never spent more than four years in a single place growing up.' That experience exposed Marcus to the rich diversity within Zimbabwe – he lived in rural towns, urban neighbourhoods and farming communities.

Marcus didn't grow up with a television at home, so music became his escape. He would play records at home. He listened to everything from music from the Democratic Republic of Congo to American music (mostly Boys II Men, Brandy, Monica, and other R&B artists). His grandparents and many of his family members were great singers involved in the church choir. At age 12, Marcus joined the church choir as a tenor, and travelled around the country, singing in different churches. That sparked his interest in the logistical side of music. 'It was a lot of people, almost 50 people in a choir... when we travelled, there's transport, accommodation, running the actual event, running sheets with time... the organisation of everything fascinated me.' As he grew older, Marcus became interested in live music performances beyond the choir. Any time there was a music concert in Harare, he would sneak out of the house at night to attend. Later, when his uncle started a nightclub, he would volunteer there. Through that experience, he started to slowly develop relationships in the music industry.

Growing up, Marcus excelled academically – but he was bored by it. He had no passion or interest for what he was learning in the classroom. When he turned 18 years old, Marcus dropped out of school. However, he was still engaged in intellectual pursuits. He took several courses during his free time and remains an avid reader. 'For the past 20 years of my life, I have probably read a book every two weeks.' He got a job at the local media group that was involved in publishing the Herald, Zimbabwe's largest daily newspaper. The group also had a printing subsidiary and an advertising subsidiary. Marcus joined the staff of about 700 people as a junior accounting clerk. Over time he became an assistant to the buyer and ended up being promoted to the acting group chief buyer when a vacancy presented itself.

On the side, Marcus worked part-time in the music industry. Along with some partners, they would organise concerts in community halls in neighbourhoods with emerging artists. In 2007, he started helping a band called Bongo Love. The band's genre of "Afrocoustics" fuses

guitar and traditional African acoustic instruments – the mbira from
Zimbabwe, the marimba from Mozambique, the djembe from West
Africa and the Afro-Cuban conga. Marcus was helping them with
their global tours – everything from obtaining visas to logistics. 'It
was my introduction to artist management.'

Eventually, Marcus left the Herald and focused full-time on
music. He started managing a Zimbabwean band called Makoomba.
Originally from the Chinotimba township next to Mosi-oa-Tunya
(the world's largest waterfall, or what the colonialists called Victoria
Falls), the band reflects its border town origins in the diversity of its
music – singing in English, Tonga, Nyanja, Ndebele and Shona – and
employing a mix of traditional and modern instruments and fusing
the African world sound cultures of funk, reggae, Afrorock, Afrobeat
and soukous. The band has won critical success locally and globally
with one critic calling them 'quite simply the most impressive band
Zimbabwe has produced in recent memory.' Marcus and the band
have been busy – they performed 75 concerts in 2017 alone and have
toured in over 60 countries worldwide. One of Marcus' proudest
moments was when they played with Hugh Masekela at the annual
Harare International Festival of the Arts.[241]

In 2009, Marcus met Valerie Kabov, who was doing research
in Zimbabwe. Amidst Zimbabwe's economic crisis, they both felt
there was an urgent need for emerging visual artists to exhibit their
work and develop their skills and experiment and innovate in an
environment free from ideological or commercial pressures. 'In Zim,
there are very few galleries and in fact there was no commercial
gallery, so you can only imagine the impact on the artist's ability to
sell and survive off their work.' There were three national galleries
in three major cities, leaving aspiring artists in other cities and towns
with nothing. Marcus realised that artists lacked the creative freedom
to do what they really wanted to do 'because a lot of funding is very
conditional, it comes with strings attached and pushes a particular

message.' He recalled one period when 'all the artists in Harare suddenly started painting about HIV/AIDS... that wasn't natural... it was clear it was geared towards attracting funding... and the people see through that as well; the artist ceases to be an artist and starts being part of an advertising campaign.'

Thus, First Floor Gallery was born and started with humble beginnings, using a spare room next to a tailor's workshop in an old art deco building in the city centre. It was established as an independent gallery that is owned and run by the artists. The Gallery as a policy does not accept any donations or aid. 'We are self-sufficient and fund ourselves... for us, it's primarily about creative freedom, dignity, and ownership... no one "owns" us.' For Marcus, it's so important for Africans to own their intellectual property and their narratives. 'I don't say this with any ill will, but many of the African portals today – Africa Now, Okay Africa, This is Africa, etc. – they are all headquartered outside Africa... Sometimes they focus on issues that many of us on the ground can't relate to... on issues that only people who live under the gaze of the other and the countries they have moved to are preoccupied with... how do we shape the narrative about Africa by us Africans on the ground.'

The gallery has a three-step approach towards developing artists; what Marcus calls their 'three Ds'. The first step is discovery. The gallery focuses on finding emerging artists with potential – there is great emphasis on reaching far and wide – across the nooks and crannies of Zimbabwe, and across Africa, to find talent. They established a residency program and have hosted emerging artists from Angola, DRC, Zambia and South Africa. Marcus really cares about finding artists who otherwise may not have an opportunity to develop their potential. The second step is to develop the talent. This part requires investing in training and materials for the artists to produce their art. The final step is to deliver to market. Here, the gallery figures out the best way to market the artists and their product and aims to get the artist to a position where they are financially successful.

The business model of the gallery is to charge 30% of artist proceeds from art sold at local exhibitions and 50% from international exhibitions (since those require a lot more investment from the gallery). This revenue stream then funds the work of the gallery and its educational programs. The gallery has produced many success stories – both creatively and financially. For example, Troy Makaza, whose exhibition *Forever Neverland* I saw when I met Marcus.

Troy was born in 1994 in Harare to a low-income family. Marcus and his team discovered Troy in 2013 and took him through the gallery's program. Troy evolved and started to create art woven from painted silicone strings accented with bright colours, critiquing Zimbabwe's social and political situation and examining contemporary themes. Passionate about art, he obtained a National Certificate in Fine Art from the National Gallery of Zimbabwe in 2015. The gallery sponsored his work for exhibition at the National Gallery of Zimbabwe in 2014. By 2015, they had taken his work to South Africa. In 2016, Troy was featured in five exhibitions in Zimbabwe and South Africa. By 2017, Troy's exhibitions went beyond Africa, and featured all over the world in France, England, USA and Australia, among others. Troy had become a global star. At local exhibitions, Troy sells out his pieces – about seven on average – earning about $25,000 per piece. 'In Zimbabwe, that's significant income for anyone... I've watched him buy his first car and buy his first piece of land... it's amazing to watch our artists become financially successful and independent.' Other artists in the gallery fetch as much as $20,000 per art piece at international exhibitions.

Marcus laments the lack of a strong domestic audience for the arts in Zimbabwe. 'In colonial times, art spaces were only for elites... they were colonial white spaces... we had all these signs like "no trespassers" that were directed at us... people were not welcome or invited to the art spaces... those feelings are still there, and we have to tear them down.' The gallery has tried to support the growth of the local art community by building bridges between artists and local communities. It has participated in urban renewal and has brought art exhibitions to "ghetto communities" like Mbare where many community members had never experienced an art exhibition before.

Despite the difficulties Zimbabwe faces, Marcus is optimistic about the future for his country. He believes in the resiliency and creativity of the young people of Zimbabwe. He is particularly inspired by Strive Masiyiwa (Zimbabwe's richest man and most successful entrepreneur) and his wife Tsitsi Masiyiwa (one of Africa's leading philanthropists and Chair of the African Philanthropy Forum) and spoke passionately about the impact they are having in Zimbabwe through their Higherlife Foundation. The Foundation has operations in Zimbabwe, Burundi and Lesotho where it has directly supported more than 250,000 vulnerable children through scholarships.

I spoke to Tsitsi after my interview with Marcus about his optimistic outlook on Zimbabwe. She agreed with his perspective and related, 'We started the Foundation in 1996 in response to the drastic deterioration in the livelihoods of children who had lost their parents to HIV/AIDS. It was imperative to us that these children get an education, so that they could fulfil their potential and be in a position to meaningfully contribute to their nations. After 20 years of working with disadvantaged communities and seeing lives transformed, I feel our journey has just begun. The investment we have made in our youth will continue to pay off for years to come. This is why I am hopeful for our nation of Zimbabwe: we have seen orphans and vulnerable children become successful individuals that lift up entire communities. What more will the children we invest in today become? Higherlife Foundation will continue investing in

Africa's people — our human capital — because we believe that when given the right opportunities, people have unlimited potential to transform their communities and ultimately their nations.'

Through art, Marcus is empowering young creatives to transform themselves and their communities. 'I want to help build a different Zimbabwe for my [five-year old] son.'

12

DOROTHY GHETTUBA

TELLS AFRICAN STORIES

DOROTHY GHETTUBA, OUR LAST CREATIVE, TOOK ME BACK TO Nairobi. She was the last entrepreneur I interviewed for the book in early 2019. By then, I had interviewed over 20 entrepreneurs based in Nairobi and because of my investment in Stawi, I was spending a lot of time in Nairobi, visiting up to six times a year. I had grown to love the city and it felt like a second home.

In Nairobi, the hotel Dusit became my favourite hang-out spot and my go-to for business meetings and social gatherings, so much so that my friend Beverly would tease me, 'Do you have shares in Dusit? You are always hanging out there.' I was devastated by the news of the terror attack in the Dusit complex on January 15th, 2019. Among the 21 victims who lost their lives was my dear friend Jason Spindler. Jason was an American living in Nairobi who had survived the September 11th terrorist attacks in New York City. He was the founder of I-DEV, a strategy and investment advisory firm focused on emerging markets. Jason and I were working on a project to invest in African tech entrepreneurs before he died. He introduced me to many entrepreneurs in Nairobi and was supportive of this project to tell African stories.

Dorothy Ghettuba also tells African stories but using the power of film and television. She set off on this mission with no formal television training and no practical experience in film production. Dorothy was born in Kenya in 1978 and had an older sister and two younger brothers. She fondly remembers her parents dressing their two daughters up in the same clothes. 'My older sister hated it.' Dorothy was rebellious in school, 'a young rascal' she called herself. She would often play truant in school, much to her parent's chagrin. They ultimately sent her to a boarding school, Serare School, at age 11. 'I guess they thought I needed an environment that could harness all my energy in a positive way.'

Boarding school was a transformative experience for Dorothy. Serare had small class sizes with only 14 students in a class. 'I couldn't really misbehave anymore because the teacher could see you.' While the school had an environment that encouraged academic excellence, it also allowed children to participate in the creative arts and encouraged creative expression. Dorothy thrived in the arts. She had grown up with music and dance and she found an outlet for her energies in the creative arts. She participated in poetry and music competitions. 'I came into my element completely... I was always performing... I had found my passion.'

Dorothy continued this passion for the arts when she enrolled at the Alliance Girls High School, an all-girls secondary school. She spent her four years there as an active member of the Choir and the Drama clubs. After graduating from high school, she told her parents that she wanted to attend UCLA to pursue theatre and film. 'My parents said no and my UCLA dreams were dead on arrival.' After high school, Dorothy moved to Australia where she studied at Wollongong University. 'I couldn't study acting, so I studied Law and I did not enjoy it at all.' Then, the family moved to Canada in 2002, which gave her an opportunity to transfer her credits to Andrews University where she studied Communications.

After university, Dorothy moved back to Canada and started working in Toronto for a venture capital firm. Whilst attending church, she joined an African acapella group. 'It was a necessity for me to find a way to express myself creatively.' What started as a small group of four people singing in church every now and then morphed into a group of seven Africans from Zambia, Kenya, Zimbabwe and Ghana singing all over Canada as well as across Africa. She then moved to Alberta to work for the Alberta Cancer Board commuting four hours by flight to Toronto so she could continue singing. In 2007, they planned an international tour in Kenya and Zambia. During their visit to Zambia, after a successful musical tour, they decided to visit the famous waterfalls, Mosi-oa-Tunya, from the Zambian side. Unbeknownst to them, their bus driver had been working the night before. Not wanting to pass on an opportunity to make some more money, he agreed to drive them to the falls. He fell asleep at the wheel and nearly crashed into an oncoming oil truck. He swerved and crashed into a tree, but luckily all the passengers survived.

Dorothy was shaken. 'It was a sobering moment and I asked myself, what if I had died today, would I be able to say that I had lived my best life ever? My answer was no.' As soon as she returned to Canada, she resigned from her job. Her mother was not happy with that decision and she made that clear. 'When I told her that I was trying to find myself, my mother pointed out that I was nearly 30 years old and I should have found myself by now.' Defiant, Dorothy moved back to Toronto to pursue life as an actress. She got a talent agent and started doing the auditioning rounds.

Dorothy was frustrated because she auditioned many times but couldn't land a gig. A friend in the industry advised her that the rule of thumb is to audition over a hundred times before getting any call-back because the 'casting agents have to get to know you.' Eventually Dorothy landed her first gig which was doing a voice over for a toothpaste ad on radio. Dorothy was ready to give up when she finally got a call to audition for a stage musical play. 'I was excited because it played to my strengths and I really thought I had nailed it... I was devastated when I didn't get the role... I saw the other girls and I *knew* I performed better than them.' She told her acting coach who counselled her that talent is only one component of the decision-making process and how she looked played a huge role in the decision. She was frustrated because 'these things are out of my control and roles for people of colour were few and far between.'

She complained to her mother who simply responded 'Well, if these people don't want to put you on their TV shows, why don't you make your own TV show and put yourself in it?' And Dorothy decided she would do exactly that. She decided to do this in Kenya where she felt had great opportunities in the media and entertainment sector. She always made a point of visiting home very year. 'There is something magical about Kenya... even today, I get excited every time I land at the airport in Nairobi.'

Dorothy packed her bags and moved to Kenya in 2008. She did a lot of research in the Kenyan media space. She had noticed a TV channel that used to have low viewership ratings was now the most watched channel and wanted to understand why. 'I set up a meeting with the Managing Director who told me that the key differentiator of his channel was that it played local content... I immediately saw an opportunity to produce local content and tell local stories.' She had no production experience, however, so she worked for a local production company. 'It was a difficult but valuable experience not because I learned how to produce but because I learned how *not* to produce and the mistakes to avoid.'

Dorothy focused her time on learning everything she could about producing. 'I literally learned how to write a script using YouTube and experimenting... I wrote my first script on MS Word which is just a travesty because there's specialised software for that... I have always consumed a lot of television shows and movies since I was a kid so I binge watched shows and tried to learn from the best shows.'

'Netflix has been a game changer for me... I love the shows, I love the entertainment it provides... as a producer, it inspires me to come up with innovative ideas and concepts... I watch Netflix all the time and I have the perfect excuse "I'm doing research"... I'm inspired by Netflix because of its operational excellence, product leadership and customer intimacy.'

Dorothy is passionate about telling stories from the local African perspective. For example, in *The Crown*, one of her favourite shows, she wonders what the episode with Kwame Nkrumah (Ghana's first president) would look like if told from Nkrumah's perspective. She loved *Black Panther* because 'it painted fictitious Africa in a positive light... I am tired of poverty pornography and safari stories.' These negative views about Africa continue to persist. In January 2018, US President Donald Trump sparked controversy when he reportedly referred to certain African nations as "shithole countries" igniting protests from many African leaders and the African Union.[242] 'We are more than that... *Black Panther* told people that Africa has got stories that are interesting and hopefully it opens up many more opportunities for telling African stories.' Dorothy believes we are more than a single story and we need a diversity of stories and we can't keep recycling the same old tropes of war and poverty. 'That can't be the only narrative we sell... we can also do drama and comedy and other genres... of course *Beasts of No Nation* gets a pass because it is Idris Elba and he can do no wrong.'

In June 2009, she started her company, Spielworks Media, with her savings from Canada. She and her partner conceived an idea to create a show based on tenants in a low-income apartment building in Nairobi full of drama with a rich plot and interesting characters. She wrote a concept note for it and shared it with a network executive.

He said, 'This is great, but I need to see a script.' So, she worked on a script and he said, 'This is great, but I need to see the pilot.' She replied 'Great, can you fund it?' He laughed and explained to her that she was responsible for funding the pilot.

Dorothy hustled and raised $5,000 in financing from friends and family and filmed a pilot episode. The executive saw it and loved it and offered to pay her $1,000 per episode. 'I was both shocked and furious, I had just spent $5,000 on shooting this episode and here he was offering me $1,000.' He encouraged Dorothy to shop it around and she quickly realised that he wasn't low-balling her; many executives offered the same price. However, she met someone at the Kenya Broadcasting Corporation who offered her $3,000 per episode. 'It was less than the $5,000 that I spent, but I also knew that at scale I could cut costs and make this work... I took the deal and in September 2009 we rolled cameras.'

The show was called *Block D* and became an instant hit, catapulting Dorothy's career. She produced another show called *Lies that Bind* about a man who dies without a will, leaving behind several wives and girlfriends fighting over his assets. The show had 260 episodes and is televised all over Africa on M-Net, the Pan-African TV channel. By 2012, her company was producing four shows and then six shows simultaneously. 'We were the hottest production company in Nairobi.'

Buoyed by the early success, Dorothy went on an acquisition spree, acquiring production assets, converting two floors in a commercial building into studios. Then in 2014, she had a request for a meeting with a new executive of her largest client, who represented over 90% of her revenues. He asked for 10% kickback on the contract value. Dorothy flatly refused. 'Then in September 2014, I got an email that the contract was cancelled and that was the beginning of the end.' With most of her revenues coming from this one client, Dorothy's company imploded immediately. Dorothy had borrowed loans from the bank to finance the company's expansion. 'We were forced to close down the studio, cancel the lease and downsize the team… it was the worst time of my life.'

In December 2014, Dorothy went to her village for Christmas. 'I needed some time to think. I was devastated and kept asking myself, did my ethics just ruin my business? Was it fair to say no to the kickback and now most of my employees have lost their jobs?… It was a depressing time and I was heart-broken.'

Dorothy and I talked a lot about mental health, a topic I am passionate about. I too suffered a major business failure in 2016 that precipitated a mental health crisis. When my doctor suggested speaking to a mental health professional about my anxiety, I clammed up and shook my head in protest. I felt a profound sense of shame; I felt the weight of stigma. I could not entertain the idea of speaking to anyone about my trauma and feelings of pain. I felt suffocated by the rigid architecture of my African masculinity. In my mind, depression was not something African men experienced, it was a "white" disease.

Growing up in Ghana, mental illness only meant one thing: the "madman" with dirty, dreadlocked hair bumbling about half-naked on the streets. Yet according to the World Health Organisation, mental health is about 'being able to cope with the normal stresses of life, work productively and fruitfully, and [being] able to make a contribution to your community.' [243] Mental health 'includes our emotional, psychological and social well-being.'[244] Globally, 75% of mental illness cases can be found in low-income countries.[245] Yet, most African governments invest less than 1% of their healthcare budgets on mental health, and unfortunately, we on the African continent have a severe shortage of psychiatrists; Nigeria alone, a country of around 200 million people has fewer than 200 psychiatrists.[246] In all of Africa, 90% of our people lack access to treatment.[247] As a result, we suffer in solitude, silenced by stigma.

As Africans, we often respond to mental illness with distance, ignorance, guilt, fear and anger. When asked directly about the cause of mental illness, in a study conducted by Arboleda-Florez, 34% of African respondents cited drug misuse, 19% cited divine wrath and the will of God and 12% said witchcraft and spiritual possession. But few cited other known causes of mental illness like genetics, socio-economic status, war, conflicts, the loss of a loved one or major failures like the collapse of a business.[248] The stigmatisation against mental illness often results in the ostracising and demonising of sufferers. I went public with my struggles in a TED talk, highlighting the socio-cultural challenges African men in particular face, and encouraging a call to action for everyone to destigmatise mental illness.

'I realised that I had no choice but to bounce back and clean the mess... I saw it as an opportunity to learn. For example, I am now cognisant of the importance of having a diverse customer portfolio and I don't allow any single client to represent more than 25% of my revenues.' The setback also forced Dorothy to diversify her company's services and clientele. 'I realised I had to learn the *business* of running a business and also work on myself.' Dorothy applied for Stanford University's SEED program, a comprehensive year-long program that includes 12 months of immersive management training designed for business owners led by Stanford Graduate School of Business faculty. She also applied for and was accepted into the Archbishop Desmond Tutu Fellowship. One of Africa's most prestigious fellowship programs, the Tutu Fellowship is designed in partnership with Oxford University and provides Fellows with an intensive learning experience on the principles and application of leadership.

With these programs supporting her, Dorothy revamped the business. Fortunately, she owned all the intellectual property of the shows, so even though her company did not produce any new TV shows, it was able to generate revenues by re-selling the content to other distributors. Spielworks Media currently produces television shows (dramas, soap operas, sitcoms, talk shows and entertainment shows), tele-movies, web shows, documentaries, infomercials and commercials both for TV and for digital platforms, online and mobile. Hers client include most of the Kenyan television broadcasters, DSTV, ZUKU Africa, SABC, Canal France International, NTV, iRoko, Econet and corporate clients like the World Bank, Standard Chartered Bank, Safaricom and Fidelity Insurance. To date, the company has produced 18 television shows, 41 movies, 21 web shows, 25 entertainments shows and five documentaries, notching 14 awards and nominations including Best TV Drama Series and Best Online Content. These productions have employed over 1,500 crew and cast.

She is focused on producing high quality content that tells local stories. 'As we produce content, we have to be hyperlocal and nuanced.' Dorothy believes digital technologies have transformed the landscape for media. 'Ten years ago, I had never produced but I was able to learn using the internet... the access to information it provides is a game changer... cloud computing has also changed the game by allowing cheap access to massive storage.' Dorothy believes that technology has democratised distribution which creates new innovative ways to win. 'My competitor is now anyone with a mobile phone... we have millions of storytellers on Facebook and YouTube... it is a double-edged sword.' She highlights the success of Ghanaian producer Nicole Amarteifio in leveraging digital distribution platforms for her hit show *An African City*.

I met Nicole, and like Dorothy, she too, had no experience in production and taught herself using the internet. Nicole always had a dream of disrupting the negative images about Africa and developed the idea for her show while watching re-runs of *Sex and the City*. 'I first had the idea [for *An African City*] in 2006...', she said, 'an African version of *Sex and the City* to showcase the beauty, glamour and intelligence of the African woman. It would mirror *Sex and the City* with characters representing Carrie, Samantha, Charlotte and two Mirandas. Not only would it challenge negative stereotypes of the African woman, *An African City* would also tell the untold stories, broadcast the achievements of Africa that the Western media often fail to show. The all-African cast would have two or more nationalities. The show would trigger a conversation on issues confronting the modern African woman, especially returnees.' The show follows five single young women of African descent who relocate to Accra after spending the majority of their lives abroad. These are successful, professional women navigating their lives as returnees, dealing with romance, sexuality, power outages, work challenges, sexism, and more; all narrated through the main character, Nana Yaa, a journalist returned from New York.

Nicole thought distribution would be the easiest part of the journey. She had a great show that she was confident would be a hit. She imagined TV stations and cable companies would jump at the opportunity. She was disappointed when she didn't find much traction and met dead ends. Some conversations were promising, but ultimately no one wanted to take the risk on the show. Luckily for Nicole, there was YouTube, with its 1.3 billion users watching over 1 billion hours of content every single day.[249] On March 2nd, 2014, she uploaded episodes of the first season on the site. She was hoping to eventually get a few thousand hits from the first series, but within minutes of the first upload, there were about 3,000 hits. It went viral and took a life of its own. It hit one million views within several weeks of being uploaded. *An African City's* YouTube channel has garnered over 3.5 million views.[250]

An African City caught the attention of African satellite channels Ebony Life TV and Canal Afrique. They eventually came on board, providing partial funding for the second season. With this, Nicole and her team could make more episodes and each episode could be longer than the first season's ten minutes. The second season was also offered on VHX, a fee-based video platform, charging $19.99 per person to watch the season, and it reportedly generated more revenues in 24 hours than the previous two years on YouTube.[251]

Dorothy also highlighted the success of Issa Rae's *Awkward Black Girls* which has generated millions of views on YouTube and has landed the creator a deal with HBO. Dorothy believes that the digital revolution and the mobile phone will allow for new possibilities for African storytellers and creatives. 'There isn't really any one Africa media space... the markets are more regional and are at different stages of development... Nollywood has been very successful in building a Pan-African and global following...' Dorothy believes Nollywood is successful because 'Nigerians create content for themselves and are hyperlocal... they don't "adapt" for an international audience... they make great content for a local audience and this translates into global appeal...' She argues that the proof is in the box office where local movies in Nigeria outperform Hollywood hits. When I checked the Box Office records in February 2019, of the top 20, 7 were Hollywood movies which accounted for 40% of receipts, 2 were Bollywood movies which accounted for less than 1% of revenues, and the remaining 11 were all Nollywood movies accounting for approximately 60% of box office receipts.[252]

Dorothy is excited about the potential for bringing African stories to film. 'The other day I asked friends on social media to suggest great books they have read by African authors that would be ideal for film adaptation... within minutes I got over 50 different responses... there are as many stories as there are Africans and we haven't even scratched the surface.' Dorothy believes there is rich content in Africa's past 'our freedom fighters, our pre-colonial, colonial and post-colonial experiences... they all offer rich content for stories.'

Dorothy used to believe writing and creativity was the sole domain of humans, our last triumph over machines. 'I'm not so sure any more... I attended an event where we had to vote on which story was written by a human and which story was written by an artificial intelligence (AI) algorithm... turns out both were written by AI... I was shocked by how good the writing was.' Dorothy is convinced that Africa is a source of rich and diverse untapped stories, that if adapted for local audiences, will generate global appeal. Like Marcus Gora, her mission is to make creativity financially viable for African creatives and storytellers. 'We have to tell our own stories, because if we don't, someone else will.' Twice named in the Top 40 under 40 Women in Kenya and the Top 50 under 50 Women in Film in Africa and recently appointed Chair of the Kenya Film Commission by the President Uhuru Kenyatta of Kenya, Dorothy is making a meaningful contribution to the continent's growing creative economy.

THE TECHIES

DOROTHY SPOKE ABOUT *BLACK PANTHER*, WHICH IS ONE OF my favourite movies. The film is set in the fictitious kingdom of Wakanda in East Africa, a technologically superior nation that was never colonised by any Western power. Wakanda offers a hopeful vision of an Africa that is powerful, independent and a global leader in technology. I met Ryan Coogler, the director of *Black Panther*, at the Obama Foundation Africa Leaders' program in Johannesburg in July 2018. I suggested to him that Wakanda's focus on technology harkens back to Africa's post-independence history. The early post-independence political leaders recognised that advancements in science and technology would be critical in 'countering colonial claims that Africans were intellectually inferior and incapable of governing themselves.'[253] They saw science and technology as the key to gaining global respect and ensuring their independence. For example, in the late 1950s, Ghana's new government under the leadership of Kwame Nkrumah established its own Atomic Energy Commission to generate electricity from nuclear energy.[254] Clapperton Mavhunga, a professor at MIT and author of *Transient Workspaces: Technologies of Everyday Innovation in Zimbabwe* calls for 'a historical rethinking about the meaning, prevalence and application of technological innovation in Africa.' He adds 'What I am challenging is the idea that technology can only come from outside Africa, from the laboratories and factories. This general narrative of technology transfer – from the haves to the have-nots – is one I find troubling.'[255]

We are seeing a renaissance in advancements in science and technology on the continent that is being pioneered by young entrepreneurs. Ghanaian investor Walter Baddoo, the Managing Partner and Co-Founder of 4DX Ventures, one of the leading venture capital firms in Africa, believes that 'technology is fundamentally rewriting the laws of business in Africa. The efficiency gains from technology have dramatically lowered the cost of starting and operating businesses. Additionally, the explosion of internet access positions companies on the continent to more easily create, deliver and capture value. We are living through a complete reimagining of how businesses are built. This is by no means a new phenomenon as the same theme has been playing out across the globe (US, China and Europe) over the last two decades. The relative affordability of smartphones and easy access to mobile data has been the catalyst for Africa to join what I consider a long-term global technology revolution.' Walter is right. In Africa today, we are living through a shift from the old economy – dominated by large input costs, mechanical processes, massive fragmentation, and often political moats – to a new economy that is powered by technology driven processes, product moats, plummeting computing costs, strong aggregation business models and intellectual abstraction through machine learning and artificial intelligence. We are living through what Walter believes is 'one of the most important transitions in history perhaps only rivalled by the emergence of China over the last 20 years or the industrial revolution in the West in the mid 1800's.' Africa is leading the world in mobile money with an estimated 122 million mobile money accounts compared to 93 million in Asia and 1.7 million in Europe.[256]

Walter and his partner Peter Orth at 4DX have been investing significantly in technology start-ups across Africa over the last decade including the likes of Andela, Sokowatch, Tizeti and mPharma. While venture capital flows to Africa are insignificant compared to the $31 billion invested in China and the $69 billion invested in the U.S.,[257] venture capital funding for African start-ups has been growing exponentially in the last half decade. From a paltry $40 million in funding in 2012, it has soared to a reported $560 million in funding for 124 start-ups in 2017. In 2018, Naspers announced it was investing over $300 million in technology start-ups in South Africa alone.[258] Cyril Collon, a general partner at Partech Ventures, another venture capital firm, explained to CNN that 'the growth of the ecosystem is driven by overall positive economic trends creating a reservoir of consumers, rapid adoption of smartphones and mobile broadband, and a dynamic early stage start-up scene supported by hundreds of tech hubs.' Partech Ventures announced that it had doubled the size of its African venture fund to $143 million in early 2019.[259]

Indeed, the continent is flourishing with a growth in tech hubs. Of the estimated 314 active tech hubs across the continent, half of them are in five countries: South Africa, Kenya, Nigeria, Egypt, and Morocco. Tech hubs such as the Meltwater Entrepreneurial School of Technology (MEST) in Accra, Kinu in Dar es Salaam, Hive Colab in Kampala, iLab in Monrovia, iHub in Nairobi, iceaddis in Addis Ababa, and RLabs in Cape Town, offer training, investment, mentoring, office space, and support for start-ups.[260]

These developments have caught the attention of Silicon Valley. In 2019, Andela raised a record $100 million from Al Gore's impact investment firm, bringing its total funding to $180 million to date.[261] In the space of three years, a single technology company operating in Africa attracted four to five times more in funding than the entire technology start-up ecosystem in Africa attracted in 2012. Times are truly changing.

Major global investors are paying attention to Africa's tech promise. In April 2019, Jumia, an e-commerce platform, made history as the first Africa-focused tech company to go public in an IPO on the New York Stock exchange, raising $196 million and valuing the company at over $1.9 billion.[262] Jumia operates in 14 African countries and serves 4 million African customers. Jumia's IPO generated a lot of controversy over its "African" identity. 'Its detractors point out that the company is incorporated in Germany; its founding executives are French and worked in Paris until the office moved to Dubai. The company's tech hub is in Portugal. Marieme Jamme, a Senegalese entrepreneur, tweeted: "Jumia was set up by tech colonialists who saw an opportunity and grabbed it."'[263] Others like E Aboyeji, co-founder of Andela, argue that we should celebrate an African success story and not get into a 'meaningless and primordial debate about what an African company is in a world without borders.'[264]

The world of technology start-ups in Africa hasn't all been stories of outsized returns. With high rewards, come high risk. Even businesses that have raised significant capital and have grown market share have struggled to build profitable business models. Efritin and OLX, two start-ups, are reported to have closed their African operations.[265] Konga, one of the leading e-commerce companies in Nigeria, after raising over $70m from the likes of Swedish investment company Kinnevik and South Africa media giant Naspers at a valuation of over $300 million, was reportedly acquired by the Zinox Group in a down round, with previous investors losing over 95% of the value of their holdings.[266]

I also readily acknowledge that technology is not a panacea for all of Africa's challenges, and presents its own concerns, which we must take seriously. First, as the 2018 scandals with Facebook and Cambridge Analytica have revealed, technological innovation has greatly outpaced our privacy protections. The American Civil Liberties Union, a non-profit, argues that 'this digital footprint is constantly growing, containing more and more data about the most intimate aspects of our lives. This includes our communications, whereabouts, online searches, purchases, and even our bodies. When the government has easy access to this information, we lose more than just privacy and control over our information. Free speech, security, and equality suffer as well.'[267] This concern over privacy isn't uniquely American. Cambridge Analytica is alleged to have interfered in Nigeria's elections in 2007 and 2015.[268]

Secondly, technology presents challenges with respect to inequality. This inequality is heavily gendered. Currently, women working in science, technology, engineering and mathematics comprise a mere 20% of the global work force.[269] In a global economy which will be increasingly dominated by technology, this presents challenges with respect to achieving gender equality. Beyond gender, research from the United States present some sober findings with relevance for Africa. Many economists believe that the major driving force behind the decline in the real value of the minimum wage and changes in the U.S. wage structure is technology.[270] As Erik Brynjolfsson, a professor at MIT's Sloan School of Management puts it, 'My reading of the data is that technology is the main driver of the recent increases in inequality. It's the biggest factor.'[271] Brynjolfsson lists robots and automation, as well as a winner-take-all effect of technology as major factors in amplifying social inequality. With advancements in gene editing and human augmentations, there are concerns about a new class divide through both physical and mental upgrades.[272] Finally, even with all the advancements in digital technologies, we cannot innovate our way out of bad governance and corruption. There are limits to what technology can achieve on the continent. We still need good governance, ethical leaders, infrastructure, strong civil society and a conducive policy environment to allow Africans to reach their full digital potential.

With those important caveats out of the way, let's meet our

techies! While some of the entrepreneurs in the previous sections, the moguls, the creatives and the sociopreneurs use technology or have built technology-enabled businesses, the entrepreneurs in this section, the techies, are a different breed. They are technologists at heart. They are the coders, the developers, the hardware geeks, the inventors, the stereotypical people we imagine when we think of tech nerds, like Shuri, T'Challa's sister in Black Panther. These techies are an eccentric bunch from Rwanda, South Africa and Ghana.

13

SIYA XUZA

INVENTS NEW ENERGY TO POWER AFRICA

IN 2008, I WAS PRESIDENT OF THE HARVARD BLACK MEN'S Forum, a social organisation at Harvard College. At one of our weekly meetings, I came across Siyabulela Xuza, a young freshman from South Africa, and adopted him as my little brother. We would meet every week for lunch and Siya would pepper me with questions about everything. Wide-eyed, humble, and hungry to learn, I was amazed to find out from our mutual friend, Naseemah Mohamed Ogunnaike, that Siya had a minor planet named after him, located close to Jupiter's asteroid belt. I joked that he should be the one mentoring me and knew then that he would change the world. Siya is currently pioneering innovative ways of meeting the energy needs of the over 600 million people in Africa who do not have access to electricity.

I travelled to South Africa to meet with Siya and learn more about his story. Siya grew up in Mthatha in the Eastern Cape of South Africa which he describes as a small township with few resources. He was mostly raised by his mother. He grew up in a very large extended family that prized education. 'My grandfather was a science teacher. My grandmother was the first black female qualified pharmacist in

South Africa. My paternal grandparents were both teachers. So, I came from a background that valued education above everything. My great uncle left South Africa for the United States, built a career as an engineer and had a good life in New Jersey. My aunt also followed suit to the United States'.

As a child, Siya exhibited intellectual curiosity - always asking a lot of questions, trying to figure out how things worked, and why things were as they were. Siya was only six years old in 1994, when South Africa had its maiden democratic election. Although he was too young to understand apartheid, Siya learned about its ugliness through stories from his uncles, grandparents and other family members. At the dawn of its democracy, a lot of significant changes were expected in the new South Africa. Key among the reforms was the abolition of the inferior education system known as the Bantu education system. The Bantu education system was a segregationist education policy focused on providing education that would make Black South Africans employable only in the unskilled labour market. As one activist described it, 'This Bantu Education Act was to make sure that our children only learnt things that would make them good for what the government wanted: to work in the factories and so on; they must not learn properly at school like the white children. Our children were to go to school only three hours a day, two shifts of children every day, one in the morning and one in the afternoon, so that more children could get a little bit of learning without government having to spend more money. Hawu! It was a terrible thing that act.'[273]

Siya remembers the restriction placed on the movement of blacks. Apartheid laws defined where they could live, work and generally move within South Africa. To access certain neighbourhoods, they needed to present their identification cards to intimidating police officers. Often, when a Black South African went to the home of a white South African, it was to provide cleaning or other domestic services. After 1994, when Siya found himself as one of the first blacks in the same school as white South Africans, it was a jarring experience full of conflicting emotions.

Since the democratic election was new to most South Africans, a lot of voter education took place. One strategy the state adopted was to fly airplanes over townships and drop election pamphlets over these towns. A light airplane vroomed over Mthatha and caught the attention of little Siya. The sight and sound of the Cessna plane sparked an interest in him about the world of flight. Curious to know more, he dived into reading more about science and technology, about rockets, space and planets, and he remembers developing a love for the planet Jupiter.

As Siya grew older, he also developed a love for chemistry. He turned his mother's kitchen into his first chemical lab, experimenting with various chemicals. His mother became alarmed at her teenage son's new-found love because he was creating minor explosions in the kitchen and using her cooking utensils and equipment as lab tools. On one occasion, he nearly set the kitchen on fire and she had to scold him. He was even once investigated by the police who had concerns with the chemical experiments he was conducting, and the materials he was purchasing, as they feared he could potentially be engaged in terrorist activities. Nothing could stop Siya's curiosity and love for scientific adventure. I laughed and told Siya he was the real-life African version of Dexter from the cartoon *Dexter's Laboratory* and he didn't even need Deedee to blow up his lab.

'But over time, it became clear to me that I wanted to focus on rocket fuels, I wanted to focus on building rockets. And this is me at about 12 years or so. I didn't have the privilege or resources to order parts or chemicals from America. I decided that instead of waiting on external sources, I'm going to use what I could get from South Africa', he continued. 'Why can't Africans get into space? Can't we build our own rockets using our African intellect, our own resources?' His resolve was further strengthened by South African internet entrepreneur Mark Shuttleworth's feat in 2002, when he became the first South African to fly to space on a self-funded trip as a space tourist. This was the second self-funded space tourism endeavour in the world.[274] Siya was inspired by Shuttleworth's 10 days in space experience.

Siya set off to build a rocket starting with the rocket fuel which he felt was the most important. 'At this time, I was in high school and what had started off as something vague and in my mum's kitchen was now a very serious science project for me. I started reading ahead. I was really motivated to do anything to learn science, to take in knowledge. A lot of what motivated me was just about finding ways to apply knowledge practically. There's a difference when you study science to get an A and when you study science because you don't want to blow up your kitchen. So, I'd read ahead, I read calculus ahead of my peers,' Siya recounted.

Initially, his mother was concerned. She didn't understand why her son was so fascinated by rockets. 'Why aren't you doing what other kids do?' She reacted the same way every mother would react if she discovers that while she's at work, her son was at home playing with rocket fuel. She would sometimes get cross with Siya when dinner tasted funny because he had used the cooking utensils in his chemical experiments. Eventually, she realised her son was fixated on these experiments and decided to support him in every way possible. Siya talks about his mother in a reverent way, 'I learned everything from her – cultivating a sense of curiosity, self-discovery, striving for excellence, self-reliance and resourcefulness, among others.'

Trying to build a rocket is commendable but how does a kid even get access to the resources required? 'I had to learn to be entrepreneurial because now I was building serious rockets, I needed lots of money and I needed lots of resources like computers, equipment, chemicals. I needed to find a lot of sponsors. Initially, the people I tried to reach out to would say "Oh no, no, we don't have time for you, I can't help you." The look of some others was more like "Who's this black kid talking about building rockets and complicated chemicals for rocket fuel?" I had a lot of resistance. A lot of people shut me down. But I said to myself that I'm not going to let that stop me. I kept on looking for sponsors.'

His traditional approach to getting sponsors failed so he thought of exploring alternative means. Getting formal appointments were no longer effective. 'People's emails didn't work because their systems were blocked to me', he said. So, he gathered information on the movement of some of his prospective sponsors and met them without appointment when they were in transit. For instance, 'If I wanted to meet say the head of Microsoft, and I knew that he was flying out to Durban, I'd make sure that I'm positioned at the airport at the time his flight would take off. I would approach him and have face time with him to introduce myself and sell my project to him'. Eventually, he succeeded in getting Microsoft South Africa and a few others to sponsor him. He requested some of his sponsors to take him to places where he could get the chemicals he needed. His focus, determination and boldness amazed some. 'Who's this black kid asking me to drive him to collect chemicals to build a rocket?' His attitude motivated them to grant his requests.

Siya was still in high school in Johannesburg when he was working on this private science project. He attended St. John's College, one of South Africa's top private schools. Sometimes, he missed classes and whole school days as he went about looking for sponsors, mobilising the logistics, doing personal research, undertaking his experiments amongst others. His then principal, Roger Cameron, said of him that he was 'not the smartest as a younger child, but he was very focused and very determined'.

For Siya, 2003 was one of the greatest years of his life. First, he had the rare opportunity of meeting Nelson Mandela. 'It started off by chance. I come from Muntata and Mandela comes from Kulu which is about 45 minutes' drive from Muntata, all in the Eastern Cape. In 2003, our headmaster invited President Mandela as the guest speaker for our prize giving day. An idea came up to get one of the students to do a praise song for him. The headmaster then came to my class, informed us about Madiba's coming and then asks for a volunteer to do a praise song. It was going to be before an audience of about 5,000 people. Much to his chagrin, nobody had the confidence to stand in front of over 5,000 people. I scanned around the room. I raised my hands and said, "I'll do it." "Have you done praise singing before?" "No. But I can do it." After school that day, I went to one of my uncles and he agreed to teach me. The day came, and I delivered. That experience introduced me to the Mandela family and the Mandela Foundation. I didn't build an intimate relationship with Nelson Mandela himself because those were his frail years, but I built a strong relationship with the rest of the family.'

2003 was also the year in which he built his first rocket and launched it. Unfortunately, it failed as it exploded before launch. Siya didn't give up and kept trying. After six months and 77 failed experiments, 'In 2004, my first rocket took off, it flew about 600 feet, it wasn't perfect, but it was better than the previous year'. In 2005, he entered his first science competition. He left the venue for the competition a tad disappointed because he was given the bronze prize. He was confident that his project was worth a gold award. The innovation was in designing a functionally graded solid rocket fuel that used specific oxidiser particle sizes to achieve predetermined burn rates to control the thrust of the rocket motor. This greatly simplified the design of rocket motors, thus reducing costs. His rocket flew faster and higher because the rocket fuel he produced burnt faster and so gave the rocket more speed. Siya had invented a cheaper, safer type of rocket fuel, which became the subject of his research project titled 'African Space: Fuelling Africa's quest to space.' When I asked him how he made that breakthrough, Siya modestly said, 'My breakthrough wasn't a Eureka moment but really driven by simplicity and out of necessity. I only thought of how I could produce rocket fuel without the conventional chemicals and equipment, using the resources available in South Africa and out of it came my breakthrough. That was the context.'

Later, Siya entered another science competition - the South African Amateur Altitude – and broke the existing record after his rocket flew nearly 1000m. He also took part in the Eskom National Science Expo and walked away with the first prize. By this time, his innovation had been recognised as the most prestigious project in South Africa by the Dr. Derek Gray Memorial Award. He got an invitation to an international science fair. 'The best prize, however, was to be invited to the International Youth Science Fair in Sweden, where I met the King and Queen of Sweden as well as attending the Nobel Peace Prize ceremony in Stockholm [in 2006]'. Siya found himself in the same room with Nobel Laureates and other scientists where he was inspired, and he shared with them his dreams and passion for African-made rockets.

During one of the sessions in Sweden, he noticed an African American gentleman and started speaking to him. When the gentleman discovered that Siya was a South African, he told him how Harvard University had given the late Nelson Mandela an honorary doctorate degree. He told Siya to stay in touch. The gentleman Siya met was the legendary late Dr. Allen Counter, the founding director of the Harvard Foundation for Intercultural and Race Relations, and a renowned neurophysiologist, educator and ethnographer. Former Harvard President Derek Bok said of Dr. Counter, 'During my years as president of Harvard, no one did more than Allen to make minority students feel welcome and at home at Harvard, to promote fruitful interaction among all races, and to serve as understanding adults to whom many undergraduates could turn in order to register their concerns, answer their questions, and have their legitimate problems communicated to the Harvard administration so that they could be understood and acted upon in appropriate ways.' Dr. Counter was a wonderful mentor to me when I was at Harvard, and Siya too, would become a beneficiary of his benevolence.

Siya's participation in the International Youth Science Fair in Sweden granted him an invitation to participate in the Intel International Science and Engineering Fair in the US. This fair is considered the biggest student science fair in the world with about 1,700 students in attendance from around the world.[275] 'It was the kind of fair where you compete with other kids from countries that were leaders in innovation. It was my first time being in America. Judges came up to me, breaking me down. A U.S. military representative even came to me at one stage and seemed to say, "how did this guy come up with this?"'

Three days into the event, the judges finished their work. They started announcing the winners. Siya's eyes lit up as he recounted that experience. As confident as he was in his project, he didn't think he was going to win the first prize, but that's what happened. 'That really was a life-changing moment for me; to get a first place there, not having done this project in America, not having the resources. It showed me that it was larger than me; that give the African child an opportunity, the resources to learn and they're equally capable of global innovation and excellence... that it's some of the prejudices we have that hold us back...'

Siya was able to set this new record because of his research focus in creating rocket fuel that not only had a greater effectiveness but was also safer than what existed. In fact, NASA (National Aeronautics and Space Administration) confirmed that Siya's rocket fuel was superior to theirs. MIT's Lincoln Laboratory, which is affiliated to NASA, blew him away when they decided to name a minor planet after him. The minor planet in the main asteroid belt near Jupiter, with an orbital period of four years, was discovered in the year 2000 and renamed '23182 Siyaxuza' in recognition of Siya's achievements at the Intel International Science and Engineering Fair in the United States.[276]

Siya returned to South Africa and completed his high school education. He stayed in touch with Dr. Counter who encouraged him to apply to Harvard. He also applied to the Anglo-American Open Scholarship Panel. They offer one of the most generous scholarships in South Africa, which covers full university tuition, a stipend for room and board as well as overseas travel. Thus, it attracts a huge number of applicants and is one of the most competitive scholarships. Clem Sunter, an author who was chairperson of the scholarship panel for many years described Siya as the brightest student he had ever interviewed.[277] Fortunately for Siya, he was offered an academic scholarship to study Chemical Engineering in University of Cape Town.

However, he turned it down after he received news that he had been admitted to Harvard University on a full scholarship. In his first year at Harvard, Siya embarked on a path of self-discovery to understand himself better, discover his passion and the path to chart in life. He looked beyond rockets and tried to figure out the big questions: 'Who am I? What is my passion? Why am I passionate about Africa? Why am I pursuing a course in engineering? Is it because of the awards I have won?' In addition, he explored other subject areas other than science and technology. He took music classes, writing classes and studied Chinese. He believes that introspection led him to conclude that his passion was for Africa and her development. His passion wasn't necessarily about rockets. Rockets were simply an outlet to channel his curiosity. He did a lot of reading about Africa and the challenges the continent faces. Energy stood out for him. 'How can I use my time to make a contribution to solving Africa's energy problem?' he wondered to himself.

'I believe that the future of energy for Africa is decentralised, personalised energy applications. The model of big power plants with heavy infrastructure and complex financing agreements is not the way for Africa. Energy must be decentralised the way telecommunication has been decentralised through the invention of the mobile phones. Secondly, though Africa has solar energy in abundance, the real opportunity was in the storage of energy and not only the generation. Once energy can be stored, it becomes easier to generate, consume or sell it, just as access to the internet is.'

He shifted focus from the traditional ways of storing energy such as using batteries, to fuel cells. 'A fuel cell is an energy conversion device. At a very simplistic level, it is a generator which doesn't make a lot of noise, doesn't use diesel and is very efficient. It uses hydrogen or any derivative compounds of it and generates power by converting chemical energy into electrical energy through a redox reaction. An advantage it has over traditional storage channels is its ability to store more energy for a longer period'.

Siya completed his four-year undergraduate degree. Then he focused on a master's program working with Harvard's School of Engineering and Applied Sciences and MIT. But Siya didn't have the patience to wait for five months for government funding, so he embarked on his own fundraising drive. He got funding and equipment from all over the world including Switzerland and Denmark. His professor was impressed with his tenacity. He began work on developing a new 'nano-material' for 'personalised energy systems'. He used supercomputers and other equipment valued at over R100 million ($10 million) for this project at the Harvard Centre for Nanoscale Systems and the Massachusetts Institute of Technology Microsystems Technology Laboratory. The innovation he worked on was how to make it possible to charge mobile devices without connecting to the national grid or using a battery. It took him a year to develop this breakthrough technology. With this smart energy innovation, it is possible to trap energy from the sun and store it for a longer period because it makes use of micro-fuel cells. In effect, he deviated from the traditional path most scientists are plodding by researching into ways to build better batteries. He looked the other way for other channels of energy storage. The Journal of Electroceramics published his breakthrough findings in 2013.

With Siya's brilliance and accomplishments, he easily could have stayed in the United States and achieved great success. However, one experience in 2013 changed his perspective. Siya nearly lost his life in the Boston Marathon bombing in April of 2013, when a terrorist detonated a pair of homemade bombs in the crowd of onlookers, killing 3 people and injuring over 260.[278] Siya was close to the finish line and was shaken by the experience. This forced Siya to think deeply about what he wanted to achieve with his life. He realised it was time to go home and channel his energies in finding a solution to Africa's energy poverty. Over 600 million Africans do not have access to electricity. Chronic under-supply of affordable and reliable electricity has long been a barrier to economic growth and poverty reduction. For example, it is estimated that a kettle boiled twice a day by a family in London uses five times as much electricity as the average Malian uses per year. Or even more stark, a freezer in the United States is estimated to consume 10 times more electricity than a Liberian consumes in 1 year.[279] Africa's poor also pay among the world's highest prices for energy, exacerbating their poverty. The African Development Bank estimates that the continent loses 2-4% of GDP annually due to power shortages. This context motivated Siya to found Galactic Energy Ventures, a start-up he created to create and invest in disruptive energy solutions to meet the needs of emerging markets. Siya imagines a future when energy will be personalised, and we can generate and store our own energy and no longer rely on energy utilities. Siya wants to transform homes into power plants 'that capture the energy of the sun during the day and store some of it in fuel cells, for use at night.'[280] Such an innovation would give off-grid Africans energy independence.

Siya initially thought he could turn his fuel cell technology into a mass market product, however, he realised over time that it wasn't feasible or commercially viable. He was learning the challenges of translating lab breakthroughs and inventions to commercially viable products that can scale. 'I had to pivot because we couldn't scale the fuel cell technology in a way that would make financial sense.'

This led Siya to focus on grid-scale energy storage solutions. 'There is a gravitational shift happening all over the world from oil to battery... most of the resources needed for a battery-dominated energy ecosystem come from Africa. For example, Congo is the world's leading supplier of cobalt.' Siya's company has developed a battery storage solution using a mineral widely available in South Africa; its identity is currently a trade secret. At the time of writing, he was in the middle of a transaction with a large publicly listed South African company and therefore could not disclose details of Galactic's energy solution. 'When the transaction closes, I will share how we are going to build an innovative distributed power company using our technology.'

Siya's achievements have won him global attention. The Presidency of South Africa awarded Siya the National Award of The Order of Mapungubwe in Silver for 'his excellent contribution to scientific innovation at an early stage, proving to himself and others that through determination and hard work one can achieve new career heights.' Michelle Obama, former First Lady of the United States, in a speech comparing Siya to her husband, said: 'You can choose to answer to the peer pressure and go on with whatever everyone else is doing or you can answer to your own hopes and dreams and start working to become whatever you want to be in this life. That's what Siya Xuza did, he grew up in the township of Umthatha and his family certainly wasn't wealthy, but he studied hard in school as a teenager. He invented his own rocket fuel and won all kinds of awards and I got to meet Siya in South Africa two years ago and I got to see him again today and he just graduated from Harvard University in the United States... You see Siya and President Obama, and so many others in the South Africa and the United States, they are living proof of what the legendary South African President Mandela said. He said, 'Education is the most powerful weapon you can use to change the world.'[281] Though Siya has been granted audiences with three South African presidents, Michelle Obama, a UN Secretary-General, the King of Sweden, Nobel laureates, astronauts, Steve Wozniak, and many others, he always remembers what his mother told him: 'Even if a planet is named after you... you should always remain down to earth.'

14

DENYSE UWINEZA

BRINGS SMES INTO THE DIGITAL AGE

OUR SECOND TECH ENTREPRENEUR, DENYSE UWINEZA, TOOK me to Rwanda, a fascinating country that in many ways epitomises the promise that Africa holds if our political leadership and policy match our potential. Two and a half decades ago, Rwanda was a failed state, embroiled in a horrendous civil war that ended in the genocide against the Tutsis, resulting in the loss of almost a million lives over the space of a few months. Today, Rwanda is considered one of the fastest growing, safest and least corrupt nations in Africa under the leadership of President Paul Kagame – an iconic, effective and inspirational leader to some, and an authoritarian violator of human rights to others. In the past decade, economic growth in Rwanda has averaged 7% per year, maternal and child mortality has fallen by more than 60% and universal health coverage has been achieved. Women hold 64% of the country's parliamentary seats, the highest in any nation in the world.[282]

Rwanda is a small, hilly land-locked country in east-central Africa with a population of 12 million people and very little natural resources.[283] Starting in the 1300s, the Tutsis are believed to have migrated into what we now call Rwanda. At the time, the native inhabitants were the Twa and Hutu peoples. In the 1600s the Tutsi King Ruganzu Ndori conquered central Rwanda and many Hutu areas. Rwanda became a unified state in the 1800s until it was acquired by Germany as part of her East Africa colony, Rwanda-Urundi in 1890.[284] After the First World War, under the Treaty of Versailles, Rwanda-Urundi was made a League of Nations protectorate to be governed by Belgium. The two territories (that later become Rwanda and Burundi) were administered separately by two different Tutsi monarchs. Both Germany and Belgium were responsible for turning the traditional Hutu-Tutsi relationship into a class-based system. The minority Tutsi, who comprise 14% of the population, were given Western education and privileges over the majority Hutu (85% of the population) and became the governing class. In 1926, the Belgians even introduced an identity card system, officially and formally differentiating Hutus from Tutsis.[285]

In 1959, the Hutus rebelled against the Belgians and the ruling Tutsi elites. Tutsi King Kigeri V was forced into exile in Uganda and an estimated 150,000 Tutsis fled to Burundi.[286] In 1960, the Hutus won the elections organised by the Belgians and a year later, Rwanda declared itself a republic. The Hutus in Rwanda installed a new president, Gregoire Kayibanda, and continued fighting with Tutsis. In 1963, an estimated 20,000 Tutsis were killed following an incursion by Tutsi rebels based in Burundi. By the mid-1960s, it was estimated that half of the Tutsi population was living outside Rwanda. Hutu-Tutsi ethnic conflicts continued spasmodically over the next 30 years, with systematic policies to exclude Tutsis, including ethnic quotas in all public service employment.[287]

In 1994, Rwandan President Juvenal Habyarimana and Burundi President Cyprien Ntaryamira were both killed in a rocket attack on their plane. Habyarimana's death triggered 100 days of unprecedented violence and genocide, perpetrated mainly by Hutus against Tutsis and moderate Hutus. About 800,000 people were killed.[288] The genocide ended later in 1994, when the predominantly Tutsi Rwandese Patriotic Front (RPF), under the leadership of Paul Kagame, and operating out of Uganda and northern Rwanda, defeated the national army and Hutu militias and established a government of national unity. Rwanda organised its first local elections in 1999, and its first post-genocide presidential and legislative elections in 2003.

After the genocide, Rwanda was so devastated that it was teetering on total collapse. So many men had been killed that women then comprised 70% of the population. However, the country engineered a remarkable socio-economic turnaround, one of the fastest in global economic history.[289] Income per capita in Rwanda has doubled since 2000, and unlike its peers in the region, the country has matched economic growth with shared economic prosperity – inequality has reduced as economic growth has increased rapidly. Many government policies are focused on benefiting the lives of the rural poor. The United Nations Development Index demonstrates how remarkably successful Rwanda has been – it has improved by more than any other country in the world in the last quarter century.[290]

Much of its success has been attributed to government policy. Transparency International ranks Rwanda as the fourth-least corrupt country in Africa, with global rankings higher than developed countries such as Greece and Italy. The World Bank has ranked Rwanda as the easiest place to do business in Africa. As the Financial Times noted, 'More than 1 million people have been taken out of extreme poverty. Good roads, security, healthcare services and an efficient bureaucracy are impressive in a region where all are in short supply.'[291] Its government is staffed with technocrats who sign performance contracts with President Kagame that are specific and outline measurable outcomes. Failure to reach targets results in automatic dismissals.[292] I developed a relationship with Rwanda's then Minister of ICT and Youth, the Honourable Jean Philbert Nsengimana and he confided in me, 'the President has tasked me to create 100,000 jobs so I can't sleep. I must perform.'

Rwanda is also renowned for its gender policies. Women in Rwanda hold significant power, which is remarkable on a continent that has registered massive gender inequality. Rwanda has a women-majority led parliament, with women holding 64% of the seats, the highest proportion in the world. Furthermore, gender equality is enshrined in the Constitution, establishing a permanent legal basis to sustain the gains achieved. Women have equal access to education and resources.[293]

Many Rwanda scholars will attribute the country's progress to the leadership of Paul Kagame. As the NY Times put it: 'No country in Africa, if not the world, has so thoroughly turned itself around in so short a time, and Kagame has shrewdly directed the transformation. Measured against many of his colleagues, like the megalomaniac Robert Mugabe of Zimbabwe, who ran a beautiful, prosperous nation straight into the ground, or the Democratic Republic of Congo's amiable but feckless Joseph Kabila, who is said to play video games while his country falls apart, Kagame seems like a godsend.'[294]

Kagame has been described as deeply analytical and is known to stay up until early dawn studying progress reports from projects in rural Rwanda. He has built a powerful global network of supporters including Bill Gates and Bono and regularly attends the World Economic Forum in Davos. The Clinton Global Initiative honoured him with a Global Citizen award, and Bill Clinton said that Kagame 'freed the heart and the mind of his people.'[295] Under President Kagame, 'Rwanda has studied locations worldwide – from Jersey to Singapore – that perform against the odds and considered what to emulate. His administration has reformed business rules, offered tax incentives, promoted women, championed east African integration, attracted aid money – which still funds 38% of the budget – and provided government spending that has propelled growth.'[296]

However, there is a controversial side to the Rwanda miracle tale.

The FT alleges that under Kagame's leadership, 'the government, meanwhile, is writing its own rule book, one that is written in authoritarian ink and regularly coloured by allegations of human rights abuses, which range from the suppression of free speech to alleged murder of political rivals.'[297] For example, critics allege that one of President Kagame's former allies, who had fled to South Africa, was assassinated in his hotel room in Johannesburg in 2014 by Rwandan state agents.[298] Human Rights Watch has derided claims of violence meted against journalists and opposition figures.[299] Another controversy involving the Rwandan government has been the official documentation by international organisations such as the United Nations of its purported involvement in the destabilisation of the Democratic Republic of Congo in the late 1990s after Rwandan troops invaded DRC to fight off Hutu militias.

I was in Kigali during the period of Kagame's decision to run for a third term, which he won decisively. The U.S. and the E.U. openly condemned the move as undermining democracy and subverting the will of the people. Human rights groups conceded that the President has broad support but accuse him of suppressing the media and opposition. President Kagame passionately defended the decision in a famous Twitter spat with Ian Birrell, the British journalist, arguing that the U.S. and the Western media do not have a 'moral right' to criticise him, especially since he is following the democratically exercised will of the Rwandan people.[300] Further, many of Kagame's supporters that I met in Kigali point out the hypocrisy of Western criticism given that in Germany, Chancellor Angela Merkel is serving her fourth term in office and also that the American presidential term limit is a recent development in America's own democratic evolution: President Franklin D. Roosevelt was elected four times. For those who point out that those leaders didn't change the constitution while in office, they point to Mayor Bloomberg in New York City who effected a change while in office to allow him to run for a third term.

Kagame's supporters argue that Rwandans care more about progress, stability, good governance and capable leadership rather than term limits at this time. They also defend the stringent governance of the media on the grounds that the media was a key tool behind the genocide when genocidaires used the radio to inflame and incite ethnic tensions.[301]

Denyse was one of those fierce defenders of her President when I met her. She is scarred from the genocide, having lost many family members. Even though she was only four years old during the genocide, Denyse can never forget the brutal outcomes. Her family was devastated by the massacre; she lost her brother, cousins, her grandparents, many uncles and aunties, from both her patrilineal and matrilineal sides of the family. 'I lost so many family members... after the genocide, we didn't have anything. Even our house was destroyed.' Denyse is burdened with survivor's guilt and feels strongly that she has a moral responsibility to 'do all I can to [honour] their absence... achieve what they would have achieved if they were still alive.' This tragedy has fuelled her ambition and motivation to succeed in all spheres of life.

Deeply patriotic, Denyse is a brilliant, young woman who has had a fascination with mathematics, physics and technology since she was ten years old. 'When I was ten, I really liked math and I was good at it. At that time, we didn't have a lot of technological devices like now, but I was curious to know what was going on in the field of technology. Since my childhood, I always dreamt of going into technology. When I was in class 6, I had an idea of doing math and physics in high school.' However, when she voiced this desire in high school, she was told that 'mathematics and physics are subjects for boys, not girls.'

Denyse always exhibited intellectual curiosity growing up. Sometimes it got her in trouble, for example, when her little sister was born, Denyse didn't understand why she wasn't eating 'normal food' like the rest of the family and tried to feed her rice when she was barely a week old – she got into major trouble for that! She was also very curious about electronics. Anytime an electronic appliance broke down at home, she would try to find out what had gone wrong and how it could be fixed, never missing an opportunity to dismantle the appliance. Her parents recognised her passion for mathematics and technology, but they didn't fully appreciate its value or what kind of future she could have. Despite their humble beginnings, Denyse's parents were determined to ensure she was educated to heights they had never attained. Her father is a driver, and her mother is a trader in automobile spare parts. Both her parents are only educated up to primary school. In fact, Denyse is the first person in her family's history to have a college degree. When Denyse asked her parents why they didn't go to school beyond primary school, she was saddened by their response. Denyse's father grew up as an orphan and he had no one to support him. Her mother, on the other hand, was denied educational opportunities because of her ethnicity. Her parents impressed on her the importance of education. 'My parents didn't obtain higher education not because they were stupid, but because they didn't have any opportunity. For me that meant I had to take full advantage of my opportunity to go to school.' The first born of five children, Denyse felt obligated to serve as a role model for her younger siblings. 'I was not and am not ashamed that my parents did not receive higher education. I am here to show that even kids from poor families or orphans can become someone special,' she said.

Unlike most of the entrepreneurs in this book, Denyse's family couldn't afford a computer, so she did not grow up with one. Her first access to a computer was in her final year of high school. She was amazed when she got a chance to see and touch a computer. She remembered thinking 'wow, it looks like a TV.' Despite her late entry to the world of computers, her curious mind enabled her to quickly discover the vast potential and the enormous possibilities in the world of education and technology. One of her greatest sources of inspiration to study technology came from a friend of hers 'who was studying information technology in university. He used to tell us what they were learning, and I was inspired. So, I talked to myself and said "Denyse, you have to also learn technology." But when I shared it with my friends and family, they said it was a career for boys, not girls… I remember when I was in senior three and I told my mum I was going to do math and physics. She replied that "Denyse, I know that you are good in math but I'm not sure it is the best idea." But because I know myself [and I knew] that I could do it, I told her I was going to still press on and do it.'

Not dissuaded by their comments, Denyse forged ahead and applied to study computer science at the National University of Rwanda and was admitted on account of her exemplary grades. Denyse laments the perception that science, technology and math is only for boys; she believes it was the driver behind the low number of girls in her computer science class at the university. Of the 118 students in her class, only a third of them were girls. It was a similar situation in other science and engineering classes; her civil engineering class had only six girls.

Denyse initially struggled in computer science relative to some of her peers who had access to computers growing up. However, these barriers did not impede her progress because she was committed to proving the naysayers wrong. In her early days as a freshman, while the lecturer introduced them to the various parts of a computer, she started thinking about how a computer was manufactured. During her typing lessons, she wondered how the computer software of the typing program was developed. She learned how to code and realised she had a passion and a high aptitude for programming. Before graduation, Denyse was already developing software. One of her professors even engaged her to assist him in developing software for a client. It was a great learning experience and the professor compensated her for contributions. A light bulb lit up for Denyse, and she suddenly realised she could make a living from her love of coding.

After graduating, most of Denyse's classmates applied for jobs, but Denyse decided on a different path. Inspired by the experience with her professor, she decided she would start her own company. Apart from satisfying her own entrepreneurial urges, she also hoped to inspire other women. 'If they know that [I] was able to achieve this, then they'll say to themselves that I'm going to study not only to look for a job from the government or private sector but maybe, I can use what I learn from school to create something new.' In January 2014, at the age of 24, along with two other colleagues, Denyse founded URU Technology Limited, a software company focused on developing software, mobile apps, and websites for small and medium-sized enterprises.

Denyse and her co-founders did not have any capital to start the business, or an office, so they worked remotely from home. Denyse jokes that the only capital she had was 'coding in Java, PHP, Javascript, HTML and CSS.' With no track record or customer reference list, it was difficult to get their first client. Eventually, they succeeded in getting their first client, Salesian Missionaries, to build a customised database management system to manage all their activities in Rwanda, Burundi and Congo. The revenue from that contract gave them the capital to bootstrap the business and add another developer.

They have now developed a wide range of software applications for a diverse group of clients. One of their core software applications is a pharmacy management software to help retail pharmacies digitise their operations and manage their sales, inventory and customer relationships electronically. Many pharmacies in Rwanda are currently utilising that software. They also developed accounting software that runs on feature phones, creating opportunities for micro enterprises to have accounting tools. To expand their reach across Rwanda, they have partnered with large corporations like the telecommunication giants MTN and Airtel to support SMEs.

Denyse has never forgotten the challenges she faced in wanting to study computer science. She has been a vocal and instrumental gender activist in Rwanda, focused on empowering women. Denyse is passionate about leveraging technology to bridge the gender gap, and to provide economic opportunities to the marginalised in Rwanda. She has created large training programs to teach hundreds of school children how to code, with an emphasis on girls. She is also training rural women on using ICT and mobile phones to create economic opportunities and training them to sign up as mobile money agents; 20 women graduated in the first cohort. Denyse believes that the mobile phone is a powerful digital platform that can enable the rural poor and the marginalised to participate in the global digital economy. She is particularly passionate about empowering young girls and women with technology. This has led her to speak at several seminars and conferences in Rwanda to inspire girls and young women, using her story. In the process she discovered that many girls miss out on their opportunity to excel because they become pregnant along the way. She's launched a digital project to educate girls and young women on sexual health issues in order to reduce the number of unwanted pregnancies and the incidence of sexually transmitted diseases. For example, she has created a website called ahange.com which provides training and awareness information to girls and young women on empowerment and sexual reproductive health. Denyse also uses technology to connect with youth clubs in high schools and at the National University of Rwanda to educate them on HIV/AIDS prevention and Youth and Sexual Reproductive Health (YSRH) best practices.

Denyse worked with a social enterprise called The Women's Bakery which '[teaches] women how to make and sell nutritious, affordable breads and manage profitable bakeries in their communities.' The organisation equips women with skills and lessons to manage bakeries in their communities, including over 150 hours of training covering everything from sourcing ingredients to management tools in running the business. While the high touch in-person training has resulted in the launch of six bakeries, Denyse believes digitising the training through the mobile phone could result in an exponential scaling of impact.

In recognition of her efforts in technology and gender activism, she was honoured as one of Africa's Most Outstanding Emerging Women Leaders by MILEAD in 2015. Co-founded by Mawuli Dake, MILEAD is a leadership development program which identifies 25 extraordinary young African women between the ages of 19 – 25 years who are pursuing women empowerment initiatives from across Africa. The Fellows are chosen through a highly competitive selection process and criteria based on 'outstanding leadership promise, community service accomplishments, and commitment to the advancement of women in Africa.' They are taken through a three week long intensive personal, professional development, networking and internship program to build their capacities.[302] Denyse told me that 'I am passionate about promoting women and gender issues after observing that women and girls are marginalised by society, family and friends. This is why I completed a Master of Arts and Social Sciences degree specialising in Gender and Development at the University of Rwanda [she did this while running her business and graduated in 2014]. I have attended several gender training sessions at the international level and I am passionate about supporting our female entrepreneurs. This program means much to me, it gives an opportunity to young women to contribute to the improvement of the situation of women in Africa. It serves as a platform for Fellows to cross-examine concepts of leadership in a broad African context, cultivate the skills and experiences necessary to occupy and excel in leadership positions, and gain knowledge on cutting-edge issues critical to African women and their communities.' In 2017, Denyse was selected as one of 15 Rwandan recipients out of over 1,000 applicants for the prestigious Young African Leadership Initiative (YALI) Mandela Washington Fellowship.

For Denyse, technology is an opportunity for her, and her country to leapfrog development and to counteract the setbacks of the genocide. Ever present on her mind, she pursues excellence for herself, her family and her country, in memory of her family members and the one million who perished in the genocide.

15

FARIDA BEDWEI

POWERS MICROFINANCE WITH TECHNOLOGY

THE NEXT TECHIE AND I WERE FACEBOOK FRIENDS FOR YEARS before meeting in person. I have been amazed by her story and affectionately call her "our generation's Yaa Asantewaa" because her strength reminds me of the Ashanti queen mother who led a rebellion against the British colonial rulers in 1900. Farida Bedwei is the co-founder and Chief Technology Officer of Logiciel, the largest microfinance banking software platform in Ghana. She was named a Young Global Leader by the World Economic Forum and remains the youngest person ever to be appointed to the board of Ghana's National Communications Authority. Ghana's former president John Mahama presented her with a Special Award at the Government of Ghana National Youth Awards in 2012. She was also listed in the Inaugural 100 Most Influential Young Africans in 2016 by the Africa Youth Awards. South Africa's CEO Magazine celebrated her with the Most Influential Woman in Business and Government in Africa for the Financial Sector award in 2013. She's the first recipient of the Legacy and Legacy Ideas Award 2011, given by the organiser of Ghana's biggest motivational speaking conference. In a national poll conducted by Avance Media in 2015, she was voted the Most Influential Young Woman in Ghana.

Ghana has an interesting history. The Republic of Ghana borrows its name from a great West African Empire from medieval times, that was known by the name of its emperor, the Ghana. It was famed for its wealth in gold, its court systems, and its warriors. The Ghana Empire was broken up by 1076 in conquest by the Muslim Almoravids, a militant confederation of groups in the Sahara who combined in a holy war to convert neighbouring states. Archaeological evidence in present day Ghana suggests that the area has been inhabited since 2000 BC. By the 16th century all the modern ethnic groups in present day Ghana had settled in the region.[303]

At the end of the 17th century, the Ashantis, the largest ethnic group in Ghana, under the leadership of their king, Osei Tutu, transformed a confederacy of Ashanti states into an empire with its capital in Kumasi. Ancient folklore has it that the High Priest, Akomfo Anokye, summoned a golden stool to descend from the sky. The Golden Stool represents the unity of the Ashanti people and remains a respected national symbol today.[304]

Europeans first arrived in Ghana (then known as the Gold Coast because about 10% of the world's global gold production came from this area) in the 15th century, starting with the Portuguese, who came to trade in gold, ivory, pepper and later, slaves. A thriving slave trade existed until 1870 when the Atlantic slave trade ended. Historian Sandra Greene estimates that 12.5 million individuals were exported from West Africa to the Americas. The Portuguese built a fortress known as the Elmina Castle on the coast of the Gold Coast in 1482 as a permanent trading post to protect Portuguese trade from other European competitors and from any attacks by inland Africans. Elmina later gained notoriety for its role as a slave-holding fort in which millions of Africans were brutally chained, dehumanised and shipped off to a life of slavery in Brazil, the Caribbean and America.[305]

Eventually the British conquered and ruled the Gold Coast as a Crown Colony in the late 19th century. Under the leadership of Kwame Nkrumah, the Gold Coast fought for and won independence from the British in 1957, becoming the first black African nation to declare independence from colonial rule, and taking on a new name and identity inspired by the old African empire: Ghana. Ghana's independence sparked a wave of anti-colonial resistance across Africa. Nkrumah is one of the most respected and admired Africans, even though his legacy is mired in controversy at home. A BBC poll voted him the African of the Millennium, surpassing other great Africans like Nelson Mandela. [306]

Nkrumah became increasingly authoritarian, which fomented significant opposition. This resulted in a coup d'état, supported by America's Central Intelligence Agency. Ghana then endured a string of coups and military rule, until the assumption of power by Jerry John Rawlings in 1981, and the transition to democracy in 1992. Since then, Ghana has been globally recognised as a beacon of democracy and good governance on the continent, with free, fair and peaceful elections resulting in changes in government in 2000, 2008, and 2016.[307]

Economically, Ghana is endowed with many natural resources. Ghana is the second largest producer of cocoa in the world, after Cote d'Ivoire, and one of the largest producers of gold. She also has significant holdings in diamonds, bauxite, timber and other minerals. In 2007, Ghana discovered oil, and started producing in commercial quantities in 2010, catapulting the country into lower middle-income status. With a GDP of $47 billion and an estimated growth rate of 8.8% in 2019 (forecast to be the fastest growing economy in the world), the country of 30 million people continues to be one of the leading destinations for foreign direct investment.[308]

However, Ghana, like other rapidly growing African countries, faces enormous challenges with inclusive growth. While the strong economic growth of the past two decades helped cut the country's poverty rate in half, from 56.5% to 24.2% between 1992 and 2013, growing inequality, regional disparities and a challenging macroeconomic environment is an obstacle to its progress. 3.65 million children, almost 30% of all children in Ghana, are currently living in poverty. Poverty in Ghana is concentrated in the northern regions, where one in three people live in rural communities.[309] My hometown, Nandom, is in the Upper West Region of Ghana, which has the highest poverty incidence rate in Ghana, at over 70%. Shuttling back and forth between urban Accra and rural Nandom is a troubling tale of two countries.

Growing up, I never appreciated the beauty and breadth of my country, until I had to plan vacations for friends visiting from the United States. From the traditional weaving villages in Bonwire, wood carving communities in Kpando, colonial neighbourhoods in Jamestown, the slave trade memorials in Elmina, or the wildlife in Mole National Park, there are endless things to do and places to visit. CNN named Ghana on its list of top 19 places to visit in 2019.[310] Ghana is also famous for its writers and poets. The country has produced literary giants of international repute such as Kofi Awoonor, Ayi Kwei Armah, Ama Ata Aidoo, Efua Sutherland, J.E. Casely Hayford, Nii Ayikwei Parkes, Taiye Selasi and Ayesha Haruna Attah, among others.

When Farida was born in Lagos on April 6th, 1979, she was immediately diagnosed with jaundice and a blocked intestine. She explained to me, 'There's something in the blood known as the Rhesus factor. If you have a positive Rhesus factor and that of your partner is negative it causes jaundice in the children. I have an older sister, Ayesha, and she had jaundice as a child, but they were able to treat it with no problems because it didn't come with any other complications. Because of my blocked intestine they had to operate on me... I was in an incubator for six weeks. By the time they were going to treat the jaundice, the damage had already been done.'

Farida's parents did not realise that their daughter had a permanent physical disability until she was a year old. Her mom found out she was not meeting any of the milestones of babies her age, like sitting or crawling. So, she took Farida to a hospital in London and after conducting a test, the results confirmed that she had cerebral palsy. '[I was diagnosed with] cerebral palsy which is a brain damage that affects the cerebrum of the brain. That's the part that controls movement and speech. It generally controls everything that you do so depending on which part is damaged, some people are better off, and others are worse off than me. There are no two cerebral palsy cases that are the same. There are some people whose hearing or sight are affected and there are some who are mentally challenged because it depends on the part of the brain that was affected', she explained. The type of cerebral palsy she has affects only her body movement and muscle coordination and not her ability to learn.

Against the doctor's suggestions and despite the growing attention in the U.K. for people with disabilities, Farida's mother chose to take care of her daughter herself, instead of putting her in a group home. Farida's father worked at the United Nations Development Program (UNDP) at the time. He was assigned to Dominica, which had just suffered a devastating hurricane, and the UN was engaged in the recovery and rebuilding process. So, the Bedwei family moved to Dominica and lived there for three and a half years, the first in a series of relocations.

In their time there, Farida was home-schooled. Her mother ordered a correspondence course from the U.K. and taught her from that. She also took her to Miami every three months for physiotherapy, studying the session intensely and taking pictures so that back in Dominica, they could go through those same exercises. Farida followed this routine for four hours every day for six days in the week, followed by four hours of home-schooling.

Fortunately, her mother was not working at the time, so she was able to take care of young Farida. This has shaped her views about female empowerment: 'That's why I always tell mothers of children with cerebral palsy that there is no quick fix; you have to put in the work and time. I was lucky that my mum had the time with me because she wasn't working. If she was working, my life would have been different. That's why when it comes to women's empowerment, I'm like look, I benefitted from having a stay-at-home mom. If a woman says she wants to be a stay-at-home mom, there's nothing wrong with it.'

Farida continued, 'But these days, women are being shamed for wanting to stay at home. They are being told that they are not ambitious and that's the problem we have in our society. I always say that the best thing you can do for any woman is to let her decide what she wants to do with her life, not to dictate to her. Because if you are dictating to her then you are not better than the male chauvinist who is telling her to stay at home. Women are not feeling appreciated, because we are not able to quantify the work that they put in as stay-at-home moms and give them the due respect and appreciation they deserve.' Farida and I had a long discussion on this discrepancy in mainstream economics, where domestic work does not count towards GDP unless someone else is hired to do it. Feminist economics has been an important response to these patterns of labour market and household studies.[311] As the example of Farida's mother shows, women, and women's household activities, are made invisible by excluding them from economic accounting and not recognising them as independent actors.

After three and a half years in Dominica, Farida's family moved to the U.K. After a year, they moved again to the Comoros Island for six months. They returned to the U.K, spending time in Manchester and

Scotland. Farida was about six and a half years old then and was to enrol in school. At the time, children with disabilities with high IQ were integrated into mainstream schools and Farida was scheduled to be integrated. But before that could happen, her father got a new job at the Commonwealth Secretariat and was posted to Grenada in the Caribbean. The Bedweis had to move – again. They lived on the island for two years; her mother continued with her home-schooling.

In her home-schooling sessions, one of the challenges Farida faced was writing. Her condition made it difficult to grip a pen well enough to write. She used a manual typewriter instead, as this was the early 1980s. As computers became cheaper and more accessible, her parents bought her a home computer. It was a Word Processor with games, with the capacity to do some programming in the basic language. She used it to do her course work and to write letters to her pen pals. In her typical inspiring fashion, she said, 'I always say that if it hadn't been disability, I wouldn't be in tech because I wouldn't have had to use the computer and I wouldn't have had to develop interest [in computers]'.

The Bedweis moved for the sixth time when she turned nine. This time, they were returning to Ghana. After a couple of years, her mother registered her at a computer training institute. This was the first time she was going into a formal classroom setting. She registered for all the four courses on offer at the institute: Word Perfect, Lotus 123, Dbase 4 and Introduction to Computers. Her classmates had either completed high school or university. Most were learning to use a computer for the first time. After two or three sessions, the owner of the school approached Farida's mother with a confession: he had thought to himself that they were wasting the money bringing a girl of her age and physical challenge to learn about computers. Similarly, her classmates thought the same and expected her to hold the class back. 'But after two or three lessons, he came to the class and saw me teaching them. I ended up explaining and showing them things they didn't understand. I had a natural grasp [of the] concepts. It was easier for me to grasp the concept because I had worked on a computer before', Farida explained.

Until then, the only other child she had constant interaction with was her sister. Her mother enrolled her in the nearest junior high school, Cambridge Junior Secondary School, a government school, so Farida could make friends of her own age. Unfortunately, the school closed after the end of her first year. She then enrolled at Kaneshie Awudome 1 Junior Secondary School where she sat for her Basic Examinations Certificate Exams (middle school exams), which resulted in her admission to Achimota School, a top tier senior high school in Accra famous for its illustrious list of graduates which include former presidents and statesmen of the country. However, Achimota School was not disability-friendly and unlike junior high school, senior high school involved a lot of movements from one class to another. As her mother could not be on campus to help her, it was a real challenge for Farida. The best alternative was to skip senior high school and pursue a diploma program. With her knack for and interest in computers, she applied for a diploma in IT at the St. Michael's Computer Technology Centre. It was an international diploma organised by the Institute of Management Information Systems based in the U.K. After graduating, she started working for Omani Computers, at the age of 18. Hungry to learn more, she did the higher diploma as a part-time student.

By this time, she had been exposed to networking, software, hardware and database management. She settled on software as the area in which to specialise. However, to be a good developer, she needed experience. There were a few software companies in Ghana at the time like Soft (now SOFTtribe) and Persol. After researching into their profiles, she opted for Soft and approached the founder, Herman Chinnery Hesse. 'I went there and told the guy [Herman] I wanted to work but I had no work experience and if he gives me the opportunity I promise, he will never regret it. He said 'ok, come on board'. That's how I got started in the software environment. Up till now, I still don't know where I got the courage from.'

When Hermann introduced her to the rest of the team, she faced new insecurities: 'I remember opening the door and seeing all those guys, I was wondering what the hell has happened! I felt like flying away! I was virtually the only woman in the company apart from the administrator. And the only woman programmer in that department. And when I needed help, I had to learn to ask guys, "Can you please help me to the bathroom?" I had to get over that shyness.'

'I always tell people: if you want something, you have to do what needs to be done to get it. And you must forget about yourself, your image and you must put shyness aside. Then you have to learn how to be with the people you are working with. Believe me, I was 17 to 18 at the time. I didn't know anything about boys - suddenly I am in an environment with a lot of rowdy boys who are always talking about girls in explicit detail. It was a whole new experience for me and they used to tease me. I have never been teased so much in my life. Then, I had to learn how to be one of them and that's the only way you can survive in such an environment. I never lost my focus, I knew what I wanted and what I had to do to achieve that', she added.

When she started working with Hermann, Ghana was experiencing persistent but irregular electric power outages. This was 1998. Power was being rationed in a 12-hourly cycle. The first day Farida reported to work, the office was closed. The only person she encountered was the receptionist, who told her to return in the evening. While at Soft, she foresaw that the web and internet-based applications were going to be the next big thing in the tech space because of its network effect. After three years at Soft, she needed a new challenge and environment. She left to study E-technology at NIIT, a leading technology school in Ghana, where she learned JAVA programming and web enabled technology.

A mutual friend introduced her to Ehizogie Biniti, who was starting a software company, Rancard Solutions, building enterprise and mobile services. He introduced Farida to his co-founder, Kofi Dadzie and after the interview, they offered her a job as their second employee. She was putting her e-tech diploma to work, entering the field she thought was going to be the future. She started at Rancard as a solutions analyst. She was 22 years old at the time and rose up through the ranks, eventually becoming responsible for the development and maintenance of the mobility platform, which connected the mobile networks to the content providers. She played a lead role in the development of a content management system for the Commission for Human Rights and Administrative Justice and the development of an enterprise web-based payroll application for KPMG's Ghana office. Rancard would go on to be a leader in the technology space, later developing artificial intelligence-driven social recommendation algorithms.

Farida still felt there was a lot she could learn. She applied to do a bachelor's degree in computer science at the University of Hertfordshire in the U.K. She got admission and an exemption from the first two years. From 2004, she spent nine months in Hertfordshire. When she returned, Rancard eagerly took her back and she worked there for another five years. She also studied project management at the Ghana Institute of Management and Public Administration (GIMPA) in 2009.

After almost 10 years at Rancard, she felt it was time for a change. She had 14 years of experience in programming. She had risen to become a senior software architect. She considered venturing into a completely different field until a friend and former colleague from Rancard, Derrick Dankyi, invited her to help him start a company. Derrick was starting a microfinance company. He wanted Farida to help set up the IT department. The company, known as G-Life Financial Services, adopted a software that originated from Kenya. It was inefficient and yet expensive. She built an alternative application that made their work easier.

They named this new software g-Kudi. At the time, it was unique in that it was a cloud-based banking solution. It simplified the entire chain of their work process: from loan application to loan disbursement and loan repayment. Its other distinct feature was that it disbursed loans to customers through an SMS code on their mobile phones. With that code, the customer could receive a loan from any branch of the company.[312] When the word got out on g-Kudi, other microfinance companies wanted it, Farida and Derrick saw a business opportunity, and Logiciel was born. Farida co-founded Logiciel with Derrick to provide their (g-Kudi) software as a service for the microfinance industry to run their banking operations. It was the first to offer clouding services in the microfinance sector. It caters to both deposit-taking microfinance institutions and non-deposit taking institutions such as money lenders. It can be used on desktop computers, mobile phones and PDAs. Introducing a cloud-based system was new, so they had to face the conservative nature of the owners and managers of microfinance institutions who were initially resistant. Many wanted to see where their data was being housed and handled. They couldn't believe they could not see the physical storage.

Farida persevered and eventually Logiciel got a deal with the Association of Microfinance Companies and sold the software to 30 clients. Though there were other competitors in that space, Farida realised that they could quickly take over the market because g-Kudi was affordable and it was easy to sign on. Their flexible terms of payment were another advantage. They adopted a subscription model where clients made a lump sum payment to install followed by monthly subscription payments. Subsequently, about 250 microfinance institutions bought the software to facilitate their operations and they were processing close to $10 million in annual transactions. It has revolutionised the operations of the microfinance industry. Farida considers g-Kudi her biggest career achievement.

However, working in tech has raised some questions for her regarding its social impact. In a country with high unemployment and no welfare system to fall back on, she worries about tech making certain jobs redundant: 'Sometimes it may be better to leave certain jobs as they are so that people can get their daily bread'. These concerns also shape Logiciel's approach to the market. They could work with major banks, but they choose to work with micro-finance because it is an under-served market. 'How about the people down there? Don't they also deserve the same IT services you and I get from the banking sector? They do. There are over thousands of them, it's a mass market.'

Logiciel has grown so dominant in the microfinance industry that the Central Bank of Ghana recently visited them to vet their systems because they recognised that with so much market power, they could pose systemic risk to the banking sector if their software was compromised. Fortunately, the software passed all the tests, and they plan to continue engaging the government bodies and providing them with analytical data on the industry. For example, Farida can get a sense of overall national and regional economic activity from the money flows and transaction data on her software.

Running a rapidly growing software start-up has been a journey of growth for Farida. While she thrived writing code, she struggled sometimes with managing clients and employees: 'I still don't have it all together, it's still very difficult to manage those two parts because you must change your whole mindset. You must realise you need your clients. Managing employees is very difficult for me because I'm not an extrovert. I'm an introvert and I would rather be sitting behind my laptop writing codes. But it's something that as an employer you must learn.'

Working on the technology, rather than business side of her

company, has its advantages as a woman entrepreneur. She feels she faces fewer challenges because 'my product has communicated to you what my capabilities are, so you cannot judge me based on my appearance but rather based on my product. So for you to come back and say that because I am a woman, I cannot do this work when you have been using it for so many years, is stupid. I never thought about sexual harassment in this field but the news coming out of Silicon Valley has shaken my beliefs.'

She is equally passionate about encouraging women to pursue careers in information technology. She has pursued this in various ways in the past, notably as a former member of the erstwhile Girls in ICT Committee created by the Ministry of Communications. She is passing on her mother's lesson to persevere despite her physical disability: 'From an early age, my mother always told me to remove the words "I can't" from my vocabulary and replace them with "I'll try". And that has been my mantra throughout my entire life. I muttered it the first time I took my first step, entered mainstream school, entered a computer training school, got my first job, went away to university to be on my own for the first time in my life, wrote my first book… I tried, and I excelled. It wasn't easy but when you have nothing to lose, and people don't expect you to amount to much because of your limitations, sometimes you just have to prove to them and to yourself that you can exceed expectations.'[313]

In 2010, Farida published a novel titled *Definition of a Miracle*. The book is about an 8-year-old girl who has cerebral palsy. Farida writes: '[The world] should realise that we have the same wants, needs, expectations and emotions as any able-bodied person. We're just like everybody else – just trapped in uncooperative bodies'.[314] In 2018, Farida collaborated with Leti Arts to write and produce a comic book with the first ever superheroine with cerebral palsy – Karmzah.

16

IYINOLUWA ABOYEJI ('E')

ENABLES COMMERCE ACROSS AFRICA

OUR NEXT TECHIE, IYINOLUWA ABOYEJI, KNOWN AS 'E', IS an established serial tech entrepreneur in Nigeria. Sheel Tyle, the legendary venture capitalist (who is a personal investor in renowned start-ups Robinhood, Andela, DocuSign and Pinterest, among others) and founder of global VC firm, Amplo LP, once told me 'There's a very small category of entrepreneurs that I'll back anything they do. E is one of them.'

Over goat pepper soup in Lagos, E narrated his life story. He was born in Lagos, Nigeria and grew up in Akoka, a small suburb in Yaba. E describes himself as the most troublesome kid in his middle-class family. His father worked at a bank before moving to Shell where he worked until his retirement. He traces the seeds of his entrepreneurship to his childhood. 'I would say my entrepreneurship journey started really early. I remember this moment in my childhood where you know, normally, when visitors come to visit, they give you money and your mom will take it from you. Later when you ask for it, she would ask you, "Who pays for the food you eat?" I didn't take that. One day, when a visitor gave my mother money for me, I told her I wanted my money. She started playing the usual trick on me asking who bought this and that for you... I was like "No, I want my money". So, she was like, "You want your money? Take your money and go." I took the money and bought garden eggs with it. My goal was to sell it and make more on the street but [I] ended up getting hungry and eating them all. I was always the "fast cash guy." I wanted the money and I wanted it now.'

Like entrepreneurship, E's interest in technology also started when he was very young. His first exposure to technology was at home. His parents bought a computer and like most of the entrepreneurs we met, E used it mainly to play computer games. Then, he discovered the internet and became addicted. He spent a lot of time in cybercafés and on social media. 'I had a very special relationship with social media because at age nine, I was younger than most other people online... I had a window and an online personality that was able to discuss issues way above my age. I could be precocious on the internet and no one needed to know so it was very interesting for me. I was always contributing to development conversations. I was interested in politics very early on and social media was my outlet,' he recalled.

After high school at Loyola Jesuit College, E explored the possibility of going to college overseas. His heart was set on the United States. He took his SAT and applied to a school in the U.S. but did not gain admission. His guidance counsellor, who had attended the University of Waterloo in Canada, encouraged him to apply to the university. 'The funny thing is, I ended up not getting into Waterloo, but I had very good grades. My guidance counsellor was very shocked, and he went to Waterloo and told them they would be losing out if they didn't admit me. He got them to change the admission decision and I got into Waterloo.'

On E's first day of orientation at the University of Waterloo, he met someone who would later play an instrumental role in his entrepreneurial journey. A fellow freshman called Pierre Arys walked up to him, tapped him on the back and after introducing himself, said, 'Yo, can I stay at your place tonight? I don't have a place to stay.' E thought it was strange since he had just met him, but he eventually agreed to accommodate him in his off-campus apartment. Pierre was a computer science student and they hung out a lot until Pierre obtained student housing and moved out, and they lost touch.

At Waterloo, E was committed to his academic work. He studied very hard, scoring a 98% on a major paper, and spent all his energies in the classroom and the library. He had dreams of pursuing law. 'I was definitely going to be a lawyer... my dream was to break Canada's telco monopoly with antitrust legislation. I was going to be an antitrust lawyer and make a lot of money suing large corporations and governments.' He had it all figured out – or so he thought – till he bumped into Pierre a year later in the hallway.

Pierre had signed on to Waterloo's co-operative education program and got placed in San Francisco. Pierre had been enthralled by the "magic" of the Bay Area. He shared his experiences with E, who became very excited. At that time, Waterloo had set up its flagship entrepreneurship development program known as Velocity. Velocity incubated start-ups and provided the knowledge, tools, space and network that entrepreneurs need to carry their business ideas from ideation to commercialisation. E participated in Velocity. His interaction with Pierre and his involvement in Velocity changed his understanding of technology. Up to this point, E was mostly a consumer of technology, but he started thinking about ways in which he could be a producer of technology. He heard stories of young people, some of whom he knew, who were building technology platforms into huge companies. 'I was like, if this guy, who I was chilling with on campus can do this, me too I can do this. And that was the mind I got into tech with, and that is how I got into the tech-entrepreneurship space.'

E pivoted from academics to tech entrepreneurship. Academic work no longer interested him. He dived head first into the world of technology and entrepreneurship. With Pierre and six other friends, E co-founded his first start-up known as Bookneto. Bookneto was a social learning platform that organised and shared learning resources. The platform gave access to past questions for a fee. They built into it a Technical Reference Model (TRM) word platform that enabled the user to download the questions but not share them. Bookneto grew and became a popular platform among students in Canada. This was a time when Massive Open Online Courses (MOOC) like Coursera were gaining popularity, and there was a lot of development in the online education space.

However, Bookneto hit a major snag when the University of Waterloo drew their attention to the fact that the company was in violation of intellectual property laws. The past questions from exams which they were using to monetise were intellectual property that were owned by the professors who had developed the questions in the first place. Undeterred, E and his team changed tack. 'We pivoted to build social learning platforms for some of the professors. [Since they] own the content, they would be able to share some of their courses with people outside the university system. Then, the only way to do a course was if you are a member of the university system and that means you wouldn't know about TRMs or TLMs [The Learning Machine]. And professors wanted a way to monetise their courses, so we were a [great] option [for them].'

Bookneto 'wasn't a blowout success but it wasn't a flat-out failure either,' said E. The start-up generated enough revenues to at least pay their salaries. From his second year to final year, Bookneto consumed E. In 2012, he graduated with a B.A. in Legal Studies. He continued working on Bookneto but confessed that 'Bookneto had a whole lot of ideas around it and it was too large a team, so it didn't work out as well. I learned some important lessons there.'

After three years of working on Bookneto, E felt the urge to do something different. He also felt a strong urge to return to Nigeria.

By then, many of the co-founders had quit Bookneto because they had gotten other jobs. Eventually all the co-founders except E and Pierre quit. Pierre and E decided to move on. One of their client professors said to them, 'You guys can't just leave this behind? I've already built my entire business around you guys so if you want to leave sell me the company.' So, they sold Bookneto to him and E decided to move back to Nigeria.

Even before he relocated to Nigeria, E co-founded his second company, Fora. Fora was an online learning platform that offered short certificate courses, university courses and courses run by other professional institutions. Most of the institutions were U.S.-based. He co-founded the company with his friends Ian, Nadayar, and Brice. They initially thought of including African universities on their platform to enable distant learning but faced a lot of challenges. 'I flew back to Abuja on July 4, 2013 and I spent a lot of time talking to the Nigerian Universities Commission (NUC) trying to figure out how we could work with them. They stonewalled me, told me I needed a license and [that] they wouldn't introduce me to universities. It was this weird hedgehog thing where you had to see somebody otherwise nothing will happen.'

At that point, E had relocated to Lagos and he 'started to suffer. My parents were like dude, this start-up thing you are doing, let me just find you a job at Shell. [That will be] two generations [at Shell and] this is what Shell loves. My dad was tight with the HR of Shell, so it wasn't going to be a problem. But I refused, and they were very angry for a good reason. My dad told me to go to business school. I refused. My dad had a very interesting treatment for my stubbornness. He told me, "Clearly things are not moving on well for you, so this is what you need to do: I have a house in Bariga. You can go live there but, you need to pay rent."' E quickly agreed. However, the responsibility to pay rent every month when he had no income stream forced him to figure out how Fora could generate revenue. The team brainstormed and came up with a new product line: they provided admission support services to employees for distance learning programs and charged a success fee to the foreign universities who accepted them.

One of the early investors in Fora, Pule Taukobong, an early stage investor who co-founded the African focused venture capital firm, CRE, advised E: 'You need to look for people that have done the same business you're trying to do.' E thought about Pule's advice and thought of 2U. 2U is an educational technology company that partners with universities to offer online degree courses. E then reached out to Jeremy Johnson, a co-founder of 2U. They eventually met in Jeremy's office in New York and he agreed to mentor E.

Around this time, Fora's financial performance had fallen short of E's expectations. The company was bleeding cash and its survival was at stake. The founding team pursued some investors in Nigeria but very little materialised. The closest they got to was raising a small round from Extreme Start Ups (now Highline VC), bringing their total capital raised to $135,000, but that could only fund them for a couple of months into an uncertain future. They were at a critical crossroads. 'I had two options – pivot Fora before the cash ran out or die,' E recounted.

E turned to his new mentor Jeremy for advice and flew out to New York to meet with him. Jeremy had just returned from Nairobi where he had given a talk to the MasterCard Foundation. One of the ideas on his mind at the time was how to scale up high quality education in a cost-effective manner. Jeremy discussed with him a concept that came to him during his visit to Kenya. The idea was to create an incubator to train software developers and feed them to employers in North America. Jeremy was ready to fund it and serve on the board of this new venture. What he needed was someone to build it with him. E was immediately interested. He asked for 24 hours to discuss it with his team.

E had a productive discussion with the team at Fora. Nadayar became an outspoken champion of the proposed new venture. He convinced the team to believe in the similarities between what they were trying to achieve with Fora and Jeremy's concept. They accepted to experiment with the talent accelerator idea. The following day, they gave the green light to Jeremy. The original plan was that Jeremy would provide the seed capital and the Fora team would work on executing on it.

Initially, they pivoted the model under Fora. But after the first recruitment and bootcamp, they realised the concept was totally different from Fora. Therefore, Fora had to give way to a completely new company. They decided early on to locate the parent company in the U.S. with an office in Nigeria. Whenever E is asked why they took this decision, his response is always the same: 'Many people have asked why the parent company is based in the U.S. The truth is that while it is possible to build a global company from Nigeria, it is very, very, difficult. While I have faith that this will improve, Nigeria is a notoriously difficult place to operate and invest in from a legal point of view. So, since it has always been more important to us to change the world than to make a political point, we incorporated Andela in the U.S.'.

Andela is underpinned by a simple philosophy that brilliance is evenly distributed globally. Andela's thesis is simple: 'In the next ten years, there will be 1.3 million software development jobs created and only 400,000 domestic computer science graduates to fill them. Africa, meanwhile, is home to the largest untapped talent pool and seven of the ten fastest growing internet populations in the world.' Andela invests in Africa's most talented developers and integrates them into the world's best technology companies. It does this by leveraging a data-driven approach to building high performing engineering teams with Africa's top developers to help companies overcome the tech talent shortage and build better products, faster.

How does Andela find these developers? By organising highly selective bootcamps. Trainees then go through a four-year developer program which includes placement with global technology companies. At the end of the incubation period, some of the developers get offers with the global technology companies, and others start their own companies. But they all do so remaining in Africa. So, importantly, Andela isn't contributing to brain drain. It is a technology leadership enterprise at heart, with a goal to train a critical mass of software developers who will become a catalyst for a new wave of technology leadership across the continent. Andela is empowering young Africans to participate in the future of technology not as spectators or end-users, but as creators.

Jeremy eventually offered to quit 2U and join them as a co-founder and CEO. E was elated. 'I was very excited to have Jeremy join full-time as our CEO. First, I knew I could learn a lot from working with Jeremy. Second, 2U had just gone public and he was (and still is) easily one of the highest profile entrepreneurs in education. Raising capital for a crazy, unproven idea like ours would be a bit easier with him on board... As our remarkable success in such a short time has shown, it was the right move.'

Jeremy also convinced Christina Sass to join the Andela founding team. Christina was one of the first people Jeremy had discussed the concept with when he was in Kenya. She was pursuing a PhD program at Harvard at the time but abandoned it to join them. Thus, the founding team of Andela was formed with Jeremy, Christina and the four co-founders of Fora – E, Ian, Nadayar and Brice, with all of them playing different but essential roles. E took up the role of director for recruitment and became the face of Andela on the continent.

E explained that Andela was boosted in its infancy by the tremendous generosity of many supporters in Nigeria. For example, Andela's office for the first two months of its operation was a vacant duplex in Lagos owned by Mrs. Titi Adeoye who gave them permission to use her property at no cost. They were connected to her through one of their angel investors, Yvonne Johnson. Bosun Tijani of Co-creation Hub also gave them office space for free, and Mr. Oyedotun gave them an office in Fadeyi to use when the need arose. At one time, they needed a place to lease for a month and one of their supporters, Mr. Eke, assisted them. E was learning the power of having a network of people who can support the start-up in ways beyond just investment capital. Many of the entrepreneurs I met were active networkers. Some of them would even send cold e-mails or calls to corporate executives or investors and were surprised when they would occasionally get a favourable response. It never hurts to try.

E always jokes that it is harder to get into Andela than to get into Harvard. The selection process is made up of an aptitude test and interviews to assess the applicant's soft skills. During the first edition, 700 people applied, and they selected only six people. The second class had 4800 applicants and they selected 16. E explains that the model is designed to be highly selective. Jeremy believes that 'the more selective an education is, the more desirable it is and the better the outcome.' The highly selective recruitment process ensures that they recruit the best and coupled with quality training, their products tend to be the best in the market. After selection, they move straight into coding boot camp.

Some of the investors of Fora became investors in Andela. These include Pule Taukobong (of venture capital firm CRE) and Idris Ayodeji Bello. Some of the earliest investors in Andela included Sheel Tyle (who is also a board member) and Walter Baddoo (managing partner of 4DX Ventures). They called me and told me, 'You have to meet E and Jeremy.' After meeting E and Jeremy, I was sold, and invested as well. Andela's $14 million Series A attracted major VC investors such as Spark Capital and Omidyar Network.

However, one of the most significant milestones in the life of

Andela was its Series B in June 2016, a $24 million round that was led by the Chan Zuckerberg Initiative and was Mark Zuckerberg and Priscilla Chan's first lead investment. The round also included Google Ventures. As E celebrates these significant milestones, he hasn't forgotten that some people thought Africa wasn't a viable market. 'A lot of my closest friends told me basically, "We don't invest in Africa." [These were] people that I expected to support me. [They] will support me on any other thing but not this,' he said. The Zuckerberg investment was monumental not just for Andela, but for the ecosystem. When the CEO of Facebook made his first lead investment in an African technology company, it became a powerful validation for start-ups across the continent. A little over a year later, in October 2017, Andela would make the news again, raising $40 million in its Series C led by CRE and marking the largest venture capital round ever led by an African VC firm. It would make the news again in January 2019, raising $100 million, raising its total capital raised to $180 million and becoming one of the most valuable technology start-ups operating on the continent, reportedly worth close to $1billion dollars.[315]

Despite the great work they were doing training software developers, E became concerned about the state of the larger African environment. 'Is the environment one that an Andela entrepreneur would thrive in? Is a market where entrepreneurship does not grow, and established companies don't digitise a viable market for our fellows to work in?' he asked himself. He observed that one of the missing pieces in Nigeria's internet ecosystem was the lack of digital payments.

Olugbenga Agboola ('GB'), a Wharton and MIT Sloan-trained financial technology engineer who had core financial services technology experiences was also frustrated with the payment ecosystem. GB was a product manager at Google, where he worked on their payment product, Wallet. He also worked on Access Bank's digital banking as Head of Innovation and Product Management. GB and E decided to work together.

'What we thought about was, how do we build or create a world where everyone is able to connect to the digital economy and thrive in that economy as equals. A world where you can use your Nigerian card in London and it will be successful. You can pay for Spotify or the smallest merchant in Ghana can pay for Facebook with Airtel Mobile Money wallet. How do you enable that world? That is the question we are trying to answer because we believe that if everybody is connected to the digital economy, it would be a better place. Our mission basically is, how do we build payment infrastructure or technology that connects Africa to the digital economy and even more importantly as we do that, how do we build a payment system that is for Africa?' E said. 'The question is, how do we then build something that is for Africa with its peculiarities of multiple payment markets like mobile money and bank accounts with different channels...?'

Eight weeks after Andela raised $24 million in funding from Mark Zuckerberg, E left Andela to co-found Flutterwave as CEO with GB as CTO and a founding team of ex-bankers, engineers and entrepreneurs. The timing was deliberate as they wanted to leverage on the goodwill that Andela's success had brought to start and grow another success story. I ran into Sheel Tyle and he told me about E's plans for Flutterwave. As was the case with Andela's rounds, I suspected the round would be oversubscribed, so on behalf of Golden Palm Investments, I wired $300,000 into E's account before he even sent me the documents, despite his protestations.

So, what is Flutterwave and why has it created all this buzz? Flutterwave is a company providing universal technology that enables businesses and consumers to make and accept payments anywhere in Africa. It is an aggregator of all payment platforms such as bank accounts, cards, mobile money, and other mediums such as ATM, web, mobile, agents, and USSD. With over $380 billion in non-cash payments made in Africa every year through highly fragmented payment infrastructures, Flutterwave is simplifying payments with one single API.

In 2017, Flutterwave was admitted into Silicon Valley's elite accelerator program known as Y Combinator. It's an accelerator that invests in early stage start-ups. E graduated from Y Combinator in summer of 2017. As of August 2019, Flutterwave has attracted over $50 million in funding from global investors including Goldman Sachs, Visa, 4DX Ventures, Mastercard, Greycroft Partners, Green Visor Capital, Y Combinator, Raba Capital, Fintech Collective, CRE Ventures, Omidyar Network and some of the founders of Andela, among others. Joe Saunders, former Chairman and CEO of Visa joined its board in October 2018. To date, Flutterwave has processed over $2.5 billion in payments and has processed over 100 million transactions across 30 African countries. Flutterwave is a partner to 50 banks in Africa and over 1,200 developers have built products leveraging Flutterwave's technology. Its customers include Uber and Booking.com. Flutterwave was named one of the most innovative companies in Africa by Fast Company in 2018.

In June 2018, Flutterwave announced a partnership with Tempo Money Transfer to introduce blockchain-based payments in Nigeria. In announcing the deal, E said that 'Our partnership with Tempo is a fantastic example of the kind of innovation Flutterwave is enabling on the Stellar blockchain technology to bring down remittance costs and connect Africa to the global economy.' E believes cryptocurrencies empower the individual to allocate capital more effectively than traditional institutions. 'There is a lot of wastage in the capital market. We have a lot of VCs not returning capital. Capital is a big waste because of networks, specific networks. But with blockchain, what's happening is, people are now controlling their allocation of capital. They don't need some big licensed bank to do the allocation of capital on their behalf and take ridiculous returns in return. All they need is to decide that this is how I will allocate my capital and they can do it by themselves without even making an investment decision, just by simply taking a position. That by itself is going to change the dynamics of capital in the digital economy'.

E is convinced that technology will disrupt politics and governance in the same way it is disrupting commerce and other sectors of the economy. 'Social media is an amazing tool which can be used to great benefits. But you have to also understand that social media platforms are not platforms because they allow us to create content but because they are aggregators of data.' He believes Nigeria's 2015 election was won partly because the governing party had a certain level of understanding of the importance of data and the deployment of technology. He says APC embarked on 'an extensive data operation... polling unit by polling unit, people were calling to say 'vote for Buhari. There were robocalls being made for people to vote for Buhari [and] people thought there was that personal connection.'

In October 2018, E stepped down as CEO of Flutterwave and passed the reigns of the company to his co-founder GB. He is still actively involved in helping Flutterwave expand globally. He stands tall as a powerful voice for the ecosystem, an avid angel investor and adviser to several start-ups in Nigeria and across Africa. When the Vice-President of Nigeria launched the Nigerian Industrial Policy and Competitiveness Advisory Council, a body set up to design and supervise policies to help Nigeria accelerate its industrialisation, its members included leaders of Nigeria's private sector: obvious candidates like industrial magnate Aliko Dangote, Africa's richest man, and emerging leaders like our techie, E.

17

GREGORY ROCKSON

DISRUPTS THE PHARMA INDUSTRY

OVER A DECADE AGO, A FRIEND OF MINE, KWAKU AKUFFO introduced me to a young, dynamic man called Gregory Rockson. All three of us would regularly attend the Africa Business Conference at Harvard Business School, a student-run conference that attracts over 1,500 attendees from all over the world. It is also one of the biggest social events in America for young African professionals, with the conference organising an annual party often headlined by leading African artists. Kwaku was always hopeful he was going to meet his future wife at one of these parties.

I became friends with Greg, but we fell out of touch after some time. In 2013, while I was travelling around the continent meeting entrepreneurs, I was making a stop in Lusaka, Zambia, to meet with the ZamSolar team, a solar start-up. At the airport, as I was exiting, I saw a convoy of SUVs and men in suits coming to pick up someone important. I walked by the "VIP" and he looked familiar. 'Greg?' He immediately turned, exclaimed, 'Sangu, what are you doing here?' and we embraced. We exchanged numbers and promised to meet up at a local bar to catch up. At the bar, I got to understand why Greg was in Zambia and what the convoy was (he was being picked by the government for a project with the Ministry of Health). When he explained his start-up idea to me, I was immediately sold and tried to convince him to let me invest. As Greg often laughs about now, I even took him to an ATM machine and offered to pay him a deposit on shares up front. I called my investment committee partner, Alex Marlantes, that very night and told him about Greg and his new idea. Alex booked a flight from San Francisco and came to Ghana where we planned to meet with Greg and his founding team.

Greg, the youngest of five siblings, grew up in Tema, an industrial and coastal city that is 25 kilometres from Ghana's capital, Accra. Greg's family experienced life-threatening challenges before his birth. In 1981, there was a coup d'état in Ghana. Greg's father, a soldier, was thrown in prison by the new military leadership for not supporting the coup. He managed to escape out of jail and fled into exile in neighbouring Togo. In response, the military government seized all his property in Ghana, and overnight the Rockson family lost everything.

They were forced to start from scratch, and Greg's mother, a teacher, became the breadwinner of the family. Though teaching was a stable job, her modest income was barely enough to provide all their needs. Greg remembers her strength and resilience and recounts the one time he saw her break down: 'There was one time I remember she didn't see me. [It was] one of those days that [it was] hard for her. She went down and [was] crying. I was about to go in and I said no. [So] I stood by the door and I secretly saw her crying. That's the first time I saw that she was struggling. What this did to me as a child was, I learnt to be content; I was never a child that asked for things because I always knew that I didn't need to ask them. They didn't give it to me because I knew they didn't have it. If they had it, they [would have given] it to me.'

Despite the financial challenges his family had to endure, his parents believed deeply in the power of education. Greg recounts trying to crack a joke with his dad by saying he wished he could leave him a trust fund, so he could fund his dreams. His father, a retired soldier, replied simply: 'The trust fund I left you is the education I gave you.' His parents sacrificed the little they had to ensure that Greg and his siblings got the best possible education. Greg for example, attended one of the best senior high schools in Ghana, Prempeh College, notable for alumni such as former President John Kufuor. He fondly remembers a childhood tradition of his father buying a newspaper as early as 5am and making sure little Greg read it before leaving for school.

His father groomed Greg as a leader in the church. His parents were devout Catholics and Monday nights were reserved for Bible study. In their church, Bible study was organised in small groups. The group Greg's family joined grew to become the biggest group in the church, numbering 60 to 70 members. His father was elected as leader of the group. Whenever his father had to travel out of town, instead of deputising his leadership to another adult in the group, he would task young Gregory to lead. This taught Greg a lot about leadership and boosted his self-confidence. It also made him dream of becoming a Catholic priest in the future.

Like most of the entrepreneurs in the book, Greg, despite his family's financial struggles, was fortunate to have access to a computer at home. A family friend had donated an old desktop computer to his older sister after she had she scored 12. As in the senior high school final examinations. Greg remembers playing games on the computer and falling in love with the PC. Then the internet came to Ghana and changed his life. Greg became a research junkie and would use the internet to learn about everything. At about 12 years old, he developed an obsession for finding a cure for HIV/AIDS. He would spend all his savings at an internet café conducting hours of research on the epidemic. 'I just believed that I would find the cure for AIDS.' He even helped set up a non-profit to help children living with HIV/AIDS in Ghana.

In Ghana at the time, students usually take a gap year between senior high school and university. During this time, Greg was introduced to computer programming through the Kofi Annan ICT Centre which had just opened in Accra. He enrolled as one of the first nine students who participated in their computer programming course offering training in C++. 'It was fascinating for me how you could translate a file into a code.' However, he wasn't just interested in learning to code, but was focused on the applications of the code, and by figuring out ways to apply the coding, he was learning to solve problems. This problem-solving approach would later come to define his working style.

At the very young age of 16, Greg gained admission to the University of Ghana as a pre-med student studying bio-medical engineering. However, after his first semester at the University of Ghana, he applied and gained admission to Westminster College, a small liberal arts college in Missouri, and moved to the U.S. in 2009. While his original intention was to continue as a pre-med student, he switched to pursue a bachelor's degree in political science. The newspaper tradition with his father had sparked a life-long interest in political affairs. 'I like politics', he confesses. 'I think that everyone should be into politics. Politics define the global social making.'[316]

Meanwhile, after his first semester at Westminster College, Greg felt Missouri was too small for his ambitions. He managed to convince his college to agree to an innovative plan that would allow him to study in different universities and have his credits transferred to Westminster. The first academic program he participated in was a New York State government program through which he worked in the office of the representative of Harlem, the Honourable Keith Wright for six months.

This was also the period when Obamacare, President Obama's signature healthcare law, was passed in the U.S. Congress. 'When it passed in congress, I thought that while I would have liked to practice medicine, I could do more as an individual if I could help improve the policy side of healthcare. Helping increase its access to more people was more valuable to me, so I started studying public policy.'[317] Inspired by Obamacare, Greg applied and was admitted to the Junior Summer Institute of the Public Policy International Affairs Fellowship (PPIA) at the Woodrow Wilson School of Public and International Affairs at Princeton University. The goal of the program is "to prepare students from diverse backgrounds – including underrepresented racial and ethnic minorities and students from families with lower socio-economic status – for graduate study and careers in public policy."[318] After the summer program at Princeton, Greg left the United States for Europe as a Rotary Scholar for a one-year program at the University of Copenhagen.

Around this time, technology was powering global connectivity in unprecedented ways. Uber, Twitter, Facebook and other technology companies were on the global ascent. Greg wanted to better understand this ecosystem. He sought a waiver from Westminster College to spend his final semester in San Francisco in order to learn first-hand the 'magic' of Silicon Valley. He had to find an academic program for his final semester. Greg applied to the Centre for the Next Generation. Co-founded by philanthropist Tom Steyer, the Centre is focused on policy research on two key thematic areas: Energy & Climate and Children & Families. In San Francisco, Greg split his time between public policy work at the Centre and spending a lot of time with technology entrepreneurs. He attended lots of events and built personal relationships with many stakeholders in the ecosystem. He began to explore potential careers in technology.

One early morning, he sat down in a Starbucks coffee shop in downtown San Francisco, trying to figure out the next chapter of his life. He had applied for a job at some tech companies and had already attended two interviews at Google. It looked promising. 'I had a good feeling that I would receive a job offer, but something just did not sit right with me', he said.[319] 'Around 9am, I received an email from a friend which had a link to an investigative article titled 'Dirty Medicine' on *CNNMoney*. It tackled the issue of criminal fraud in Ranbaxy Laboratories, an Indian multinational pharmaceutical company. This article marked my return to Africa and my quest to use big data to help African governments develop better drug surveillance and monitoring systems. The piece on Ranbaxy outraged me. The author writes that in a conference call with a dozen company executives, one brushed aside fears about the quality of the AIDS medicine Ranbaxy was supplying for Africa. "Who cares?" the executive said. "It's just blacks dying."'

'I felt insulted personally by that statement... I became angrier because I feel we had allowed that to happen. Because, while the U.S. [Food and Drug Administration] sanctioned Ranbaxy and some of the production plants were closed, not a single African regulator issued any warning. I wrote to a lot of regulatory institutions in Africa asking, "What are you going to say about Ranbaxy?" I didn't get a single response.' This news report fuelled his interest in the pharmaceutical industry. Greg immersed himself in understanding the workings of the industry.

During the research, he came across a story in the local Ghanaian newspaper that compelled him to narrow his focus and created the seeds for what would become mPharma. The story was about a Ghanaian woman with a chronic heart condition. She had been admitted to a hospital in Accra on an emergency. The doctors prescribed the drug to save her life. However, the drug was not easily accessible, and her family members had to rush from pharmacy to pharmacy, with the doctors calling everywhere trying to locate the drug. By the time they managed to find a pharmacy that stocked the drug, it was too late – the woman had passed away.

Greg was devastated by this story. 'The story of this woman didn't make sense to me. I can order food, order a taxi, book a hotel room in real time. Why do doctors have to rely on phone calls to locate drugs? Why do they have to write prescriptions on paper to order them? What about the follow-up appointments? Once the patient leaves the consulting room, that's generally the end of the relationship with the doctor. The doctor to patient ratio in Africa is roughly one per 15,000. Doctors do not have the time to follow up with every patient.'[320] Greg moved from asking questions to thinking of solutions. He started researching and brainstorming. He found out that only four countries in Sub-Saharan Africa have proper drug monitoring systems in place. Thus, African drug regulators have little to no means of harnessing effective pharmacovigilance capabilities. Doctors in turn, are unfamiliar with the practice, overburdened by the low doctor-to-patient ratio, and wary of any potential legal or malpractice liabilities. Pharmaceutical companies also lack any incentives since only 17% of African countries mandate them to conduct post-marketing surveillance. Greg realised that 'we need a better way to collect, store and process data on adverse drug effects. We need to develop a population-based approach to drug monitoring. Luckily, the tools to build these solutions are right in front of us. Today, with Africa leapfrogging the world when it comes to mobile technology, we can turn every individual into a data collector.'[321] mPharma's conception had begun.

As a founding member of the Copenhagen hub of the Global Shapers, Greg got invited to the World Economic Forum in Davos in 2012. At WEF he met Dr. Daniel Vasella, then Chairman and CEO of Novartis. Dr. Vasella was passionate about Africa and pushed for Novartis to invest heavily there. Greg reached out to Dr. Vasella for advice and he would later invest in mPharma and join its board of directors. Greg knew he would need to build a world class team to execute his idea. Later, in a conversation with a friend he made in Copenhagen, the friend said, 'I have a friend in my class who is also a good designer and would be very interested to be a part of the things you are working on.' He introduced Greg to Dan Shoukimas, a liberal arts senior at Connecticut College who was studying abroad in Denmark. Greg recruited him as a co-founder. 'I started talking with Dan and he also says, "I have a very good friend [and college classmate] who is a programmer and will be very interested in this." I was like "Sure introduce us," and that's how Greg found James Finucane, the third co-founder. They started discussions over email and Skype in 2012, but never met in person until April of 2013. Before they had even met in person, both co-founders had already agreed to move to Ghana with Greg to help him start mPharma.

Gregory believes the most important and best decision he ever took since he conceived mPharma was his choice of co-founders. This is 'because I have come to realise that you need to have the same value system as your co-founders in order to make anything work. You must be motivated by the same things. You cannot have one motivated by the problem and one motivated by money. Clashes will happen. And if you are motivated by the same thing, you will always overcome whatever problems you face. In many ways, we are so similar yet different. Similar in the sense that we share the same views, so we don't have to debate but so different in the sense that we can each not do anyone's job. I cannot do Danny's job as a designer. I'm not a designer. Danny cannot do James's job as a programmer. They both can't do my job leading the organisation and the business. And that has led to a strong partnership that even in the toughest of days, we are able to see a much higher ideal beyond whatever the short-term struggles are and that keeps us moving.'

They moved to Ghana in 2013, working out of Greg's family home in Tema. They had a great idea, but didn't have a lot of money, and faced many difficulties convincing stakeholders in Ghana. It was a herculean task convincing retail pharmacies and hospitals to come on board. Coming on board required giving mPharma access to their inventory, and some of the healthcare providers refused to cooperate, claiming "trade secrets." Greg confesses that, looking back, in their first four months, they really didn't know what they were doing. Fortunately, Greg had met a high-ranking diplomat from Zambia in Geneva during the World Health Assembly and had pitched some of his ideas for mPharma. This diplomat was very excited and invited Greg to visit Zambia for meetings with the health ministry about a potential pilot. This was when I met Greg at the airport in Lusaka with the VIP entourage. Greg's trip to Zambia had been very successful and the Zambian government expressed its willingness to partner with mPharma on a pilot project. Greg had one problem though: mPharma did not have any capital.

By this time, my partner, Alex Marlantes, flew to Ghana from San Francisco and we planned a meeting with Greg, Dan and James at the Golden Tulip Hotel in Accra. We discussed their ideas for mPharma for several hours, with Greg drawing images on a napkin to illustrate the proposed business model. Alex and I were enthralled by the idea. We had both studied pharmacy benefit managers in the United States and knew the potential was in the billions of dollars. But we were worried. This was an untested team of young men in their early '20s with zero work experience. I'll never forget what Alex told me: 'Sangu, this is a binary investment for us. Either it's going to be a zero or this will be one of the best investments we will ever make. If they succeed, mPharma will easily become one of the most impactful companies to emerge out of the African continent.' We decided to invest in mPharma. Greg initially rejected our offer and countered with a multi-million-dollar valuation that was 50%

higher than what we proposed. We thought it was unjustified given that the company didn't even have a product; all they had was an idea. Greg claimed there were lots of other investors he could talk to who would invest and gave us 48 hours to decide. We agreed to the crazy valuation, but insisted on warrants, which would give us the right to buy additional shares in the future. We then wired $150,000 and became the first investor in mPharma. Several years later, Greg, who has become a very close friend, would confess to me that he was completely bluffing; not only did mPharma not have any other investors at the time, but they were running out of cash and could only survive for another ten days without the capital infusion.

For the initial pilot, they built an e-prescription software and were able to extract an enormous amount of data to track drugs on a dashboard as well as establish a real-time disease surveillance system. When a patient goes to see a doctor, the prescription is sent electronically to the patient's phone via SMS. Additionally, when the prescription pops up on the patient's phone, it comes with all the pharmacy locations where the patient can obtain the drug. Moreover, the patient-doctor relationship is further enhanced because either of them can contact each other for follow-up or feedback via phone after the first contact.

Then, mPharma added another layer to its service, offering remote management of the inventory of retail pharmacies and hospital pharmacies through proprietary technology infrastructure. They have developed several tools that enable them to collect and process data from each pharmacy in their network. The key data they collect is patient level prescriptions and dispensation. This is then aggregated and used to forecast demand and manage inventory for hospitals and retail pharmacies.

As Greg explained: 'The drug supply chain in Africa is built on a "Push" data model. This means, distributors must wait to receive a purchase order from providers before supplying drugs to them. The

Push model is built on siloed data systems between distributors and providers. As a result, both parties are unable to forecast demand which leads to frequent stock-outs. We have designed a "Pull" model, based on an integrated data system that gives distributors real time access to anonymised patient level dispensation data from providers. Instead of waiting for a provider to send a purchase order before supplying drugs, a distributor can use the dispensation data they receive to set appropriate re-order levels. A new purchase order is automatically triggered when the stock reaches the reorder level and prompts the distributor to supply drugs without needing the input of the provider. The financial interests of the provider are aligned with those of the distributor if the stock is provided on a consignment basis.'[322]

The data obtained is also a treasure trove for health ministries and pharmaceutical companies. It is the solution to the pharmacovigilance question that prompted the founding of mPharma. The tools in the company's data architecture enable them to easily monitor drug use for strategic policy and business decisions. The data generated also helps the pharmacy to better manage its inventory and operations. The data generated is sold as a separate service to pharmaceutical companies and governments.

However, Greg and his team noticed from the data that there was a massive divergence between the number of prescriptions and the number of drug dispensations. Upon investigation, they realised that a substantial number of patients were going to the pharmacies, but were not buying the drugs, deterred by high pricing. A study by the World Health Organisation revealed that some drugs are marked up by as much as 300%.[323] Greg and his team realised the problem wasn't just the access and availability of drugs; affordability was increasingly becoming the biggest issue.

The mPharma team needed more research and resources to solve this problem. They applied to Microsoft's Ventures Accelerator

Program, which is a four-month incubator program that offers early stage start-ups or first-time entrepreneurs' mentorship, technical assistance and access to professional contacts. Participants are also offered Microsoft services worth $60,000 for their first year of operations. As part of the Accelerator Program, Greg and his co-founders relocated from Accra, Ghana to Microsoft's research and development (R&D) site in Tel Aviv, Israel. Greg noted, with disappointment, that their presence 'outside Africa' during that time played a key role in securing many of the deals they inked with large corporations; being based in Tel Aviv gave them a badge of credibility. mPharma later joined the Alchemist, a top Silicon Valley enterprise accelerator, becoming the first African start-up to do so. The accelerator is backed by some of the leading venture capitalists and technology companies in the Valley including Cisco, Khosla Ventures, and Andreessen Horowitz.[324]

So, what does mPharma really do? As Greg puts it, 'our proprietary supply chain software enables us to implement vendor managed inventory for independent healthcare providers in Africa. This model enables mPharma to create a tightly coupled pharmacy monolith – on a continent that has a highly fragmented pharmacy retail market – with leverage over pricing, distribution and reimbursements. mPharma has created several different technological solutions for data collection: Thea, a CRM tool that gives facilities the ability to perform claim submission and management; SyncDB, an onsite integration that allows for a facility to automatically sync select parts of their database to mPharma's integration layer; our integrations REST API that allows facilities to integrate with mPharma through HTTP; and an excel spreadsheets tool that a facility may use to keep track of their dispensations. mPharma's collection process unifies these disparate and distinct data sources into one cohesive data set which allows us to build a data driven supply chain infrastructure.'

For patients, mPharma has created a financing solution called

Mutti which allows patients to use credit to purchase drugs for chronic conditions. For third party payers, such as insurers, they can partner with mPharma and benefit from reduced drug prices (by as much as 30%). For hospitals, the high cost of drugs requires significant and on-going capital investment in inventory to keep in-house pharmacies stocked with drugs. This deprives hospitals from cash that they can use to invest in new technologies or expand capacity. mPharma sources and buys drugs from the world's top manufacturers and stocks the shelves for the hospital, freeing up significant working capital for the hospital. Finally, for drug manufacturers who want access to new and existing patient populations in Africa, mPharma offers a Market Access as a Service (MaaS) solution to leverage the data the company collects to create meaningful insights for drug companies. mPharma offers insights on drug utilisation patterns, anonymised prescription, dispensation and disease trends and customised tailored payments plans for increased access. The company has signed some of the largest global pharmaceutical giants including Novartis and Pfizer.

mPharma is currently serving about 100,000 patients every month across Africa through its services, operating in Ghana, Nigeria, Zambia, Zimbabwe and Kenya, and manages inventory for over 340 healthcare facilities. These technological innovations have won mPharma global fame. In 2015, mPharma won the 2015 World Health Summit Start-up Track in Berlin, which recognises 'outstanding ideas and innovative business concepts that have the potential to revolutionise healthcare and improve global health.'[325] In 2016, the company won a $50,000 Impact Award in the economic empowerment category of internet.org's Facebook-led initiative called the Innovation Challenge in Africa. Award winners are usually ideas, apps, websites or online services that create value in Africa through either empowerment or education. mPharma won the award for increasing affordability of drugs, increasing access to drugs and its flexible micro-payment system.[326] In 2018, Fast Company named mPharma the number one most innovative company in Africa, and Greg graced the cover of Forbes as one of its 30 under 30 entrepreneurs in healthcare. In 2019, mPharma was awarded $1.5 million from the Skoll Foundation and honoured as part of the 'select group of social entrepreneurs whose innovations have already had significant, proven impact on some of the world's pressing problems.'[327]

In the last quarter of 2017, mPharma formalised a ground-breaking partnership with the Red Cross, resulting in the opening of a string of Red Cross pharmacies all over Africa starting from Zimbabwe. Through its Quality-Rx program, mPharma is going beyond the large pharmacy retail shops and partnering with thousands of small community pharmacies, providing them with zero-interest loans and technology support. Commenting on the round, Greg stated: 'It is estimated that the 10 largest pharmacy retail chains in Kenya, Nigeria and Ghana have a combined total of only 186 outlets, while there are over 15,000 mom and pop pharmacies in these countries. We can serve more patients and bring down drug costs if mom and pop pharmacies are able to better manage their inventory. We built mPharma to do exactly this.'[328]

With the value of pharmaceutical spending in Africa expected to hit $45 billion by 2020, Gregory explains that the goal of mPharma is to position itself to be 'the largest dispenser of chronic drugs for patients in Africa. We will accomplish this by offering the lowest drug prices and health benefits plans for patients across the continent.'[329] Greg believes the key three markets of Nigeria, Kenya and Ethiopia, which he jokingly calls the "Holy Trinity," could drive revenues to over $150 million.

While Greg initially struggled to raise capital, mPharma has now become the darling of global investors. To date the company has raised over $35 million in venture financing. Its investors include some of the world's leading venture capitalists and family offices, including 4DX Ventures; the Bharti Mittal family, owners of Airtel; Social Capital; and legendary venture capitalist Jim Breyer, whose investment in mPharma was his first ever in Africa. Through Golden Palm Investments, I have invested over $1 million in mPharma and participated in every round of financing and continue to serve on mPharma's board of directors. I keep reminding Alex that our fateful bet on three untested 20-something-year-olds remains the boldest and greatest investment we have ever made. The story of Greg and mPharma stands out as a powerful reminder of the potential for African entrepreneurship in the digital age.

CONCLUSION

CONGRATULATIONS! YOU MADE IT TO THE END OF THE BOOK.
I hope, like me, you have been inspired by the lives and examples of
these young entrepreneurs and gained some insight into the socio-
cultural and historical context that shaped them. They present
case studies of opportunity that should draw the attention of
policymakers, government officials, scholars, investors and budding
entrepreneurs. Great challenges lie ahead. Over a billion Africans
will be born between now and 2050, when Africa's population
will reach 2.5 billion. I believe most of Africa's political leaders are
catastrophically unprepared for this demographic explosion. Yet, I
remain optimistic, and have never been more excited for the future.
Technology is democratising opportunity, and young entrepreneurs
are innovating in exciting ways. I have already raised red flags over
the glorification and over-hyping of entrepreneurship. Nevertheless,
it holds great promise for solving the youth unemployment challenge.
My travels across the 45 African countries and interviews with over
600 entrepreneurs left me with some insights. I'd like to discuss three
key takeaways.

The first insight is on **education**. Across every single country I
visited, almost every entrepreneur I met listed finding talent and
human capital as among their top three challenges. Many of the
entrepreneurs I interviewed highlighted a skills gap between the
demands of industry and what students are learning in the classroom.

This calls for comprehensive education reform and new models to tackle the human capital challenge. As I mentioned in Saran Jones' chapter, Liberia had a national crisis when 100% of its students failed the university entrance exam. I have seen the power of innovative models for education and will give two examples.

While I was hiring employees for my company, I kept coming across exceptional students who had one institution in common: Ashesi University. Ashesi was founded in 2002 by Patrick Awuah, Jr., an engineer who quit his job at Microsoft in Seattle to move back home to Ghana and start a university to solve what he identified as a leadership problem. Ashesi's vision is 'an African renaissance driven by a new generation of ethical, entrepreneurial leaders. [Ashesi aims] to educate such leaders and to drive a movement in African higher education to scale up the education of such leaders.' Ashesi started from humble beginnings in a rented home in 2002 with a founding class of 30 students. Today, Ashesi operates on over 100 acres of land, enrols over 1,000 students and has over 1,200 alumni. At the heart of Ashesi's pedagogy is a multidisciplinary core curriculum that develops critical thinking, creative problem solving, ethical reasoning, and effective communication skills. Ashesi offers studies in Humanities and Social Sciences, Business Administration, Management Information Systems, Computer Science, Computer Engineering, Mechanical Engineering and Electrical Engineering.

From starting Africa's first student-run honour code system (no invigilators in the exam room) to running far-reaching social ventures, to founding companies that build software for millions of users, Ashesi's students and alumni are having impact that is gaining global recognition. Nearly 100% of Ashesi's graduates receive job offers, start businesses or enter graduate school within 6 months of graduation. In 2012, Ashesi University was ranked among the top 10 most respected organisations in Ghana (a first for an education institution) in a survey of 300 CEOs conducted by PricewaterhouseCoopers (PwC) and Business and Financial Times. In 2016, Ashesi was selected by the World Bank to host the Ghana Climate Innovation Centre, a business accelerator to help scale start-ups working on climate change solutions. In 2017, Ashesi was awarded the World Innovation Summit in Education Prize, one of the world's biggest prizes in education. Beyond the impact on its own students and alumni, Ashesi has also been leading a coalition of like-minded institutions and universities across Africa, sharing best practices and collaborating on pedagogical innovation and curriculum reform. Patrick recognises that the scale of our challenges requires a collaborative approach because no single institution can solve the challenges in education and leadership. For example, Ashesi is mentoring the African Development University in Niger (with a student body of 70% women), co- founded by Harvard Kennedy School alumnus Kader Kaneye, who incubated the idea during his studies at the Harvard Innovation Lab to 'create talent to design and drive the transformation of Niger, the Sahel region and the continent.'

Another interesting model for tackling our education challenges, is being pioneered by Ghanaian TED Fellow and TIME 100 laureate, Fred Swaniker. Fred established the African Leadership University (ALU) with campuses in Mauritius and Rwanda. Started in 2015 with 173 students in the inaugural class, ALU today has 300 students in each campus. ALU is a different type of university. Instead of conventional classes, the school prepares an individualised, student-focused leadership curriculum that is designed to develop and test skills. Fred and his team interviewed over 150 employers researching the missing skills in college graduates. They identified seven "meta skills" (including critical thinking, analytical reasoning, leading yourself, leading others and managing projects). Then, they came up with 135 learning outcomes that will help develop these skills which every student learns in the first year. In addition, students all undergo mandatory internships as part of their university experience. ALU offers degrees in Business Management, Social Sciences, Computer Science, Entrepreneurship, Global Challenges, International Business and Trade and a master's degree in Business Administration. However, students don't declare majors.

As Fred explained it, 'Traditionally universities have schools that are built in silos, the school of business, school of law, etc. but we think in order to solve the world's greatest problems you need to adopt a much more interdisciplinary approach. We created our schools around seven grand challenges that Africa is going to face in the next 50 years and seven great opportunities [urbanisation, climate change, infrastructure, healthcare, education, job creation and governance].' So, for example, students in the school of urbanisation will study a mix of architecture, civil engineering, urban planning and technology all focused on solving the urbanisation challenge that Africa will face in the coming years. Fred also developed a unique income sharing model for tuition. 'Instead of a fixed amount they need to pay with interest you would get from a loan, [students] commit to paying back a fixed percentage of their income, let's say 7-10% for 10 years and then they are done.' Fred has an ambitious mission to create 3 million new generation African leaders by 2060 by opening ALU campuses in 25 cities across Africa. It sounds 'crazy', but Fred argues that 'tertiary enrolment rates in Africa are only 8%, in India it's about 24%... just to catch up to India's level of tertiary enrolment we would need to build 135 universities the size of Harvard every single year for the next 15 years. When you are in that kind of environment, you can't do things the normal way.'[330] The likes of Patrick and Fred need the support of governments, philanthropists and international institutions focused on solving the education challenge. We can't scale entrepreneurship in a digital age without the requisite human capital.

The second insight is on **financial capital**. In Silicon Valley, which is flushed with an oversupply of venture capital, the mantra is 'don't worry about money, just focus on the best ideas.' Almost every entrepreneur I met laughed at this. For them, in a world of nascent venture capital, access to capital can make the difference between success and failure. I know this from my own work at Golden Palm Investments – for every dollar we invested in an African start-up, there were nine other compelling high-quality companies we could have invested in (and several thousand more who are looking for capital). We need to implement policies that will promote the equity financing of start-ups. For example, we should consider allocating a small percentage of pension funds towards seeding local venture capital funds. African assets under management, estimated at $634 billion, have been growing at a remarkable pace and are projected to reach $1.1 trillion in 2020.[331] We should also consider tax policy that removes any taxes on capital gains for long term investments in start-ups to incentivise investments in start-ups. There are still too few venture capitalists focused on Africa. We need more capital to fund our young and emerging entrepreneurs. With much less capital than their counterparts in other parts of the world, this book has shown entrepreneurs who are able to deliver incredible social and economic value.

We need capital that will support the growth of big companies. Acha Leke et al. in *Africa's Business Revolution* argue that 'Africa's relative lack of big companies matters not just for shareholders but for society, because these firms are the primary drivers of economic growth.' They add that these big companies, which they term business baobabs, 'enliven their local economies: they contribute disproportionately to higher wages and taxes, productivity improvement, innovation and technology dissemination.' McKinsey conducted a study from 2014 to 2016 that revealed that the top 20% of companies were responsible for 90% of the economic value created in the world, which they defined as the profit a company makes after repaying its investors. However, a lot of existing programs available for African entrepreneurs do not enable the creation of business baobabs. I applaud philanthropists like Tony Elumelu, Chairman of United Bank for Africa and the founder of the Tony Elumelu Foundation. Elumelu has committed $100 million to training and funding 10,000 African entrepreneurs over 10 years with a goal to realise $10 billion in revenue and create 1 million jobs. That means he expects each entrepreneur on average to generate $1 million in revenue and to create 100 jobs. Each entrepreneur in his program receives $5,000 in investment capital. While $100 million is a significant amount and an extraordinary gesture of generosity, $5,000 is a small sum for an entrepreneur who is expected to create $1 million in revenue, in the absence of follow-on capital. Might the program have greater success of reaching its goals for economic impact by focusing on a smaller group of higher impact entrepreneurs? Could the $100 million have a greater impact by giving $1 million to the best 100 ideas and entrepreneurs, giving them enough capital to scale? Micro-finance and micro-investing will not create business baobabs. We need to think big and invest big in start-ups most likely to become baobabs.

We also need to pay attention to diversity and inclusion in our allocation of capital. Apart from the obvious social and moral imperative, there is a compelling economic case. A 2007 study found that Fortune 500 companies in the top quartile for female board representation outperform those in the lowest quartile by at least 53% return on equity.[332] An Illinois State Board of Investment survey of emerging managers (defined as investment managers who are minorities, women or disabled) from 2006 to 2013 showed impressive outperformance over the time period against the relevant benchmarks.[333] There are already some Africans funds that are taking leadership here. Alitheia is a pioneer investment VC firm run by Tokunbo Ishmael, one of the few women VC investors on the continent. Alithea has already invested in three FinTech companies, Paga, Lidya and Oradian, which are focused on driving financial inclusion, especially among women. We need more Ishmaels and Alitheias.

The final insight is on the **role of government.** At many conferences on entrepreneurship in Africa that I have attended, people condemn African governments and advise entrepreneurs to avoid government at all costs. There is some merit to those considerations. However, my experience and my research lead me to the conclusion that we simply cannot achieve the optimal level of development without involving government. The private sector in many African countries is small compared to government. No private company, no matter how large, can match the scale and legitimacy of national governments. Despite its flaws, government plays a valuable role in promoting the public good. Data over the last 30 years demonstrate that several government programs have improved the lives of many citizens. We also need government to provide the vital regulations to protect citizens. There is a prominent role for government to play.

African governments need to adopt policies to enable start-ups to scale. Some governments, for example the government of Rwanda, have already created partnerships with Andela, granting them tax holidays and co-investing in their model to train developers. Such public-private partnerships focused on training a tech workforce is critical to succeed in the new global digital economy. In addition, African central banks need to create opportunities for FinTech companies like Flutterwave to gain payment licenses to power and enable more merchants. Why shouldn't mPharma be managing the drug inventory at public hospitals for national governments and using their technology to deliver cost savings to the national treasury? The digital economy requires investments in network infrastructure and energy. The growth in digital technologies will also allow Africa to make remarkable advances in productivity.

Beyond the role that government can play in partnering with start-ups and helping them scale, I believe it is important for young entrepreneurs to consider public service. We need public service entrepreneurs. David Sengeh is a classic example of success in his new role as Chief Innovation Officer of Sierra Leone. Could Siya be a future Minister of Energy, Greg a future Health Minister, Saran a future Minister of Water, or Patricia a future President? With a median age of 19.5, and the average age of its ten oldest presidents at 78, and only one female president, Africa's leaders don't represent its youthful demography. This needs to change.

I believe in Africa. I believe in our young people. And I believe we will forge a different narrative for our children and our grandchildren.

REFERENCES

INTRODUCTION

1   The Economist. (2000). *The hopeless continent.* [online] Available at: https://www.economist.com/node/21519234 [Accessed 3 May 2018].

2   Gilles Pison, G. (2017). *There's a strong chance a third of all people on earth will be African by 2100.* [online] Quartz. Available at: https://qz.com/1099546/population-growth-africans-will-be-a-third-of-all-people-on-earth-by-2100/ [Accessed 11 Apr. 2018].

3   Akyeampong, E. and Fofack, H. (2015). *Five centuries ago Africa was booming: it can rise again.* [online] the Guardian. Available at: https://www.theguardian.com/commentisfree/2015/sep/09/africa-rising-people-economies [Accessed 11 Apr. 2018].

4   Forbes.com. (2018). *Africa's Billionaires List.* [online] Available at: https://www.forbes.com/africa-billionaires/list/#tab:overall [Accessed 11 Apr. 2018].

5   The Economist. (2011). *Africa rising; The Hopeful Continent.* [online] Available at: https://www.economist.com/node/21541015 [Accessed 2 May 2018].

6   Akyeampong, E. and Fofack, H. (2015). *Five centuries ago Africa was booming.* [Accessed 11 Apr. 2018].
    To learn more about the relationship between Europe and Africa, read Walter Rodney's *How Europe Underdeveloped Africa.*

7   Edinger, H. and Davies, M. (2017). *Africa: How business needs to plan for the changing continent.* [online] Deloitte Insights. Available at: https://www2.deloitte.com/insights/us/en/economy/global-economic-outlook/2017/q2-africa.html [Accessed 17 Apr. 2018].

8   World Bank. (2016). *While Poverty in Africa Has Declined, Number of Poor Has Increased*. [online] Available at: http://www.worldbank.org/en/region/afr/publication/poverty-rising-africa-poverty-report [Accessed 11 Apr. 2018].

9   Yuan Sun, Irene. *The Next Factory of the World: How Chinese Investment is Reshaping Africa*. Harvard Business Review Press, 2017

10 Gsma.com. (2018). *The Mobile Economy*. [online] Available at: https://www.gsma.com/mobileeconomy/wp-content/uploads/2018/02/The-Mobile-Economy-Global-2018.pdf [Accessed 19 Dec. 2018].

11 Manyika, J., Cabral, A., Moodley, L., Moraje, S., Yeboah-Amankwah, S., Chui, M. and Anthonyrajah, J. (2013). *Lions go digital: The internet's transformative potential in Africa*. [online] McKinsey & Company. Available at: https://www.mckinsey.com/industries/high-tech/our-insights/lions-go-digital-the-internets-transformative-potential-in-africa [Accessed 3 May 2018].

12 *Africa internet Users, 2018 Population and Facebook Statistics*. [online] Available at: https://www.internetworldstats.com/stats1.htm [Accessed 11 Apr. 2018].

13 Ojobo, T. (2016). *Investments in Telecoms hit $68b in Nigeria*. [online] Ncc.gov.ng. Available at: https://www.ncc.gov.ng/stakeholder/media-public/news-headlines/118-investments-in-telecoms-hit-68b-in-nigeria [Accessed 19 Dec. 2018].

14 Leke, Acha et al. (2018), *Africa's Business Revolution*. Harvard Business Review Press.

15 Ibid

16 Leke, A. and Yeboah-Amankwah, S. (2018). *Africa: A Crucible for Creativity*. [online] Harvard Business Review. Available at: https://hbr.org/2018/11/africa-a-crucible-for-creativity [Accessed 19 Dec. 2018].

17 Leke, Acha et al. (2018), *Africa's Business Revolution*. Harvard Business Review Press.

18 Ibid

19 Dapaah, B. (2014). *How bamboo bikes gave women a new future in Ghana*. [online] World Economic Forum. Available at: https://www.weforum.org/agenda/2014/03/bamboo-bikes-ghanas-women-riding-high/ [Accessed 30 May 2019].

Cathcart-Keays, Athlyn (2015). *It's money lying in the streets: meet the woman transforming recycling in Lagos*. [online]. Available at https://www.theguardian.com/cities/2015/oct/21/money-lying-streets-meet-woman-transforming-recycling-lagos-wecyclers [Accessed July 19, 2019].

20 BlackPast.org. (n.d.). *Musa, Mansa (1280-1337) | The Black Past: Remembered and Reclaimed.* [online] Available at: http://www.blackpast.org/gah/musa-mansa-1280-1337 [Accessed 4 May 2018].

21 Sow, M. (2018). *Figures of the week: Africa's growing youth population and human capital investments.* [online] Brookings. Available at: https://www.brookings.edu/blog/africa-in-focus/2018/09/20/figures-of-the-week-africas-growing-youth-population-and-human-capital-investments/ [Accessed 30 May 2019].

ASPIRING MOGULS: INTRODUCTION

22 Bughin, J., Chironga, M., Desvaux, G., Ermias, T., Jacobson, P., Kassiri, O., Leke, A., Lund, S., Wamelen, A. and Zouaui, Y. (2016). *Lions on the move II: Realising the potential of Africa's economies.* [online] McKinsey & Company. Available at: https://www.mckinsey.com/global-themes/middle-east-and-africa/lions-on-the-move-realising-the-potential-of-africas-economies [Accessed 11 Apr. 2018].

23 Ibid

24 Chatterjee, S. and Mahama, J. (2017). *Promise Or Peril? Africa's 830 Million Young People By 2050.* [online] UNDP in Africa. Available at: http://www.africa.undp.org/content/rba/en/home/blog/2017/8/12/Promise-Or-Peril-Africa-s-830-Million-Young-People-By-2050.html [Accessed 12 Apr. 2018].

25 Afdb.org. (2016). *Jobs for Youth in Africa: Strategy for Creating 25 Million Jobs and Equipping 50 Million Youth 2016-2025.* [online] Available at: https://www.afdb.org/fileadmin/uploads/afdb/Documents/Boards-Documents/Bank_Group_Strategy_for_Jobs_for_Youth_in_Africa_2016-2025_Rev_2.pdf [Accessed 12 Apr. 2018].

26 Dayo Olopade (2014) *The Bright Continent.* USA: Houghton Mifflin Harcourt

27 Kermeliotis, T. and Veselinovic, K. (2014). *The numbers that show Africa is buzzing with entrepreneurial spirit.* [online] CNN. Available at: http://edition.cnn.com/2014/05/13/business/numbers-showing-africa-entrepreneurial-spirit/index.html [Accessed 12 Apr. 2018].

28 Kelley, D., Singer, S. and Herrington, M. (2016). *Global Entrepreneurship Monitor 2015/2016 Report*. [online] GEM Global Entrepreneurship Monitor. Available at: http://gemconsortium.org/report/49480 [Accessed 12 Apr. 2018].

29 MasterCard Social Newsroom. (2018). *Africa a world leader in women business owners: Mastercard Index of Women Entrepreneurs*. [online] Available at: https://newsroom.mastercard.com/mea/press-releases/ africa-a-world-leader-in-women-business-owners-mastercard-index-of-women-entrepreneurs/ [Accessed 30 May 2019].

30 African Development Bank. (2013). *Recognising Africa's Informal Sector*. [online] Available at: https://www.afdb.org/en/blogs/afdb-championing-inclusive-growth-across-africa/post/recognising-africas-informal-sector-11645/ [Accessed 12 Apr. 2018].

31 IMF. (2016). *Factsheet - Debt Relief Under the Heavily Indebted Poor Countries (HIPC) Initiative*. [online] Available at: https://www.imf.org/ en/About/Factsheets/Sheets/2016/08/01/16/11/Debt-Relief-Under-the-Heavily-Indebted-Poor-Countries-Initiative [Accessed 12 Apr. 2018].

32 Doingbusiness.org. (2019). *Ranking of economies - Doing Business - World Bank Group*. [online] Available at: http://www.doingbusiness. org/rankings [Accessed 5 Nov. 2018].

ERIC MUTHOMI CREATES VALUE FROM BANANAS

33 Rice, X. (2008). *Death toll nears 800 as post-election violence spirals out of control in Kenya*. [online] the Guardian. Available at: https:// www.theguardian.com/world/2008/jan/28/kenya.international [Accessed 12 Apr. 2018].

34 Worldpopulationreview.com. (2018). *Population of Kenya 2018*. [online] Available at: http://worldpopulationreview.com/countries/ kenya-population/ [Accessed 12 Apr. 2018]. Kenya-information-guide. com. (n.d.). *Nairobi's economy - a large contributor to Kenya's GDP*. [online] Available at: http://www.kenya-information-guide.com/nairobi-business.html [Accessed 12 Apr. 2018].

35 Imf.org. (2014). *Report for Selected Countries and Subjects*. [online] Available at: http://www.imf.org/external/pubs/ft/weo/2014/02/ weodata/weorept.aspx?pr.x=67&pr.y=13&sy=2014&ey=2019&scsm= 1&ssd=1&sort=country&ds=.&br=1&c=664&s=NGDPD%2CNGDP DPC%2CPPPGDP%2CPPPPC&grp=0&a [Accessed 12 Apr. 2018].

36 Bughin, J., Chironga, M., Desvaux, G., Ermias, T., Jacobson, P., Kassiri, O., Leke, A., Lund, S., Wamelen, A. and Zouaui, Y. (2016). *Lions on the move II: Realising the potential of Africa's economies.* [online] McKinsey & Company. Available at: https://www.mckinsey.com/global-themes/middle-east-and-africa/lions-on-the-move-realising-the-potential-of-africas-economies [Accessed 11 Apr. 2018].

37 Food and Agriculture Organisation of the United Nations. (n.d.). *Key facts on food loss and waste you should know!* [online] Available at: http://www.fao.org/save-food/resources/keyfindings/en/ [Accessed 12 Apr. 2018].

38 Ntale, C. (2013). *Where does aid money really go – and what is it spent on?* [online] CNN. Available at: http://edition.cnn.com/2013/10/09/opinion/where-does-aid-money-really-go/index.html [Accessed 12 Apr. 2018].

39 World Health Organisation International. (2017). *Levels and Trends in Child Malnutrition: UNICEF / WHO / World Bank Group Joint Child Malnutrition Estimates.* [online] Available at: http://www.who.int/nutgrowthdb/jme_brochoure2017.pdf [Accessed 12 Apr. 2018].

40 Roxburgh, C., Dorr, N., Leke, A., Tazi-Riffi, A., Wamelen, A., Lund, S., Chironga, M., Alatouik, T., Atkins, C., Terfous, N. and Zeino-Mahmalat, T. (2010). *Lions on the move: The progress and potential of African economies.* [online] McKinsey & Company. Available at: https://www.mckinsey.com/global-themes/middle-east-and-africa/lions-on-the-move [Accessed 12 Apr. 2018].

41 Stawiindustries.com. (n.d.). *Stawi Foods and Fruits Limited.* [online] Available at: http://stawiindustries.com/ [Accessed 12 Apr. 2018].

42 Otuoma, P. (2014). *Farmers embrace chicken pea in short rains to boost yearly yields.* [online] Farmbizafrica.com. Available at: http://farmbizafrica.com/~farmbiza/index.php?option=com_content&view=article&id=1613:farmers-to-sell-their-cereals-through-receipt-system-taming-exploitive-middlemen&catid=26&Itemid=144 [Accessed 12 Apr. 2018].

43 Food and Agriculture Organisation of the United Nations. (n.d.). *Key facts on food loss and waste you should know!* [online] Available at: http://www.fao.org/save-food/resources/keyfindings/en/ [Accessed 12 Apr. 2018].

44 WWF Global. (n.d.). *Nature Challenge Africa*. [online] Available at: http://wwf.panda.org/who_we_are/wwf_offices/regional_office_for_africa/our_solutions/naturechallengeafrica/ [Accessed 12 Apr. 2018].

45 Enablis.org. (2013). *Enablis - Enablis supports entrepreneurs in Africa*. [online] Available at: http://www.enablis.org/newsmedia/news/enablis-and-ilo-to-award-best-business-plans-in-national-competition.aspx#.Ws96uIjFLIV [Accessed 12 Apr. 2018].

46 Data.worldbank.org. (n.d.). *Fertility rate, total (births per woman) | Data*. [online] Available at: https://data.worldbank.org/indicator/SP.DYN.TFRT.IN?view=chart [Accessed 19 Dec. 2018].

47 Neslen, A. (2018). *Nestlé under fire for marketing claims on baby milk formulas*. [online] The Guardian. Available at: https://www.theguardian.com/business/2018/feb/01/nestle-under-fire-for-marketing-claims-on-baby-milk-formulas [Accessed 30 May 2019].

48 S., T. (2015). *Why does Kenya lead the world in mobile money?*. [online] The Economist. Available at: https://www.economist.com/blogs/economist-explains/2013/05/economist-explains-18 [Accessed 12 Apr. 2018].

49 Iwuoha, J. (2013). *Eric Muthomi – The Kenyan lawyer who built a successful business from a simple 'banana idea' - Smallstarter Africa*. [online] Smallstarter Africa. Available at: http://www.smallstarter.com/get-inspired/eric-muthomi-stawi-foods-kenya/ [Accessed 12 Apr. 2018].

50 Nsehe, M. (2013). *30 Under 30: Africa's Best Young Entrepreneurs*. [online] Forbes. Available at: https://www.forbes.com/sites/mfonobongnsehe/2013/02/23/30-under-30-africas-best-young-entrepreneurs/2/#27b366e7601b [Accessed 12 Apr. 2018].

51 CNN. (2014). *Law graduate turns bananas into flour - CNN Video*. [online] Available at: https://edition.cnn.com/videos/business/2014/01/01/spc-african-start-up-stawi-foods-fruits.cnn [Accessed 12 Apr. 2018].

PATRICIA NZOLANTIMA BUILDS AN ADVERTISING GIANT

52 World Population Review. (2016). *DR. Congo Population 2017*. [online] Available at: http://worldpopulationreview.com/countries/dr-congo-population/ [Accessed 13 Apr. 2018].

53 Rosen, A. (2013). *The Origins of War in the DRC*. [online] The Atlantic. Available at: https://www.theatlantic.com/international/archive/2013/06/the-origins-of-war-in-the-drc/277131/ [Accessed 13 Apr. 2018].

54 The historian Patrick Manning estimates that 4 million African lives were lost during the transatlantic slave trade from 1500 – 1900. See Patrick Manning, 'The Slave Trade: The Formal Demographics of a Global System' in Joseph E. Inikori and Stanley L. Engerman (eds), *The Atlantic Slave Trade: Effects on Economies, Societies and Peoples in Africa, the Americas, and Europe* (Duke University Press, 1992), pp. 117-44. Many historians estimate that about 11 million people were killed during the Holocaust. *Documenting Numbers of Victims of the Holocaust and Nazi Persecution* [online] United States Holocaust Memorial and Museum. Available at: https://encyclopedia.ushmm.org/content/en/article/documenting-numbers-of-victims-of-the-holocaust-and-nazi-persecution

55 *Hochschild, Adam (1999). King Leopold's Ghost: A Story of Greed, Terror, and Heroism in Colonial Africa (1st ed.).* Boston: Houghton Mifflin.

56 BBC News. (2019). *Democratic Republic of Congo profile*. [online] Available at: https://www.bbc.com/news/world-africa-13286306 [Accessed 30 May 2019].

57 McGreal, C. (2008). *The roots of war in eastern Congo*. [online] The Guardian. Available at: https://www.theguardian.com/world/2008/may/16/congo [Accessed 30 May 2019]. Eastern Congo Initiative. (n.d.). *History of the Conflict*. [online] Available at: http://www.easterncongo.org/about-drc/history-of-the-conflict [Accessed 30 May 2019].

58 World Bank. (n.d.). *DR. Congo Overview*. [online] Available at: http://www.worldbank.org/en/country/drc/overview [Accessed 13 Apr. 2018].

59 African Development Bank. (n.d.). *Democratic Republic of Congo Economic Outlook*. [online] Available at: https://www.afdb.org/en/countries/central-africa/democratic-republic-of-congo/democratic-republic-of-congo-economic-outlook/ [Accessed 30 May 2019].

60 UNDP Human Development Reports. (2018). | *Human Development Indices and Report: 2018 Statistical Update*. [online] Available at: http://hdr.undp.org/en/2018-update [Accessed 19 Dec. 2018].

61 Global Business Report. (2014). *Mining in Democratic Republic of Congo: A Journey to Africa's Mineral Heartland*. [online] Available at: http://gbreports.com/wp-content/uploads/2014/09/DRC_Mining2013. pdf [Accessed 13 Apr. 2018].

62 Encyclopedia Britannica. (1998). *Kongo people*. [online] Available at: https://www.britannica.com/topic/Kongo-people [Accessed 13 Apr. 2018].

63 African Development Bank. (2018). *Democratic Republic of Congo Economic Outlook*. [online] Available at: https://www.afdb.org/en/ countries/central-africa/democratic-republic-of-congo/democratic-republic-of-congo-economic-outlook/ [Accessed 19 Dec. 2018].

64 Meridian Team (2012). *2012 Innovation Summit and Mentoring Partnership for Young African Leaders | Meridian International Center*. [online] Meridian.org. Available at: http://www.meridian. org/project/2012-innovation-summit-and-mentoring-partnership-for-young-african-leaders/ [Accessed 13 Apr. 2018].

65 Uber.com. (n.d.). *Making career moves? Sign up to be an Uber Driver or get a ride to the airport | Uber*. [online] Available at: https://www. uber.com/en-GH/ [Accessed 16 Apr. 2018].

66 Bensinger, G., Farrell, M. and Hoffman, L. (2018). *Uber Proposals Value Company at $120 Billion in a Possible IPO*. [online] The Wall Street Journal. Available at: https://www.wsj.com/articles/uber-proposals-value-company-at-120-billion-in-a-possible-ipo-1539690343 [Accessed 19 Dec. 2018].
Isaac, M., Merced, M. and Sorkin, A. (2019). *How the Promise of a $120 Billion Uber I.P.O. Evaporated*. [online] New York Times. Available at: https://www.nytimes.com/2019/05/15/technology/uber-ipo-price. html [Accessed 30 May 2019].

67 Eveleth, R. and LaFrance, A. (2019). *Are Taxis Safer Than Uber?* [online] The Atlantic. Available at: https://www.theatlantic.com/technology/ archive/2015/03/are-taxis-safer-than-uber/386207/ [Accessed 30 May 2019].

YUSUF RANDERA-REES INCUBATES MICRO-ENTREPRENEURS

68 Data.worldbank.org. (n.d.). *GDP per capita (current US$) | Data*. [online] Available at: https://data.worldbank.org/indicator/NY.GDP. PCAP.CD?year_high_desc=false [Accessed 16 Apr. 2018].

69 Statistics South Africa. (n.d). *Population characteristics*. [online] Available at: http://www.statssa.gov.za/?cat=15 [Accessed 19 Dec. 2018].

70 World Bank. (n.d.). *South Africa Overview*. [online] Available at: http:// www.worldbank.org/en/country/southafrica/overview [Accessed 16 Apr. 2018].

71 Ibid

72 Goodman, P. (2018). *South Africa Sees Fresh Start for Economy, With the Same Challenges*. [online] Nytimes.com. Available at: https://www. nytimes.com/2018/02/15/business/south-africa-economy-ramaphosa. html?rref=collection%2Ftimestopic%2FSouth%20Africa&mtrref=un defined&gwh=7554CE6C23C1BE66D4849B0812035B3F&gwt=pay [Accessed 16 Apr. 2018].

73 Chutel, L. (2019). *Johannesburg's hipster gentrification project is at risk of crumbling*. [online] Quartz Africa. Available at: https:// qz.com/africa/1589532/how-maboneng-ended-up-being-auctioned-in-liquidation-sale/ [Accessed 30 May 2019].

CHINNY OGUNRO DESIGNS AFRICA'S HEALTHCARE FUTURE

74 Worldpopulationreview.com. (2018). *Nigeria Population 2018*. [online] Available at: http://worldpopulationreview.com/countries/nigeria-population/ [Accessed 13 Apr. 2018].

75 Google. (2018). *World Development Indicators-Google Public Data Explorer*. [online] Available at: https://www.google.com.gh/publicdata/ explore?ds=d5bncppjof8f9_&met_y=ny_gdp_mktp_cd&hl=en&dl= en#!ctype=l&strail=false&bcs=d&nselm=h&met_y=ny_gdp_mktp_ cd&scale_y=lin&ind_y=false&rdim=country&idim=country:NGA&i fdim=country&hl=en_US&dl=en&ind=false [Accessed 19 Dec. 2018].

76 O'Neill, J. (2007). *THE N-11: MORE THAN AN ACRONYM*. [online] Goldmansachs.com. Available at: http://www.goldmansachs.com/our-thinking/archive/archive-pdfs/brics-book/brics-chap-11.pdf [Accessed 13 Apr. 2018].

77 Abubakar, A. (2016). *Country Profile: Nigeria*. [online] Harvard Divinity School. Available at: http://rlp.hds.harvard.edu/files/hds-rlp/ files/nigeria_country_profile_1.pdf [Accessed 13 Apr. 2018].

78 Institute for Economics and Peace (2017). *Global Terrorism Index 2017: Measuring and Understanding the Impact of Terrorism.* [online] Visionofhumanity.org. Available at: http://visionofhumanity.org/app/uploads/2017/11/Global-Terrorism-Index-2017.pdf [Accessed 13 Apr. 2018].

79 Lustig, R. (2016). *Boko Haram's forgotten victims return to a humanitarian disaster.* [online] The Guardian. Available at: https://www.theguardian.com/world/2016/nov/20/boko-haram-forgotten-victimd-humanitarian [Accessed 16 Apr. 2018].

80 Slang for Lagos.

81 United Nations population division database. [online]. http://www.un.org/en/devleopment/desa/population/publications/datbase/index.shtml [Accessed May 31, 2019].

82 Adegbeye, O. (2017). *Transcript of 'Who belongs in a city?'.* [online] Ted.com. Available at: https://www.ted.com/talks/olutimehin_adegbeye_who_belongs_in_a_city/transcript [Accessed 13 Apr. 2018].

83 Ehrhart, H., Le Goff, M., Rocher, E. and Jan Singh, R. (2014). *Does Migration Foster Exports? Evidence from Africa.* [online] World Bank. Available at: https://openknowledge.worldbank.org/bitstream/handle/10986/16810/WPS6739.pdf?sequence=1 [Accessed 19 Dec. 2018].

84 Duvivier, R., Burch, V. and Boulet, J. (2017). *A comparison of physician emigration from Africa to the United States of America between 2005 and 2015.* [online] NCBI. Available at: https://www.ncbi.nlm.nih.gov/pmc/articles/PMC5485566/ [Accessed 28 Dec. 2018].

85 Ighobor, K. (2016). *Diagnosing Africa's medical brain drain.* [online] UN. Available at: https://www.un.org/africarenewal/magazine/december-2016-march-2017/diagnosing-africa%E2%80%99s-medical-brain-drain [Accessed 19 Dec. 2018].

86 Casimir, L. (2018). *Data show Nigerians the most educated in the U.S..* [online] Houston Chronicle. Available at: https://www.chron.com/g00/news/article/Data-show-Nigerians-the-most-educated-in-the-U-S-1600808.php?i10c.encReferrer=aHR0cHM6Ly93d3cuZ29vZ2xlLmNvbvbS5naC8%3d&i10c.ua=1&i10c.dv=14 [Accessed 19 Dec. 2018].

87 Fischler, M. (2015). *Dix Hills, N.Y.: Large Lots and Good Schools.* [online] The New York Times. Available at: https://www.nytimes.com/2016/01/03/realestate/dix-hills-ny-large-lots-and-good-schools.html [Accessed 19 Dec. 2018].

88 sites.tufts.edu. (2015). *Nigeria: Civil war | Mass Atrocity Endings.* [online] Available at: https://sites.tufts.edu/atrocityendings/2015/08/07/ nigeria-civil-war/ [Accessed 19 Dec. 2018].

89 USAID. (2018). *Power Africa Fact Sheet: Nigeria.* [online] Available at: https://www.usaid.gov/powerafrica/nigeria [Accessed 28 Dec. 2018]. Okere, R. (2018). *More hurdles to attaining regular electricity supply in Nigeria.* [online] The Guardian Nigeria Newspaper. Available at: https:// guardian.ng/energy/more-hurdles-to-attaining-regular-electricity-supply-in-nigeria/ [Accessed 28 Dec. 2018].

90 Clemens, M. and Pettersson, G. (2008). *New Data on Africa Health Professionals Abroad.* [online] NCBI. Available at: https://www.ncbi. nlm.nih.gov/pmc/articles/PMC2254438/ [Accessed 28 Dec. 2018].

91 Woetzel, J., Krishnan, M., Dobbs, R., Manyika, J., Kutcher, E., Devillard, S., Labaye, E., Ellingrud, K. and Madgavkar, A. (2015). *How advancing women's equality can add $12 trillion to global growth.* [online] Mckinsey Global Institute. Available at: https://www.mckinsey. com/featured-insights/employment-and-growth/how-advancing-womens-equality-can-add-12-trillion-to-global-growth [Accessed 30 May 2019].

THE SOCIOPRENEURS: INTRODUCTION

92 World Bank. (2017). *Commodity prices likely to rise further in 2018: World Bank.* [online] Available at: http://www.worldbank.org/en/news/ press-release/2017/10/26/commodity-prices-likely-to-rise-further-in-2018-world-bank [Accessed 9 Apr. 2018].

93 Dzawu, M. (2018). *Stocks in Economy With Best Growth Forecast Lead the World.* [online] Bloomberg.com. Available at: https://www. bloomberg.com/news/articles/2018-01-31/optimism-in-accra-turns-ghana-stocks-into-january-world-beaters [Accessed 9 Apr. 2018].

94 World Bank. (2018). *Global Economic Prospects.* [online] Available at: http://www.worldbank.org/en/publication/global-economic-prospects [Accessed 9 Apr. 2018].

95 Kayumba, C. (2018). *Exit of Zuma, Mugabe, Desalegn shows power is with the 'elite'.* [online] The East African. Available at: http://www. theeastafrican.co.ke/rwanda/Opinion/Zuma-Mugabe-Desalegn-power-exit/1433246-4321702-14uowtu/index.html [Accessed 9 Apr. 2018].

96 Hodal, K. (2016). *Nearly half all children in sub-Saharan Africa in extreme poverty, report warns.* [online] the Guardian. Available at: https://www.theguardian.com/global-development/2016/oct/05/nearly-half-all-children-sub-saharan-africa-extreme-poverty-unicef-world-bank-report-warns [Accessed 9 Apr. 2018].

97 The World Bank. (n.d.). *Poverty & Equity Data Portal.* [online] Available at: http://povertydata.worldbank.org/poverty/region/SSF [Accessed 19 Dec. 2018].

98 Delaney, K. (2018). *Bill and Melinda Gates: The world's priority should be poverty reduction in Africa.* [online] Quartz. Available at: https://qz.com/1392813/bill-and-melinda-gates-the-worlds-priority-should-be-poverty-reduction-in-africa/ [Accessed 19 Dec. 2018].

99 International Monetary Fund (2013). *Regional Economic Outlook: Sub-Saharan Africa. Building Momentum in a Multi-Speed World.* International Monetary Fund, Washington, DC.

100 Martinez, M. and M. Mlachila (2013) *The Quality of the Recent High-Growth Episode in Sub-Saharan Africa.* International Monetary Fund, Washington DC (IMF Working Paper; WP/13/53).

101 Ibid

102 Ilo.org. (2016). *Youth unemployment challenge worsening in Africa.* [online] Available at: http://www.ilo.org/addisababa/media-centre/pr/WCMS_514566/lang--en/index.htm [Accessed 10 Apr. 2018].

103 Afdb.org. (2016). *Jobs for Youth in Africa.* [online] Available at: https://www.afdb.org/fileadmin/uploads/afdb/Images/high_5s/Job_youth_Africa_Job_youth_Africa.pdf [Accessed 10 Apr. 2018].

104 Martin, Roger L., and Sally Osberg. *Social entrepreneurship: The case for definition.* Vol. 5. No. 2. Stanford: Stanford social innovation review, 2007.

DAVID SENGAH INNOVATES FROM WAR

105 Encyclopedia Britannica. (n.d.). *Sierra Leone | Culture, History, & People - Civil war.* [online] Available at: https://www.britannica.com/place/Sierra-Leone/Civil-war [Accessed 10 Apr. 2018].

106 Kamara, E. (n.d.). *History - Visit Sierra Leone.* [online] VSL Travel. Available at: https://www.visitsierraleone.org/background-information/history/ [Accessed 30 May 2019].

107 BBC News. (2018). *Sierra Leone country profile*. [online] Available at: http://www.bbc.com/news/world-africa-14094194 [Accessed 10 Apr. 2018].

108 Globalreligiousfutures.org. (n.d.). *Religions in Sierra Leone | PEW-GRF*. [online] Available at: http://www.globalreligiousfutures.org/countries/sierra-leone#/?affiliations_religion_id=0&affiliations_year=2010&region_name=All%20Countries&restrictions_year=2015 [Accessed 10 Apr. 2018].

109 Cia.gov. (n.d.). *The World Factbook — Central Intelligence Agency*. [online] Available at: https://www.cia.gov/library/publications/the-world-factbook/geos/sl.html [Accessed 10 Apr. 2018].

110 Www1.wfp.org. (n.d.). *Sierra Leone | World Food Programme*. [online] Available at: http://www1.wfp.org/countries/sierra-leone [Accessed 10 Apr. 2018].

111 Web.archive.org. (n.d.). *Sierra Leone Overview*. [online] Available at: https://web.archive.org/web/20110511080815/http://www.sl.undp.org/sloverview.htm [Accessed 10 Apr. 2018].

112 Www1.wfp.org. (n.d.). *Sierra Leone | World Food Programme*. [online] Available at: http://www1.wfp.org/countries/sierra-leone [Accessed 10 Apr. 2018].

113 World Bank. (n.d.). *Sierra Leone*. [online] Available at: http://www.worldbank.org/en/country/sierraleone [Accessed 10 Apr. 2018].

114 Barry, J. (2017). *Sierra Leone Buries Over 300 Mudslide Victims in Mass Graves*. [online] Nytimes.com. Available at: https://www.nytimes.com/2017/08/16/world/africa/sierra-leone-mudslides-floods-burial-freetown.html?rref=collection%2Ftimestopic%2FSierra%20Leone&action=click&contentCollection=world&region=stream&module=stream_unit&version=latest&contentPlacement=6&pgtype=collection [Accessed 10 Apr. 2018].

115 Worldpopulationreview.com. (n.d.). *Population of Cities in Sierra Leone 2018*. [online] Available at: http://worldpopulationreview.com/countries/sierra-leone-population/cities/ [Accessed 10 Apr. 2018].

116 Hrw.org. (1999). *Human Right Abuses Committed by RUF Rebels*. [online] Available at: https://www.hrw.org/legacy/reports/1999/sierra/SIERLE99-03.htm [Accessed 10 Apr. 2018].

117 Denov, Myriam (2010). *Child Soldiers; Sierra Leone's Revolutionary United Front*. New York: Cambridge University Press.

118 Seas.harvard.edu. (2008). *Undergraduates develop 'dirt-powered' microbial fuel cells to light Africa | Harvard John A. Paulson School of Engineering and Applied Sciences.* [online] Available at: https://www. seas.harvard.edu/news/2008/05/undergraduates-develop-dirt-powered-microbial-fuel-cells-light-africa [Accessed 10 Apr. 2018].

119 Buntz, B. (2013). *Artificial Limbs: Then, Now, and in the Future.* [online] MDDI Online. Available at: https://www.mddionline.com/artificial-limbs-then-now-and-future [Accessed 10 Apr. 2018].

120 NBC News. (2014). *Innovator's Prosthetic Socket Aids Boston Marathon Victims.* [online] Available at: https://www.nbcnews. com/science/science-news/innovators-prosthetic-socket-aids-boston-marathon-victims-n75386 [Accessed 10 Apr. 2018].

121 Sengeh, D. (2012). *DIY Africa: Empowering a new Sierra Leone.* [online] CNN. Available at: https://edition.cnn.com/2012/11/14/tech/diy-africa-empowering-a-new-sierra-leone/index.html [Accessed 10 Apr. 2018].

ANDREW MUPUYA PIONEERS PAPER BAGS

122 VOA. (2009). *Protesters Come Out Against Uganda's Lord's Resistance Army.* [online] Available at: https://www.voanews.com/a/a-13-2009-05-12-voa50-68643392/407922.html [Accessed 13 Apr. 2018].

123 Grossman, S. (2012). *'Kony 2012' Documentary Becomes Most Viral Video in History.* [online] Time Magazine. Available at: http://newsfeed. time.com/2012/03/12/kony-2012-documentary-becomes-most-viral-video-in-history/ [Accessed 13 Apr. 2018].

124 Pflanz, M. (2012). *Joseph Kony 2012: growing outrage in Uganda over film.* [online] The Telegraph. Available at: https://www.telegraph.co.uk/news/worldnews/africaandindianocean/uganda/9131469/Joseph-Kony-2012-growing-outrage-in-Uganda-over-film.html [Accessed 13 Apr. 2018].

125 Wilson, T. (2018). *Reggae star Bobi Wine mobilises Uganda's disillusioned youth | Financial Times.* [online] Financial Times. Available at: https://www.ft.com/content/1c1c55b0-d165-11e8-a9f2-7574db66bcd5 [Accessed 19 Dec. 2018].

126 BBC News. (2016). *Profile: Uganda's Yoweri Museveni.* [online] Available at: http://www.bbc.com/news/world-africa-12421747 [Accessed 13 Apr. 2018].

127 The World Bank. (n.d.). *Uganda | Data.* [online] Available at: https://data.worldbank.org/country/uganda [Accessed 19 Dec. 2018].

128 Deloitte. (2016). *Uganda Economic Outlook 2016: The Story Behind the Numbers.* [online] Available at: https://www2.deloitte.com/content/dam/Deloitte/ug/Documents/tax/Economic%20Outlook%202016%20UG.pdf [Accessed 13 Apr. 2018]. World Bank. (n.d.). *Uganda Overview.* [online] Available at: http://www.worldbank.org/en/country/uganda/overview [Accessed 13 Apr. 2018].

129 UN Uganda. (2017). *Press Release on HIV Situation in Uganda February 23 2017 | UN IN UGANDA.* [online] Available at: http://www.un-ug.org/press-releases/press-release-hiv-situation-uganda-february-23-2017 [Accessed 13 Apr. 2018]. Kelly, A. (2008). *Background: HIV/Aids in Uganda.* [online] the Guardian. Available at: https://www.theguardian.com/katine/2008/dec/01/world-aids-day-uganda [Accessed 13 Apr. 2018].

130 Ibid

131 Ugandawildlife.org. (n.d.). *Uganda Wild Life.* [online] Available at: http://www.ugandawildlife.org/ [Accessed 13 Apr. 2018].

132 Whitaker, M. (2007). *Why Uganda hates the plastic bag.* [online] BBC. Available at: http://news.bbc.co.uk/2/hi/programmes/from_our_own_correspondent/6253564.stm [Accessed 13 Apr. 2018].

133 Vidal, J. (2018). *The plastics crisis is more urgent than you know. Recycling bottles won't fix it.* [online] The Guardian. Available at: https://www.theguardian.com/commentisfree/2018/mar/28/plastic-crisis-urgent-recycling-bottles-no-fix [Accessed 19 Dec. 2018].

134 Wright, M., Kirk, A., Molloy, M. and Mills, E. (2018). *The stark truth about how long your plastic footprint will last on the planet.* [online] The Telegraph. Available at: https://www.telegraph.co.uk/news/2018/01/10/stark-truth-long-plastic-footprint-will-last-planet/ [Accessed 19 Dec. 2018].

135 Parker, L. (2018). *We Depend On Plastic. Now, We're Drowning in It..* [online] National Geographic. Available at: https://www.nationalgeographic.com/magazine/2018/06/plastic-planet-waste-pollution-trash-crisis/?user.testname=lazyloading:c [Accessed 19 Dec. 2018].

136 https://www.jaworldwide.org/aboutja/ [Accessed 19 Dec. 2018]

137 Babikwa, D. (2017). *The Status of the Management of Polythene Bags in Uganda and Policy Direction.* [online] Wastemanagementconference. com. Available at: http://wastemanagementconference.com/ EAWMC%202017%20Presentations/The%20status%20of%20 plastic%20waste%20management%20in%20uganda-Dr.%20 Daniel%20Babikwa,%20Director,%20NEMA%20Uganda.pdf [Accessed 13 Apr. 2018].

138 International Labour Organisation. (2015). *ILO Youth Entrepreneurship Facility Youth-to-Youth Fund in East Africa: Public-Private Partnership.* [online] Available at: http://www.ilo.org/pardev/partnerships/public-private-partnerships/factsheets/WCMS_409910/lang--en/index.htm [Accessed 13 Apr. 2018].

139 African Leadership Academy. (2012). *Andrew Mupuya named as 2012 Anzisha Grand Prize Winner.* [online] Available at: http://www. africanleadershipacademy.org/andrew-mupuya-named-as-2012-anzisha-grand-prize-winner/ [Accessed 17 Apr. 2018].

140 Ferd. (2012). *Ferd - The Ferd Award for Social Entrepreneurship 2012.* [online] Available at: https://ferd.no/en/sosiale_entreprenorer/nyheter/ ferd_award_for_social_entrepreneurship_2012 [Accessed 13 Apr. 2018].

141 JA-YE Europe. (2012). *The Ferd Award for Social Entrepreneurship -2012.* [online] Available at: http://share.jayeapps.com/jaye.europe/-/ the-ferd-award-for-social-entrepreneurship--2012-236/ [Accessed 13 Apr. 2018].

142 Great Lakes Safaris. (2013). *Uganda Youth Entrepreneur Challenge.* [online] Available at: http://safari-uganda.com/news/uganda-youth-entrepeneur-challenge/ [Accessed 13 Apr. 2018].

143 Dolan, K. (2016). *Africa's Most Promising Entrepreneurs: Forbes Africa's 30 Under 30 For 2016.* [online] Forbes. Available at: https://www. forbes.com/sites/kerryadolan/2016/06/06/africas-most-promising-entrepreneurs-forbes-africas-30-under-30-for-2016/#36d0d94d1f43 [Accessed 13 Apr. 2018].

SARAN KABAN JONES WATERS A NATION

144 Data.worldbank.org. (n.d.). *Liberia | Data.* [online] Available at: https:// data.worldbank.org/country/Liberia [Accessed 10 Apr. 2018].

145 BBC News. (2018). *Liberia country profile.* [online] Available at: http:// www.bbc.com/news/world-africa-13729504 [Accessed 10 Apr. 2018].

146 Kpatindé, F. (2006). *A tale of two camps: bustling Buduburam and quiet Krisan.* [online] UNHCR. Available at: https://www.unhcr.org/news/latest/2006/7/44c7783e4/tale-camps-bustling-buduburam-quiet-krisan.html [Accessed 3 Jun. 2019].

147 Ft.com. (n.d.). *The mixed legacy of Liberia's Ellen Johnson Sirleaf.* [online] Available at: https://www.ft.com/content/1dabec18-f530-11e7-8715-e94187b3017e [Accessed 10 Apr. 2018].

148 MacDougall, C. (2018). *Ibrahim Prize for African Leadership Goes to Liberia's Ellen Johnson Sirleaf.* [online] Nytimes.com. Available at: https://www.nytimes.com/2018/02/12/world/africa/liberia-sirleaf-ibrahim-prize.html?mtrref=undefined&gwh=AFC32F5736CB61B7D3A77A752BE778C0&gwt=pay [Accessed 10 Apr. 2018].

149 Ibid

150 BBC News. (2013). *Liberia students all fail university admission exam.* [online] Available at: http://www.bbc.com/news/world-africa-23843578 [Accessed 10 Apr. 2018].

151 Kristof, N. (2017). *A Solution When a Nation's Schools Fail.* [online] New York Times. Available at: https://www.nytimes.com/2017/07/15/opinion/sunday/bridge-schools-liberia.html?mtrref=www.google.com.ng&assetType=opinion&auth=login-email [Accessed 17 Apr. 2018].

152 Pilling, D. (2017). *Inside Liberia's controversial experiment to outsource education.* [online] Financial Times. Available at: https://www.ft.com/content/291b7fca-2487-11e7-a34a-538b4cb30025 [Accessed 17 Apr. 2018].

153 Ratcliffe, R. and Hirsch, A. (2019). *UK urged to stop funding 'ineffective and unsustainable' Bridge schools.* [online] The Guardian. Available at: https://www.theguardian.com/global-development/2017/aug/03/uk-urged-to-stop-funding-ineffective-and-unsustainable-bridge-academies [Accessed 30 May 2019].

154 Adegbeye, O. (2017). *Transcript of 'Who belongs in a city?'* [online] Ted.com. Available at: https://www.ted.com/talks/olutimehin_adegbeye_who_belongs_in_a_city/transcript [Accessed 10 Apr. 2018].

155 "Water, Sanitation and Hygiene," https://www.unwater.org/water-facts/water-sanitation-and-hygiene [Accessed Friday July 19, 2019].

156 Ibid

157 Ibid

158 "Water, Sanitation and Hygiene,' https://www.unicef.org/liberia/water-sanitation-and-hygiene [Accessed Friday, July 19, 2019].

159 "Water, Sanitation and Hygiene," https://www.unwater.org/water-facts/water-sanitation-and-hygiene [Accessed Friday July 19, 2019].

160 Participatory rural appraisal (PRA) or participatory learning approach (PLA) is an approach used by NGOs and other agencies involved in international development. The approach aims to incorporate the knowledge and opinions of rural people in the planning and management of development projects and programs.

161 Centers for Disease Control and Prevention. (2017). *2014-2016 Ebola Outbreak in West Africa | History | Ebola (Ebola Virus Disease) | CDC.* [online] Available at: https://www.cdc.gov/vhf/ebola/history/2014-2016-outbreak/index.html [Accessed 27 Dec. 2018].

M'HAMED KOUIDMI LEVERAGES TECHNOLOGY TO CREATE JOBS

162 BBC News. (2016). *Algeria profile.* [online] Available at: http://www.bbc.com/news/world-africa-14118853 [Accessed 10 Apr. 2018].

163 Mauro, J. (2016). *Sibling continues bishop's mission to improve Muslim-Christian relations - The Monitor.* [online] Trentonmonitor.com. Available at: http://www.trentonmonitor.com/main.asp?SectionID=4&SubSectionID=88&ArticleID=13683 [Accessed 10 Apr. 2018].

164 BBC News. (2016). *Algeria profile.* [online] Available at: http://www.bbc.com/news/world-africa-14118853 [Accessed 10 Apr. 2018].

165 World Bank. (2016). *Algeria | Data.* [online] Available at: https://data.worldbank.org/country/algeria [Accessed 17 Apr. 2018].

166 BBC News. (2016). *Algeria profile.* [online] Available at: http://www.bbc.com/news/world-africa-14118853 [Accessed 10 Apr. 2018].

167 Alami, A. (2015). *In Algeria, Entrepreneurs Hope Falling Oil Prices Will Spur Innovation.* [online] Nytimes.com. Available at: https://www.nytimes.com/2015/05/03/world/africa/algerian-entrepreneurs-see-opportunity-in-oil-price-plunge.html?rref=collection%2Ftimestopic%2FAlgeria&mtrref=undefined&gwh=86F9E00A1E1C230E5F5FB5E2D97C331F&gwt=pay [Accessed 10 Apr. 2018].

168 World Bank. (n.d.). *Algeria Overview.* [online] Available at: http://www.worldbank.org/en/country/algeria/overview [Accessed 10 Apr. 2018].

169 Ibid

170 BBC News. (2016). *Algeria profile.* [online] Available at: http://www.bbc.com/news/world-africa-14118853 [Accessed 10 Apr. 2018].

171 World Bank. (2016). *Poverty has Fallen in the Maghreb, but Inequality Persists.* [online] Available at: http://www.worldbank.org/en/news/feature/2016/10/17/poverty-has-fallen-in-the-maghreb-but-inequality-persists [Accessed 10 Apr. 2018].

172 Ibid

173 BBC News. (2014). *Where is it illegal to be gay?.* [online] Available at: http://www.bbc.com/news/world-25927595 [Accessed 10 Apr. 2018].

174 Busari, S. (2017). *The women risking their lives to fight homophobia in Africa.* [online] CNN. Available at: https://www.cnn.com/2017/10/20/africa/africa-gay-attitudes-change-minds/index.html [Accessed 10 Apr. 2018].

175 Banning-Lover, R. (2017). *Where are the most difficult places in the world to be gay or transgender?.* [online] the Guardian. Available at: https://www.theguardian.com/global-development-professionals-network/2017/mar/01/where-are-the-most-difficult-places-in-the-world-to-be-gay-or-transgender-lgbt [Accessed 10 Apr. 2018].

176 Owunna, M. (2017). *A Photographer Captures LGBTQ Africans Around The Globe.* [online] GOOD. Available at: https://www.good.is/features/lgbtq-african-immigrants-mikael-owunna [Accessed 10 Apr. 2018].

177 Nichols, M. (2013). *Gambian president says gays a threat to human existence-20130928.* [online] Yahoo.com. Available at: https://www.yahoo.com/news/gambian-president-says-gays-threat-human-existence-20130928-122519635.html [Accessed 10 Apr. 2018].

178 Reuters. (2014). *Gambia's Jammeh calls gays 'vermin', says to fight like mosquitoes.* [online] Available at: https://www.reuters.com/article/us-gambia-homosexuality/gambias-jammeh-calls-gays-vermin-says-to-fight-like-mosquitoes-idUSBREA1H1S820140218 [Accessed 10 Apr. 2018].

179 Fletcher, J. (2016). *Born free, killed by hate.* [online] BBC News. Available at: http://www.bbc.com/news/magazine-35967725 [Accessed 10 Apr. 2018].

180 Wesangula, D. (2017). *On the run from persecution: how Kenya became a haven for LGBT refugees.* [online] the Guardian. Available at: https://www.theguardian.com/global-development-professionals-network/2017/feb/23/on-the-run-from-persecution-how-kenya-became-a-haven-for-lgbt-refugees [Accessed 10 Apr. 2018].

181 Gehring, J. (2017). *LGBT Catholics & the Francis Papacy |
     Commonweal Magazine*. [online] Commonwealmagazine.org. Available
     at: https://www.commonwealmagazine.org/lgbt-catholics-francis-
     papacy [Accessed 10 Apr. 2018].
182 Greene, R. (2016). *Pope to church: Accept gays, divorced Catholics*.
     [online] CNN. Available at: https://edition.cnn.com/2016/04/08/europe/
     vatican-pope-family/index.html [Accessed 10 Apr. 2018].
183 Gibson, D. (2016). *Is Pope Francis alone on apologizing to gays?*. [online]
     National Catholic Reporter. Available at: https://www.ncronline.org/news/
     vatican/pope-francis-alone-apologizing-gays [Accessed 10 Apr. 2018].
184 World Bank. (2016). *Poverty has Fallen in the Maghreb, but Inequality
     Persists*. [online] Available at: http://www.worldbank.org/en/news/
     feature/2016/10/17/poverty-has-fallen-in-the-maghreb-but-inequality-
     persists [Accessed 10 Apr. 2018].
185 Daoud, K. (2016). *Opinion | Black in Algeria? Then You'd Better Be
     Muslim*. [online] Nytimes.com. Available at: https://www.nytimes.
     com/2016/05/03/opinion/kamel-daoud-black-in-algeria-then-youd-
     better-be-muslim.html?rref=collection%2Ftimestopic%2FAlgeria&m
     trref=undefined&gwh=AA02A0EE44D72CAAB49B2E9AFE4F3278
     &gwt=pay&assetType=opinion [Accessed 10 Apr. 2018].

THE CREATIVES: INTRODUCTION

186 Lopes, C. (2015). Creativity is the new gold: Africa needs to do a few
     smart things to unlock the jackpot. [online] MG Africa. Available at:
     http://mgafrica.com/article/2015-08-27-creativity-is-the-new-money/
     [Accessed 5 Apr. 2018].
187 Santiago, J. (2015). *What is creativity worth to the world economy?*.
     [online] World Economic Forum. Available at: https://www.weforum.
     org/agenda/2015/12/creative-industries-worth-world-economy/
     [Accessed 5 Apr. 2018].
188 Austen-Peters, B. (2017). How art can be a force for development in
     Africa. [online] Aljazeera.com. Available at: https://www.aljazeera.com/
     indepth/opinion/art-force-development-africa-170926083535422.html
     [Accessed 5 Apr. 2018].
189 Mohammed, O. (2015). *With a billion Africans set to shop online, a
     new wave of start-ups is looking to cash in*. [online] Quartz. Available
     at: https://qz.com/478714/africas-emerging-consumer-class-is-a-boon-
     for-the-continents-online-retailers/ [Accessed 5 Apr. 2018]

190 Hruby, A. (2018). *Tap creative industries to boost Africa's economic growth.* [online] Financial Times. Available at: https://www.ft.com/content/9807a468-2ddc-11e8-9b4b-bc4b9f08f381 [Accessed 17 Apr. 2018].

191 Ibid

192 Rao, M. (2016). *Meet the Shonda Rhimes of Ghana.* [online] Marie Claire. Available at: https://www.marieclaire.com/culture/a22729/shonda-rhimes-of-ghana-nicole-amarteifio/ [Accessed 5 Apr. 2018].

193 Gbadamosi, N. (2017). *Africa's fashion millennials cash in on world's internet addiction.* [online] CNN Style. Available at: https://www.cnn.com/style/article/africa-e-commerce-fashion/index.html [Accessed 28 Dec. 2018].

194 Merriam, A. (1959). Characteristics of African Music. *Journal of the International Folk Music Council, 11,* 13-19. doi:10.2307/834848

195 The Development Economics Research Group on International Trade. (2001). *Workshop on the Development of the Music Industry in Africa.* [online] Available at: http://siteresources.worldbank.org/INTCEERD/Resources/CWI_music_industry_in_Africa_synopsis.pdf [Accessed 28 Dec. 2018].

196 Hruby, A. (2018). *The African music industry is gaining global interest.* [online] Axios. Available at: https://www.axios.com/the-african-music-industry-is-gaining-global-interest-45987188-f6f2-4be5-bfc1-c8f7e1114c8f.html [Accessed 28 Dec. 2018].

ABAI SCHULZE RECONNECTS TO HER ROOTS

197 BBC News. (2018). *Ethiopia country profile.* [online] Available at: http://www.bbc.com/news/world-africa-13349398 [Accessed 5 Apr. 2018].

198 Ibid

199 Jeffery, J. (2018). *It's East Africa's capital of cool: Ready to go?* [online] CNN Travel. Available at: https://edition.cnn.com/travel/article/things-to-do-addis-ababa-ethiopia/index.html [Accessed 6 Apr. 2018].

200 Goodwin, L. (2018). *Ethiopian Coffee Culture - Legend, History and Customs.* [online] The Spruce Eats. Available at: https://www.thespruceeats.com/ethiopian-coffee-culture-765829 [Accessed 28 Dec. 2018].

201 Goodwin, L. (2018). *Everything to Know About an Ethiopian Coffee Ceremony.* [online] The Spruce Eats. Available at: https://www.thespruceeats.com/ethiopian-coffee-ceremony-765830 [Accessed 28 Dec. 2018].

202 BBC News. (2018). *Ethiopia country profile.* [online] Available at: http://www.bbc.com/news/world-africa-13349398 [Accessed 5 Apr. 2018].

203 BBC News. (2018). *Ethiopia gets first female president.* [online] Available at: https://www.bbc.com/news/world-africa-45976620 [Accessed 28 Dec. 2018].

204 G., T. (2018). *How Ethiopia and Eritrea made peace.* [online] The Economist. Available at: https://www.economist.com/the-economist-explains/2018/07/17/how-ethiopia-and-eritrea-made-peace [Accessed 28 Dec. 2018].

205 Burke, J. (2018). *'These changes are unprecedented': how Abiy is upending Ethiopian politics.* [online] The Guardian. Available at: https://www.theguardian.com/world/2018/jul/08/abiy-ahmed-upending-ethiopian-politics [Accessed 28 Dec. 2018].

206 World Bank. (2017). *Overview.* [online] Available at: http://www.worldbank.org/en/country/ethiopia/overview [Accessed 6 Apr. 2018].

207 Constable, P. (2014). *African immigrant population doubling each 10 years; Washington, Maryland and Virginia high on list.* [online] Washington Post. Available at: https://www.washingtonpost.com/local/african-immigrant-population-doubling-each-decade-washington-area-among-highest/2014/10/01/efbada70-498f-11e4-891d-713f052086a0_story.html?utm_term=.d5fe84c339b5 [Accessed 6 Apr. 2018].

208 Africa Center for Economic Transformation. (2016). *Unemployment in Africa: no jobs for 50% of graduates – ACET.* [online] Available at: http://acetforafrica.org/highlights/unemployment-in-africa-no-jobs-for-50-of-graduates/ [Accessed 28 Dec. 2018].

209 Ashoka | Everyone a Changemaker. (n.d.). *Social Entrepreneurship.* [online] Available at: https://www.ashoka.org/en/focus/social-entrepreneurship [Accessed 6 Apr. 2018].

210 Zaaf Collection. (n.d.). *ABOUT | Zaaf Collection.* [online] Available at: https://www.zaafcollection.com/zaaf-founder-zaaf-team/ [Accessed 6 Apr. 2018].

211 Eastaugh, S. (2015). *Can you guess the world's top tourism destination for 2015?* [online] CNN Travel. Available at: https://edition.cnn.com/travel/article/ethiopia-worlds-best-tourism-destination/index.html [Accessed 6 Apr. 2018].

212 Kuo, L. (2016). *Only China, Syria, and Iran rank worse in internet freedom than Ethiopia.* [online] Quartz. Available at: https://qz.com/838908/internet-freedom-in-ethiopia-is-the-fourth-worst-in-the-world-after-iran-syria-and-china/ [Accessed 6 Apr. 2018].

213 Busari, S. (2016). *Ethiopia declares state of emergency amid protests.* [online] CNN. Available at: http://www.cnn.com/2016/10/09/africa/ethiopia-oromo-state-emergency/ [Accessed 6 Apr. 2018].

214 https://www.theguardian.com/world/2018/jul/08/abiy-ahmed-upending-ethiopian-politics

215 Freedomhouse.org. (2015). *Ethiopia.* [online] Available at: https://freedomhouse.org/report/freedom-net/2016/ethiopia#sdfootnote1sym [Accessed 6 Apr. 2018].

216 Stevis-Gridneff, M. (2018). *Ethiopia Opens Door to the World With Unprecedented Privatization Plan.* [online] The Wall Street Journal. Available at: https://www.wsj.com/articles/ethiopia-opens-door-to-the-world-with-unprecedented-privatization-plan-1528275922 [Accessed 28 Dec. 2018].

217 Freedomhouse.org. (2015). *Ethiopia.* [online] Available at: https://freedomhouse.org/report/freedom-net/2016/ethiopia#sdfootnote1sym [Accessed 6 Apr. 2018].

218 Ibid

219 African Leadership Network (ALN). (2015). *AAE2015 Recognises Outstanding Social Entrepreneurs.* [online] Available at: http://africanleadershipnetwork.com/2015/10/23/aae2015-recognises-outstanding-social-entrepreneurs/ [Accessed 9 Apr. 2018].

220 Tonyelumelufoundation.org. (2015). *Tony Elumelu Foundation.* [online] Available at: http://www.tonyelumelufoundation.org/programme/wp-content/uploads/2015/03/TEEP_1000_NAMES_.pdf [Accessed 9 Apr. 2018].

221 Lionesses of Africa. (2016). *In Focus: Meet Africa's Leading Women-led Artisan Enterprises.* [online] Available at: http://www.lionessesofafrica.com/blog/2016/9/1/in-focus-meet-africas-leading-women-led-artisan-enterprise [Accessed 17 Apr. 2018].

DANA KHATER EXPORTS EGYPTIAN FASHION

222 Tucker, A. (2016). *Space Archaeologist Sarah Parcak Uses Satellites to Uncover Ancient Egyptian Ruins.* [online] Smithsonian. Available at: https://www.smithsonianmag.com/innovation/space-archaeologist-sarah-parcak-winner-smithsonians-history-ingenuity-award-180961120/#Q46guBkdCg8QgxLx.99 [Accessed 9 Apr. 2018].

223 BBC News. (2018). *Egypt country profile.* [online] Available at: http://www.bbc.com/news/world-africa-13313370 [Accessed 9 Apr. 2018].

224 Data.worldbank.org. (n.d.). *Egypt, Arab Rep. | Data.* [online] Available at: https://data.worldbank.org/country/egypt-arab-rep [Accessed 9 Apr. 2018].

225 Worldpopulationreview.com. (2017). *World Cities/Cairo Population.* [online] Available at: http://worldpopulationreview.com/world-cities/cairo-population/ [Accessed 9 Apr. 2018].

226 Databank.worldbank.org. (2016). *CountryProfile.* [online] Available at: http://databank.worldbank.org/data/views/reports/reportwidget. aspx?Report_Name=CountryProfile&Id=b450fd57&tbar=y&dd=y& inf=n&zm=n&country=EGY [Accessed 9 Apr. 2018].

227 Rlp.hds.harvard.edu. (n.d.). *The Arab Spring in Egypt.* [online] Available at: https://rlp.hds.harvard.edu/faq/arab-spring-egypt [Accessed 9 Apr. 2018].

228 Ibid

229 Alsaafin, L. (2018). *Abdel Fattah el-Sisi narrowly misses 100 percent of vote in Egypt.* [online] Aljazeera.com. Available at: https://www. aljazeera.com/news/2018/04/abdel-fattah-el-sisi-narrowly-misses-100- percent-vote-egypt-180402112319879.html [Accessed 9 Apr. 2018].

230 Databank.worldbank.org. (n.d.). *CountryProfile.* [online] Available at: http://databank.worldbank.org/data/views/reports/reportwidget. aspx?Report_Name=CountryProfile&Id=b450fd57&tbar=y&dd=y& inf=n&zm=n&country=EGY [Accessed 9 Apr. 2018].

231 Walsh, D. (2017). *Smartphones in Egypt Bring Biting Humor but Also Scrutiny.* [online] Nytimes.com. Available at: https://www.nytimes. com/2017/11/08/technology/personaltech/promise-perils-technology- egypt.html?rref=collection%2Ftimestopic%2FEgypt [Accessed 9 Apr. 2018].

232 Flat6labs.com. (2013). *Coterique | Flat6Labs.* [online] Available at: http://www.flat6labs.com/company/coterique-2/ [Accessed 9 Apr. 2018].

233 Flat6labs.com. (n.d.). *Cairo | Flat6Labs.* [online] Available at: http:// www.flat6labs.com/location/cairo/#top [Accessed 9 Apr. 2018].

234 Cristofolletti, T. (2017). *Gender Equality and Women's Empowerment | Egypt | U.S. Agency for International Development.* [online] Usaid. gov. Available at: https://www.usaid.gov/egypt/gender-equality-and- womens-empowerment [Accessed 9 Apr. 2018].

MARCUS GORA PROMOTES CONTEMPORARY ARTISTS

235 Ingham, K., Sanger, C. and Bradley, K. (2018). *Zimbabwe | history - geography*. [online] Encyclopedia Britannica. Available at: https://www. britannica.com/place/Zimbabwe [Accessed 28 Dec. 2018].

236 Delaney, J. (2007). *To the Mountains of the Moon: Mapping African Exploration, 1541-1880*. [online] Princeton University Library. Available at: https://libweb5.princeton.edu/visual_materials/maps/ websites/africa/maps-southern/southern.html [Accessed 3 Jan. 2019].

237 BBC News. (2018). *Zimbabwe profile*. [online] Available at: https:// www.bbc.com/news/world-africa-14113618 [Accessed 3 Jan. 2019].

238 Ibid

239 'Hanke S., & Kwok, A. (2009) 'On the Measurement of Zimbabwe's Hyperinflation', Cato Journal, 29 (2)' (PDF) [Accessed 27 November 2018].

240 Ibid

241 Romero, A. (2016). *Artist Profile: Mokoomba | World Music Central.org*. [online] Worldmusiccentral.org. Available at: https://worldmusiccentral. org/2016/03/20/artist-profile-mokoomba/ [Accessed 4 Jan. 2019].

DOROTHY GHETTUBA TELLS AFRICAN STORIES

242 Davis, J., Stolberg, S. and Kaplan, T. (2018). *Trump Alarms Lawmakers With Disparaging Words for Haiti and Africa*. [online] Nytimes.com. Available at: https://www.nytimes.com/2018/01/11/us/politics/trump-shithole-countries.html [Accessed 9 Apr. 2018].

243 World Health Organisation (WHO) (2010). *Mental Health: Strengthening our response*. Geneva: WHO. Available from www.who. int/mediacentre/factsheets/fs220/en/

244 Medlineplus. (n.d.). *Mental Health*. [online] Available at: https:// medlineplus.gov/mentalhealth.html [Accessed 30 May 2019].

245 Amuyunzu-Nyamongo, Mary. 'The social and cultural aspects of mental health in African societies.' *Commonwealth Health Partnerships* (2013): 59-63.

246 Monteiro, Nicole M. 'Addressing mental illness in Africa: Global health challenges and local opportunities.' *Community Psychology in Global Perspective* 1.2 (2015): 78-95. See also,

Jenkins, R., Kydd, R., Mullen, P., Thomson, K., Sculley, J., Kuper, S., Carroll, J., Gureje, O., Hatcher, S., Brownie, S., Carroll, C., Hollins, S. and Wong, M. (2010). International Migration of Doctors, and Its Impact on Availability of Psychiatrists in Low and Middle Income Countries. *PLoS ONE*, [online] 5(2), p.e9049. Available at: https://journals.plos.org/plosone/article?id=10.1371/journal.pone.0009049 [Accessed 3 Jun. 2019]. (data on Nigeria)

See also, Carey, B. (2015). *The Chains of Mental Illness in West Africa.* [online] New York Times. Available at: https://www.nytimes.com/2015/10/12/health/the-chains-of-mental-illness-in-west-africa.html?_r=0 [Accessed 30 May 2019].

247 Lamichhane, Jagannath. 'Get pragmatic to tackle mental health stigma.' *SciDev.Net.* SciDev.Net, 16 Mar. 2016. Web. 20 Jan. 2017.

248 Amuyunzu-Nyamongo, Mary. 'The social and cultural aspects of mental health in African societies.' *Commonwealth Health Partnerships* (2013): 59-63.

249 Etherington, D. (2017). *People now watch 1 billion hours of YouTube per day.* [online] TechCrunch. Available at: https://techcrunch.com/2017/02/28/people-now-watch-1-billion-hours-of-youtube-per-day/ [Accessed 9 Apr. 2018].

250 Andress, J. and Schamisso, B. (2017). *Ghana's Rich Culture; Past & Present.* [online] Newsy. Available at: https://www.newsy.com/topics/ghana-s-rich-culture-past-present/ [Accessed 9 Apr. 2018].

251 Abdulai, J. (2016). *Six Things We Learned About An African City | Circumspecte.* [online] Circumspecte. Available at: https://circumspecte.com/2016/02/interview-african-city-behind-scenes/ [Accessed 9 Apr. 2018].

252 Nigeria Box Office. [online]. Available at: http://www.ceanigeria.com/box-office [Accessed 24 July 2019].

THE TECHIES: INTRODUCTION

253 Singh, N. (2018). *What 'Black Panther's' Wakanda can teach us about Africa's history — and its future.* [online] The Washington Post. Available at: https://www.washingtonpost.com/news/monkey-cage/wp/2018/02/28/what-black-panthers-wakanda-can-teach-us-about-africas-history-and-its-future/?utm_term=.53fd65ea93e7 [Accessed 4 Jan. 2019].

254 Ibid

255 Dizikes, P. (2014). *The overlooked history of African technology.* [online] MIT News. Available at: http://news.mit.edu/2014/clapperton-mavhunga-book-african-technology-1006 [Accessed 30 May 2019].

256 Leke, Acha et al. (2018), *Africa's Business Revolution.* Harvard Business Review Press.

257 Gebre, S. (2017). *Silicon Valley Loses Out on Africa Startups, TechCrunch Says.* [online] Bloomberg. Available at: https://www.bloomberg.com/news/articles/2017-10-13/silicon-valley-missing-out-on-african-startups-techcrunch-says [Accessed 4 Jan. 2019].

258 Kareem, Y. (2018). *Naspers is spending over $300 million seeking its first major African tech start-up wins.* [online] Quartz Africa. Available at: https://qz.com/africa/1439105/naspers-invests-314-million-in-south-africa-tech-startups/ [Accessed 4 Jan. 2019].

259 Bright, J. (2019). *Partech is doubling the size of its African venture fund to $143 million.* [online] TechCrunch. Available at: https://techcrunch.com/2019/01/31/partech-is-doubling-the-size-of-its-african-venture-fund-to-143-million/?guccounter=1&guce_referrer_us=aHR0cHM6Ly93d3cuZ29vZ2xlLmNvLnVrLw&guce_referrer_cs=Qj2_S18c-lxqewewuWzCOg [Accessed 30 May 2019].

260 Giles, C. (2018). *Record-breaking funding for African tech startups in 2017, says report.* [online] CNN. Available at: https://edition.cnn.com/2018/02/23/africa/increase-investment-african-tech-startup/index.html [Accessed 4 Jan. 2019].

261 Brustein, Joshua (2019), *Al Gore's Firm Leads $100 Million Investment in African Outsourcing Startup.* [online]. Available at https://www.bloomberg.com/news/articles/2019-01-23/al-gore-s-firm-leads-100-million-round-in-african-startup-andela. [Accessed July 24, 2019].

262 Bowker, J. (2019). *Jumia Surges on U.S. Debut as Africa's Amazon Goes Public.* [online] Bloomberg. Available at: https://www.bloomberg.com/news/articles/2019-04-12/jumia-raises-196-million-as-africa-s-amazon-lists-in-new-york [Accessed 30 May 2019].

263 Pilling, D. (2019). *Complaints that Jumia is not African ring hollow.* [online] Financial Times. Available at: https://www.ft.com/content/95e28f88-719a-11e9-bf5c-6eeb837566c5 [Accessed 30 May 2019].

264 Ibid

265 Akinosun, G. (2018). *Investing in African startups: The good, the bad, and the hopeful.* [online] Techpoint.Africa. Available at: https://techpoint.ng/2018/02/08/investing-african-startups/ [Accessed 4 Jan. 2019].

266 Matuluko, M. (2018). *It seems Kinnevik and Naspers lost a combined 93% ROI in Konga.* [online] Techpoint.Africa. Available at: https://techpoint.ng/2018/02/05/kinnevik-naspers-konga-investment/ [Accessed 4 Jan. 2019].

267 American Civil Liberties Union. (n.d.). *Privacy & Technology.* [online] Available at: https://www.aclu.org/issues/privacy-technology [Accessed 4 Jan. 2019].

268 Onuah, F. (2018). *Nigeria to probe alleged Cambridge Analytica involvement in....* [online] Reuters. Available at: https://www.reuters.com/article/us-facebook-cambridge-analytica-nigeria/nigeria-to-probe-alleged-cambridge-analytica-involvement-in-elections-presidency-idUSKCN1H913U [Accessed 4 Jan. 2019].

269 Davidson, A. (2018). *Gender inequality is alive and kicking in technology.* [online] The Conversation. Available at: http://theconversation.com/gender-inequality-is-alive-and-kicking-in-technology-92539 [Accessed 4 Jan. 2019].

270 National Bureau of Economic Research. (2003). *Technology and Inequality.* [online] Available at: http://www.nber.org/reporter/winter03/technologyandinequality.html [Accessed 4 Jan. 2019].

271 Rotman, D. (2014). *What Role Does Technology Play in Record Levels of Income Inequality?.* [online] MIT Technology Review. Available at: https://www.technologyreview.com/s/531726/technology-and-inequality/ [Accessed 4 Jan. 2019].

272 Hernæs, C. (2017). *Is technology contributing to increased inequality?.* [online] TechCrunch. Available at: https://techcrunch.com/2017/03/29/is-technology-contributing-to-increased-inequality/ [Accessed 4 Jan. 2019].

SIYA XUZA INVENTS NEW ENERGY TO POWER AFRICA

273 Overcomingapartheid.msu.edu. (n.d.). *South Africa: Overcoming Apartheid.* [online] Available at: http://overcomingapartheid.msu.edu/sidebar.php?id=65-258-2 [Accessed 8 Jan. 2019].

274 Spacedaily.com. (2002). *Millionaire Ready To Holiday On International Space Station*. [online] Available at: http://www.spacedaily.com/news/tourism-02f.html [Accessed 11 Apr. 2018].

275 Intel. (n.d.). *Intel International Science and Engineering Fair (Intel ISEF)*. [online] Available at: https://www.intel.com/content/www/us/en/education/competitions/international-science-and-engineering-fair.html [Accessed 11 Apr. 2018].

276 Digital, D. (2013). *Siyabulela has a planet named after him*. [online] News24. Available at: https://www.news24.com/Drum/Archive/siyabulela-has-a-planet-named-after-him-20170728 [Accessed 11 Apr. 2018].

277 Sunter, C. (2009). *Planet Siyaxuza by Clem Sunter*. [online] Awesome SA. Available at: http://www.awesomesa.co.za/?article&global%5b_id%5d=22&global-Planet%20Siyaxuza%20by%20Clem%20Sunter [Accessed 11 Apr. 2018].

278 Ray, M. (2018). *Boston Marathon bombing of 2013 | terrorist attack, Massachusetts, United States*. [online] Encyclopedia Britannica. Available at: https://www.britannica.com/event/Boston-Marathon-bombing-of-2013 [Accessed 8 Jan. 2019].

279 Kende-Robb, C. (2016). *Africa's energy poverty is keeping its people poor*. [online] World Economic Forum. Available at: https://www.weforum.org/agenda/2016/09/africa-s-energy-poverty-is-keeping-its-people-poor [Accessed 8 Jan. 2019].

280 Magano, K. (2014). *Siya Xuza: Mthata's Own Rocket Scientist – The Journalist*. [online] The Journalist. Available at: http://www.thejournalist.org.za/kau-kauru/siya-xuza-mthatas-rocket-scientist [Accessed 8 Jan. 2019].

281 Youth Village. (2016). *Michelle Obama Talks About Siya Xuza and Compares His Journey To That Of Her Husband, President Obama*. [online] Available at: http://www.youthvillage.co.za/2016/01/pic/ [Accessed 8 Jan. 2019].

DENYSE UWINEZA BRINGS SMES INTO THE DIGITAL AGE

282 'Why Kagame's Bid to Serve a Third Term Makes Sense for Rwanda.' Quartz, Quartz, 11 Mar. 2016, qz.com/637207/why-kagames-bid-to-serve-a-third-term-makes-sense-for-rwanda/ [Accessed 29 Apr. 2017].

283 BBC. *Rwanda Country Profile*. BBC News. BBC, 05 Jan. 2017 [Accessed 27 Apr. 2017].

284 Ibid

285 *Rwanda: A Historical Chronology*. PBS. Public Broadcasting Service, n.d. [Accessed 27 Apr. 2017].

286 'The World Factbook: RWANDA.' Central Intelligence Agency. Central Intelligence Agency, 12 Jan. 2017 [Accessed 27 Apr. 2017].

287 *Rwanda: A Historical Chronology*. PBS. Public Broadcasting Service, n.d. [Accessed 27 Apr. 2017].

288 BBC. *Rwanda Country Profile*. BBC News. BBC, 05 Jan. 2017 [Accessed 27 Apr. 2017].

289 Mason, Katrina. (2015). *Kagame Seeks Lasting Economic Miracle for Rwanda*. Financial Times, [online], Available at: www.ft.com/content/3cdd59b0-ded5-11e4-b9ec-00144feab7de. [Accessed 28 Apr. 2017]. Market, To The. *22 Years After the Rwandan Genocide*. The Huffington Post, [online] 7 Apr. 2016, www.huffingtonpost.com/to-the-market/22-years-after-therwanda_b_9631032.html. [Accessed 28 Apr. 2017].

290 *A Hilly Dilemma*. The Economist, The Economist Newspaper, 10 Mar. 2016, www.economist.com/news/middle-east-and-africa/21694551-should-paul-kagame-be-backed-providing-stability-and-prosperity-or-condemned?zid=309&ah=80dcf288b8561b012f603b9fd9577f0e [Accessed 28 Apr. 2017].

291 Manson, Katrina. *Kagama Seeks Economic Miracle* [Accessed 28 Apr. 2017]

292 *A Hilly Dilemma*. The Economist, The Economist Newspaper, 10 Mar. 2016, www.economist.com/news/middle-east-and-africa/21694551-should-paul-kagame-be-backed-providing-stability-and-prosperity-or-condemned?zid=309&ah=80dcf288b8561b012f603b9fd9577f0e [Accessed 28 Apr. 2017].

293 Topping, Alexandra. *Rwanda's Women Make Strides towards Equality 20 Years after the Genocide*. The Guardian, Guardian News and Media, 7 Apr. 2014, www.theguardian.com/global-development/2014/apr/07/rwanda-women-empowered-impoverished [Accessed 28 Apr. 2017].

294 Gettleman, Jeffrey. *The Global Elite's Favorite Strongman*. The New York Times, The New York Times, 7 Sept. 2013, www.nytimes.com/2013/09/08/magazine/paul-kagame-rwanda.html [Accessed 28 Apr. 2017].

295 Ibid

296 *A Hilly Dilemma*. The Economist, The Economist Newspaper, 10 Mar. 2016, www.economist.com/news/middle-east-and-africa/21694551-should-paul-kagame-be-backed-providing-stability-and-prosperity-or-condemned?zid=309&ah=80dcf288b8561b012f603b9fd9577f0e [Accessed 28 Apr. 2017].

297 Manson, Katrina. *Kagama Seeks Economic Miracle* [Accessed 28 Apr. 2017].

298 Baker, Gerard, and Matina Stevis. *Rwanda's Paul Kagame Urges Africans Not to Emulate West*. The Wall Street Journal, Dow Jones & Company, 7 Mar. 2017, www.wsj.com/articles/rwandas-paul-kagame-urges-africans-not-to-emulate-west-1488925440 [Accessed 28 Apr. 2017].

299 French, Howard W. *Paul Kagame, War Criminal?* Newsweek, Newsweek, 25 Jan. 2013, www.newsweek.com/case-against-rwandas-president-paul-kagame-63167 [Accessed 28 Apr. 2017].

300 Birrell, Ian. *My Twitterspat with Paul Kagame*. The Guardian, Guardian News and Media, 16 May 2011, www.theguardian.com/commentisfree/2011/may/16/my-twitterspat-with-paul-kagame [Accessed 28 Apr. 2017].

301 Stubbs, Thomas. *Why Kagame's Bid to Serve a Third Term Makes Sense for Rwanda*. Quartz, Quartz, 11 Mar. 2016, qz.com/637207/why-kagames-bid-to-serve-a-third-term-makes-sense-for-rwanda/ [Accessed 28 Apr. 2017].

302 moremiinitiative.org. (2015). *Call for Application 2015: Milead Fellowship*. [online] Available at: http://moremiinitiative.org/call-for-applications-2015-milead-fellowship/ [Accessed 11 Apr. 2018].

FARIDA BEDWEI POWERS MICROFINANCE WITH TECHNOLOGY

303 Encyclopedia Britannica. (2018). *Ghana | historical West African empire*. [online] Available at: https://www.britannica.com/place/Ghana-historical-West-African-empire [Accessed 4 Jan. 2019]. GhanaNation.com. (2017). *History of Ghana*. [online] Available at: https://content.ghanagrio.com/article/181-history-of-ghana-4.html [Accessed 10 Apr. 2018].

304 Ibid

305 Countrystudies.us. (n.d.). *Ghana - ARRIVAL OF THE EUROPEANS.* [online] Available at: http://countrystudies.us/ghana/6.htm [Accessed 4 Jan. 2019].

The Common Wealth. (n.d.). *Ghana : History.* [online] Available at: http://thecommonwealth.org/our-member-countries/ghana/history [Accessed 4 Jan. 2019].

306 Ibid

307 GhanaNation.com. (2017). *History of Ghana.* [online] Available at: https://content.ghanagrio.com/article/181-history-of-ghana-4.html [Accessed 10 Apr. 2018].

308 Data.worldbank.org. (n.d.). *Ghana.* [online] Available at: https://data.worldbank.org/country/ghana [Accessed 10 Apr. 2018]. See also, Naidoo, P. and Wallace, P. (2019). *Ghana Is the Star in IMF's 2019 Economic Growth Forecast.* [online] Bloomberg. Available at: https://www.bloomberg.com/news/articles/2019-04-10/ghana-is-the-star-in-imf-s-2019-economic-growth-forecast-chart [Accessed 30 May 2019].

309 Statsghana.gov.gh. (2014). *Ghana Living Standards Survey Round Six; Poverty in Ghana (2005-2013).* [online] Available at: http://www.statsghana.gov.gh/docfiles/glss6/GLSS6_Poverty%20Profile%20in%20Ghana.pdf [Accessed 10 Apr. 2018].

310 CNN Travel. (2019). *CNN Travel's 19 places to visit in 2019.* [online] Available at: https://edition.cnn.com/travel/article/places-to-visit-2019/index.html [Accessed 30 May 2019].

311 Nelson, J. (2006). *Can We Talk? Feminist Economists in Dialogue with Social Theorists.* [online] Ase.tufts.edu. Available at: http://www.ase.tufts.edu/gdae/about_us/cv/nelson_papers/Can_We_Talk.pdf [Accessed 3 Jun. 2019].

312 Said-Moorhouse, L. (2015). *The inspirational tech guru who's owning cerebral palsy like a boss.* [online] CNN. Available at: https://edition.cnn.com/2015/02/13/africa/farida-bedwei-ghanaian-software-genius/index.html [Accessed 8 Jan. 2019].

313 Ibid

314 Ibid

IYINOLUWA ("E") ABOYEJI ENABLES COMMERCE ACROSS AFRICA

315 Brustein, Joshua (2019), *Al Gore's Firm Leads $100 Million Investment in African Outsourcing Startup*. [online]. Available at https://www. bloomberg.com/news/articles/2019-01-23/al-gore-s-firm-leads-100-million-round-in-african-startup-andela. [Accessed July 24, 2019].

GREGORY ROCKSON DISRUPTS THE PHARMA INDUSTRY

316 Nean, E. (n.d.). *#SiliconValley Africa: mPharma Is Going to Disrupt the Healthcare Sector in Emerging Markets – Here's How.* [online] StartupBRICS. Available at: http://startupbrics.com/siliconvalley-africa-mpharma-healthcare-emerging-markets [Accessed 4 Jan. 2019].

317 Ibid

318 Woodrow Wilson School of Public and International Affairs. (n.d.). *PPIA Junior Summer Institute*. [online] Available at: http://wws.princeton.edu/admissions/ppia-junior-summer-institute [Accessed 4 Jan. 2019].

319 Voices of Africa. (2013). *The story of mPharma – Voices of Africa*. [online] Available at: https://voicesofafrica.co.za/the-story-of-mpharma/ [Accessed 4 Jan. 2019].

320 Ibid

321 Ibid

322 Proparco Magazine. (2013). *Improving the Quality and Accessibility of African Medicine*. [online] Available at: https://www.proparco.fr/sites/proparco/files/2018-01/proparco-RevuePSD28-african-medecine-UK.pdf [Accessed 4 Jan. 2019].

323 Sarley, D., Abdallah, H., Rao, R., Gyimah, P., Azeez, J. and Garshong, B. (2003). *Ghana: Pharmaceutical Pricing Study Policy Analysis and Recommendations*. [online] WHO. Available at: http://www.who.int/hiv/amds/en/country2.pdf [Accessed 4 Jan. 2019].

324 Ibid

325 World Health Summit. (2015). *History*. [online] Available at: https://www.worldhealthsummit.org/about-whs-/history/2015.html [Accessed 8 Jan. 2019].

326 Westminster College. (2016). *Changing the World through Social Medicine: Gregory Rockson '12*. [online] Available at: http://news.westminster-mo.edu/global/gregory-rockson-12/ [Accessed 4 Jan. 2019].

327 Skoll. (n.d.). *Skoll | Skoll Awards*. [online] Available at: http://skoll.org/ about/skoll-awards/ [Accessed 30 May 2019].

328 Ayitey, C. (2017). *mPharma Raises $6.6 million in a Series A Funding Round*. [online] Gharage. Available at: https://gharage.com/2017/11/23/ mpharma-raises-6-6-million-series-a-funding [Accessed 8 Jan. 2019].

329 Cheney, C. (2017). *The IFC wants venture capitalists to take a close look at these opportunities*. [online] Devex. Available at: https://www. devex.com/news/the-ifc-wants-venture-capitalists-to-take-a-close-look- at-these-opportunities-90485 [Accessed 8 Jan. 2019].

CONCLUSION

330 Custer, S. (2017). *Interview: Fred Swaniker, African Leadership University, Mauritius*. [online] The Pie News. Available at: https:// thepienews.com/pie-chat/fred-swaniker-africa-leadership-university/ [Accessed 8 Jan. 2019].

331 Minney, T. (2017). *How big are African pension funds? at African Capital Markets News*. [online] African Capital Market News. Available at: http://www.africancapitalmarketsnews.com/3544/how- big-are-african-pension-funds/ [Accessed 8 Jan. 2019].

332 Wagner, Harvey M. (2011). *The Bottom Line: Corporate Performance and Women's Representation on Boards (2004–2008)*. [online] Catalyst. Available at: https://www.catalyst.org/research/the- bottom-line-corporate-performance-and-womens-representation-on- boards-2004-2008/ [Accessed 8 Jan. 2019].

333 Atwood, William. "Illinois State Board of Investment TFL Webinar on Diversity and Inclusion." [online]. Available at http://iri.hks.harvard. edu/files/iri/files/tlf-diversity-and-inclusion-the-business-case-for- investors-slides.pdf. [Accessed 2 June, 2019].

ACKNOWLEDGEMENTS

I have been apprehensive to write this section, for fear of leaving out so many I have been indebted to in realising this project. But during these seven years, over 66 cities across 45 African countries, and countless 'thank yous' along the way, I would like to single out those who have played key roles in my journey.

First, I'd like to thank my Lord and Saviour, Jesus Christ for giving me the strength and perseverance to finish this project. Thank you, Lord!

I'd like to thank my mother, Amira Delle, who has been my rock of Gibraltar, and has supported me in countless ways. I am forever indebted to her. I am grateful to my father, Naa Edmund Delle Kyiir VIII for his blessings and support. I am eternally grateful for the love and support of my siblings Eguu, Banguu, John and Edmund, especially Banguu, who read the whole manuscript multiple times. I am grateful to my nephews and nieces for teaching me that this book is not exactly ideal bedtime story material; cheers to Sangu Delle Jr., Banguu Delle Jr., Maalu Delle, Viela Delle, Sage Mensah, John Paul Mensah Jr., Jamal Foli, Kofi Misa-Schuster, Benjamin Inusah and Isaac Inusah.

I could not have done this without the support of my family and close friends, who gave feedback on the manuscript and supported me in so many ways: Adom Arthur, Alexander Mora, KSM, Mavis Ampah, Nana Misa, Ama Misa, Naya Misa, Princess Emefa

Kludjeson, Adwoa Kontoh Yeboah, John Paul Mensah, Elaine Mensah, Mawena Glymin, Ndu Okereke, Darryl Finkton, Adam Demuyakor, Gerrel Olivier, Nworah Ayogu, Ayodeji Ogunnaike, Oludamini Ogunnaike, Makinde Ogunnaike, Naseemah Mohamed Ogunnaike, Kwabena Agyemang, George Nsiah, Alyssa Colbert, Elorm Baeta, Edem Baeta, Jude Addo, Kwaku Osei, Andrew Overton, Guy Assad, KJ Yamoah, Ahmed Inusah, Ramzi Inusah, Chris Golden, Sheel Tyle, Walter Baddoo, Peter Orth, Sarah Parcak, Kayode Ogunro, Jemila Abdulai, Aissata Lam, Issam Chleuh, Kashuo Bennett, the Qoboza family, Uche Pedro, Blinky Bill, Juliana Rotich, Shinn Chenn, Dalumuzi Mhlanga, Efosa Ojomo, Vivian Onano, Alfonso Costa, Chike Achebe, Tracy Han, Amandla Ooko-Ombaka, Kader Kaneye, Reverend Sister Domitilla, Father Campbell, Prophet Thompson, the Mallah family, the Soros class of 2014, Rachael Techie-Menson, Afua Rida, Dufie Addo, Sly Agbagba, Bright Gbeku, Uncle Ike Thompson, Habiba Sinare, Shmuel Brew-Butler, Eddie Addo, Eric Taylor III and Vinay Gokaldas.

I am so grateful for my support team of writers, editors and researchers. I could not have done this without Hawa Abdul Rahman, Colette Bishogo, Alex Kellogg, Barikisu Sumara – Muntari and Natasha Nyanin. I am indebted to Yaw Frimpong Tenkorang for his great assistance throughout this project and for helping me turn hundreds of hours of interviews into meaningful stories.

I am grateful for my English teachers, professors and tutors who helped nurture my writing: the late Mrs. Tsikata (Ghana International School), Samuel Amebley (University of Ghana), Lynda Pickbourn (Ghana International School/Hampshire College), Mrs. Payida (Ghana International School), Alyssa Peterson Morreale (Peddie School/Trinity Hall), Dr. Suzanne Lane (Harvard/MIT) and Luci Herman (Harvard/Stanford). I am also grateful to various professors who supported me and advised me while writing this book. At Harvard Business School: Bill Kerr, Henry McGee, Luis Viceira,

Amy Schulman and Leslie Perlow. At Harvard University's Faculty of Arts and Sciences: Henry Louis Gates, Jr., Emmanuel Akyeampong, Ntuli Qoboza-Akyeampong, Brandon Terry, Timothy McCarthy, Evelyn B. Higginbotham. At Harvard Law School: Ron Sullivan, David Wilkins, Raymond Atuguba, Bruce Mann and Lucie White. At Oxford University: Andrew Shacknove and Liz Ulmas. I am also indebted to Esi Ansah at Ashesi University and Francis Hukpati at Ghana International School.

I could not have done this without my partners at Golden Palm Investments who have supported this journey and have helped me back some amazing entrepreneurs on the continent: John Higgins, Lake Wang, Brandon Arrindell, Alex Marlantes, Ryu Goto, AJ Okereke and Bemnet Zewdie. I am also grateful to my senior colleagues at Africa Health Holdings: Chinny Ogunro, Erharuyi Idemudia, Victor Muo, Jide Adebisi and to all our colleagues in Accra, Lagos and NY.

I am thankful for my family of mentors who have all inspired me by their examples and offered great support during this journey: Raymond McGuire, Timothy Barakett, Alan Waxman, Euvin Naidoo, Thomas Buberl, Jude Bucknor, Keli Gadzekpo, Philip Sowah, Chris Hansen, Dror Bar-Ziv, George Van Amson, Carla Harris, Hakeem and Myma Belo-Osagie, Kimathi Kuenyehia, Steve Bonner, Rufus Jones, Peter Shapiro, John Green, Kofi Kwakwa and Robert Reffkin.

I leveraged various programs and networks that I am associated with to gain access to hundreds of entrepreneurs. Thank you to the Harvard Alumni Association, Paul and Daisy Soros Fellowship, TED Fellows Program, Desmond Tutu Fellowship, Africa Leadership Network, GLG Social Impact Fellowship, Forbes Africa 30 under 30, Obama Foundation Africa Leaders and the Global Shapers initiative of the World Economic Forum.

I am grateful to the Bracken Bower Prize committee for shortlisting me for the award in 2014. It inspired confidence in the project and gave me fuel to finish. Thank you!

I am immensely grateful to three people who play a key role in my health and wellness: Jen Rodgers, my personal assistant; Andrew Cassidy, my life coach; and Dr. E, my therapist.

Of course, I couldn't have done this without my amazing editor and publisher, Bibi and her whole team at Cassava Republic. I am grateful to TED for bringing us together in Tanzania during TEDGlobal in 2017. Bibi – you are a FORCE of nature. You pushed me, inspired me and encouraged me every step of the way. This project is as much yours as it is mine.

To all the young entrepreneurs across Africa – those I featured, those I met, those I didn't meet – you are the real MVPs. I am so inspired by all of you. You give me so much hope for our future.

Finally, to Afra, my best friend in the world: I really don't know how to thank you; from reading every single line and giving constructive feedback, to accommodating the incessant demands of the project. You have been my biggest champion and I am forever indebted to you.

SUPPORT *MAKING FUTURES*

We hope you enjoyed reading this book. It was brought to you by Cassava Republic Press, an award-winning independent publisher based in Abuja and London. If you think more people should read this book, here's how you can support it:

1. **Recommend it.** Don't keep the enjoyment of this book to yourself; tell everyone you know. Spread the word to your friends and family.
2. **Review, review, review.** Your opinion is powerful and a positive review from you can generate new sales. Spare a minute to leave a short review on Amazon, GoodReads, Wordery, our website and other book buying sites.
3. **Join the conversation.** Hearing somebody you trust talk about a book with passion and excitement is one of the most powerful ways to get people to engage with it. If you like this book, talk about it. Share it on Facebook, Twitter and Instagram. Take pictures of the book and share your favourite quotes . You can even add a link so others know where to purchase the book from.
4. **Buy the book as gifts for others.** Buying a gift is a regular activity for most of us – birthdays, anniversaries, holidays, special days or just a nice present for a loved one for no reason... If you love this book and you think it might resonate with others, then please buy extra copies!

5. **Get your local bookshop or library to stock it.** Sometimes bookshops and libraries only order books that they have heard about. If you loved this book, why not ask your librarian or bookshop to order it in. If enough people request a title, the bookshop or library will take note and will order a few copies for their shelves.

6. **Recommend a book to your book club.** Persuade your book club to read this book and discuss what you enjoy about the book in the company of others. This is a wonderful way to share what you like and help to boost the sales and popularity of this book. You can also join our online book club on Facebook at Afri-Lit Club to discuss books by other African writers.

7. **Attend a book reading.** There are lots of opportunities to hear writers talk about their work. Support them by attending their book events. Get your friends, colleagues and families to a reading and show an author your support.

Thank you!

Stay up to date with the latest books, special offers and exclusive content with our monthly newsletter.
Sign up on our website:
www.cassavarepublic.biz

Twitter: @cassavarepublic #ReadCassava
#ReadingAfrica
Instagram: @cassavarepublicpress
Facebook: facebook.com/CassavaRepublic

Transforming a manuscript into the book you are now reading is a team effort. Cassava Republic Press would like to thank everyone who helped in the production of *Making Futures: Young Entrepreneurs in a Dynamic Africa.*

Editorial
Bibi Bakare-Yusuf
Layla Mohamed
Lanaire Aderemi

Design & Production
Seyi Adegoke
Typesetter
R. Ajith Kumar

Sales & Marketing
Kofo Okunola
Emma Shercliff